How to Survive Without a Salary

How to Survive Without a Salary

Learning how to live the Conserver Lifestyle

---

by Charles Long

W
Warwick Publishing
www.warwickgp.com

How to Survive Without a Salary:
Learning to Live the Conserver Lifestyle
(Revised Edition)

We acknowledge the financial support of the Government of Canada through the Book Publishing Industry Development Program for our publishing activities.

ISBN: 1-894622-37-5

Published by Warwick Publishing Inc.
161 Frederick Street
Toronto, Ontario M5A 4P3 Canada
www.warwickgp.com

Distributed in Canada by:
Canadian Book Network
c/o Georgetown Terminal Warehouses
34 Armstrong Avenue
Georgetown, Ontario L7G 4R9 Canada

Distributed in the United States by:
Weatherhill, Inc.
41 Monroe Turnpike
Trumbull, CT 06611 USA

Editor of this edition: Jennifer Iveson
Layout: Melinda Tate
Cover Design: Clint Rogerson

Printed and bound in Canada

Contents

Preface

There's something about this so-called global economy that reminds me of the sanitary worker who falls in a cesspool. To his great relief he discovers a bump on the bottom where, if he stands on his tip-toes and stretches his neck, he can just keep his mouth above the surface of the muck. To his great dismay he also discovers that taking any step in any direction only makes his predicament worse. He refuses all offers of help, muttering through clenched lips, "Don't make a wave . . . Don't make a wave . . . ."

Consider this: Ten years ago, as the Internet went mainstream, students and anyone else considering a career were advised to get into computers. And indeed, many of those who followed that advice quickly landed jobs that offered great salaries and stock options and perks like being able to bring your dog to work. But less than a decade later, many of those same people ended up unemployed for months, even years, after the dot-com boom went bust. The great economic focus on the high-tech industry meant that when it faltered, the stock market faltered too, causing a rippling effect that reached all sectors.

And this: The North American Free Trade Agreement accelerated the shift of jobs from the high-wage north to low-wage Mexico. The Mexican economy blossomed, until currency speculators plucked the rose and drove the peso over the cliff, erasing all the good news gains.

And, inevitably, this: Despite unprecedented growth and profits, real personal incomes have fallen. The gap between rich and poor keeps widening. Even the good waves turn out to be bad news for anybody standing on the bottom.

Is it any wonder that the old dream of career has gone flatter than last year's birthday balloon? You remember the dream: learn some useful skill, put it to use in a steady job, get a few promotions, a few raises, earn a decent living and retire on a pension at sixty-five. The idea that any job would just keep getting better was strong enough to support a belief in the career "ladder." One rung at a time, and always up.

Those old enough to have enjoyed a good start on the ladder have found it's not all it was cracked up to be. The generations following behind the Baby Boomers have had trouble getting even one foot on the bottom rung. Meanwhile, the wave makers of the financial world have replaced the once-solid ground beneath the ladder with quicksand.

As career ladders start sinking, some careerists tighten their grip on the ladder, demanding that the union or the government do something, competing with fellow ladder clingers for a firmer foothold, doing everything but acknowledge that the ladder itself is sinking. Others are beginning to see where the "tighter grip" survival strategy will lead.

While the ladder sinks for individuals, the corporate economy gets better and better. We've seen a recurring pattern since the late 1980s: Profits go up, exports go up, and stock markets hit record highs. Government deficits finally start to fall, interest rates hit bottom, and inflation flirts with zero. Then the Boardroom celebrates its recovery with an orgy of downsizing, re-engineering, re-structuring, and generally reaming out the payroll to keep itself afloat.

One excuse always trotted out for these periodic downsizing sessions is "global competition." But what does global competition really mean? We know jobs disappear, but do shareholders tighten their belts? Put a freeze on dividends? Downsize the executive suite? Or does global competition cut at less exalted levels? Let's put a face on it. A real person like Iqbal Masih.

Iqbal was small, sickly and all of four when he was sold to a carpet maker in a Pakistani village. He spent the next six years chained to a loom, working fourteen hours a day, six days a week, fed too little and beaten for his mistakes. At the age of ten, Iqbal slipped his chain and escaped. He spent the next two years telling other child workers that their bondage was illegal, that they were free to walk away from the beatings, the abuse and the crippling work that would kill half of them before they reached the age of twelve. Iqbal helped 3,000 children escape from the tanneries, textile factories and steel mills that drove Pakistan's successful entry into the global economy. Then he was killed, shot by an unknown assassin in April of 1995.

Iqbal's 3,000 fellow escapees did not stop the tide. There are still ten million child laborers in Pakistan. And Pakistan is not alone in its quest to find cheaper and cheaper ways to produce the goods for the world marketplace. The slave trade in Africa continues to this day. According to Kevin Bales, author of *Disposable People: New Slavery in the Global Economy,* slaves, many of whom are children, are cheaper today than at any other time in human history. The agricultural slave that cost $1,000 in Alabama in 1850 ($50,000 at today's prices) can be purchased for around $100 today. That's what global competition means.

"Competition" is a loaded word in the Western lexicon. It's an honorable, almost sporting quest to be the best. We accept competition in the workplace, even as we find ourselves competing with old friends to keep our own jobs. We celebrate competition when we go to the mall and find that prices have fallen. We understand when the boss calls us into the cafeteria to explain that half the employees have to go, because of global competition. It sounds inevitable, almost worthy. Nobody mentions that in this race for the cheapest payroll there is a four-year-old boy, chained to a loom and beaten with a cane when he falters. If that's winning, do we want to be in the race? And what is our responsibility for the Iqbals? Will their misery end if we buy their carpets, their clothing, and their steel instead of buying ours? So far it hasn't. Though there have been campaigns to end the exploitation of children in the labor market, as Pakistan's economy grows in the new world market children are still being put to work. Wages are cut. Whole factories are now designed for tiny workers, because children are cheaper than machines. It's the bottom line, you understand.

This wasn't the way it was supposed to be. Western civilization enjoyed a century of technological advances that freed workers from their former drudgery. It was messy at times, but progress seemed inevitable. Children left the Dickensian sweatshops and went to school.

Adults worked fewer hours and made more money. More money in the economy meant more for everybody. When we first imagined a world with computers and robots, we believed that, like the first Industrial Revolution, this new burst of productivity would reward us all with more leisure, more goods, and more choice. A few short decades ago it was easy to imagine a thirty-hour work week, longer vacations, and early retirement. If, with the new technology, it would take less human labor to produce more goods, we could all work less and prosper more. Remember that dream?

You know, of course, what happened. Productivity has gone up, as expected. But the average work week has grown longer, not shorter. As the need for human labor shrank, we didn't all work less; the unlucky got downsized, and those left on the payroll had to work harder, competing for the remaining jobs, taking real wage cuts even as profits grew. The choice was to work harder and longer for less, or not at all.

Another time, another place, such rank unfairness might have been a call to revolution. Not here. Not now. We bought into the myth of competition for so long that being downsized can feel like personal failure rather than a deliberate grab by a few for all the goodies. The reaction to lay-off is more likely to be shame than anger. The instinct is to hide, not fight. The victims have been persuaded to blame themselves.

The job scare is a two-edged sword. On the surface, there's the money problem. We've come to believe that a regular paycheck is the only socially acceptable way to feed and clothe the family. As restructuring takes the security out of all careers, we haven't adjusted our thinking to accommodate the new reality. On the contrary, that less-secure salary becomes even more important, because now it not only has to provide the necessities of life, it has to be big enough to cushion against possible job loss. The less certain job futures become, the more money we need and the more desperately we need it.

But money is only half the problem. The deeper cut is the psychic damage. It's a question of self esteem. We've conditioned ourselves to define self-worth by what we do at work. When the economy threatens to take that away, it doesn't matter how much money we have in the bank; a lay-off, even a possible lay-off, is a blow to the ego's solar plexus. It's a bit like being dumped by your mate. The fact that there might be a billion or so other possible mates out there, many of whom might be an improvement on the last one, doesn't make the dumpee feel one little bit better.

That psychic damage from the jobless recovery, that horrible, gut-churning anger that comes with job rejection, or even the possibility of rejection, was something we could afford to downplay in earlier editions of *How to Survive Without a Salary*. We assumed that readers would be kissing the company goodbye for their own good reasons, that the reader would be the dumper, not the dumpee. Things have changed.

Curiously, the practical advice offered in these pages has required little adjustment from one edition to the next. Solving the money problem, if anything, has become easier. In what was once called "the new economy," and is now simply today's economic reality, the way to deal with downturns was to dump people, not go out of business. As businesses cut staff, there are more and more opportunities for outsiders, freelancers, and contractors to earn an adequate living without being on anybody's payroll. Personal computers, the Internet, cellphones and the ever-evolving array of affordable technology make it even easier to free-lance as a one-person business, working at home or on a comfy beach somewhere. The practical side of surviving sans salary has always included a casual income of some kind. And casual income is a whole lot easier than it ever has been.

Likewise, the nitty-gritty of living on less has become somewhat easier. The aging of the population has taken the pressure off the housing market in most places. There are more bargains in housing and land than there were a few years ago. Smaller families in older, larger, homes have left room for shared housing. Barter and bargaining are more socially acceptable. Stalled consumer growth has forced retailers to be more aggressive with discounts and sales gimmicks. There are now more retailers in do-it-yourself and second-hand markets. The environmental movement has diverted re-useables and recyclables from landfill sites and into the hands of conservers.

On the red side of the ledger, the importance of debt remains paramount. Debt is an even bigger monster than before. Simply, consumer debt shackles the debtor to his job. When the job sinks, the debtor goes down with the job, no matter how low interest rates might be.

Surviving without a salary, for most, still means a little self-sufficiency and a lot of flexibility. Debt robs the individual of both self-sufficiency and flexibility. You can't settle the Visa bill with home-grown tomatoes and a counter-offer to barter chores. Ironically, credit companies prefer cash. The discipline to get out of debt and stay out of debt is the same now as it was before.

The biggest change from that day when I kissed my own job good-bye is the death of the traditional career. I resigned voluntarily. I was the eccentric and this, for my former colleagues, was the road not taken. For those who stayed in the mainstream, a long-term nine-to-five job was the norm. Now the idea of surviving in a single career, from apprenticeship to retirement, is the improbable stuff of dreams. Practical people don't count on the company being there for them anymore. Then, surviving without a salary was a self-appointed eccentric's folly. Now it's too often imposed. Some of the fun has gone out of the game.

That's too bad. There's no pleasure in saying I told you so. But the sad fact is that competing for the global bottom line has beaten the bejeezus out of company loyalty and the old career. It's a game that the worker can no longer win. Hard work isn't enough any more. The most that too many employees can hope for is to survive on the salary long enough to get squeezed out on reasonable terms and with enough self-respect left to realize that it's not a personal failure.

If it is society's failure, if it is a lack of political will to stop the pillage of many by the few, then what can one do? What now if not revolution?

Perhaps the most direct answer to an economy that has abandoned its workers is for workers to abandon the economy, seceding one by one to make smaller, independent economies, family arrangements, neighborhood co-ops, alternatives to the consumer machine. Become a company of one. Make your own rules, set your own goals. Be your own Board of Directors. You decide what gets cut from the costs of this mini-corporation. Fire General Motors by not buying the car? Done. Lay off Kraft? Easy. Slash the family deficit? Downsize the tax bill? Cover child care costs in-house instead of out-sourcing? Increase dividends by paying yourself instead of the mall? Why not? They've been doing it to you for years.

If the global economy has lost its way, let it go. Declare the larger economy a big mistake and start anew. This time, make it small enough to work for you.

~ 1 ~

What's the Catch?

When I admit that we have lived quite comfortably without a salary for
most of our lives, the usual response is incredulity. "What's the catch?"
friends ask, as they survey the standard array of offspring, pets, and
bulky appliances that signal a rather ordinary middle-class household.

They might be more inclined to believe it if they found us living in
the back seat of an old Ford, or subsisting on day-old bread and dandelion salad. An ancestral tycoon or rows of cannabis amongst the corn
might hint at other means of support. Government check stubs or a
framed lottery ticket would suggest a shortcut along the way.

The truth is more prosaic. There are no magic formulae or secret
sugar daddies to milk. What we do have is a lifestyle — carefully
planned and slowly built — that reduces the need for cash to a level that
can easily be met with casual income.

There really is no catch. Instead, there are many small steps taken
over the years. While not one of those steps, in itself, is unique, the
cumulative effect has been a dramatic change in the way we behave as
consumers. Though our material lives are far from Spartan, the way we
define our needs and satisfy them sets us apart from the average consumer. We are conservers.

Living without a salary is really a rather ordinary way to live. It may
seem extraordinary to those whose norm is a forty-hour week, a boss, a

mortgage, and a regular paycheck, but millions of very normal North Americans do it. Businessmen, farmers, professionals, and entrepreneurs of every stripe live without a salary.

This book is about the Conserver Lifestyle. Whether or not there's a salary is incidental. Leaving the nine-to-five behind is simply easier for conservers than it is for consumers. Lots of conservers choose to keep their jobs. But for conservers it's a choice, not a life-long necessity. Quitting the job is by no means the answer for every harried middle-class consumer.

For many — worried about layoffs, inflation, retirement funds, interest rates and medical costs — the conserver lifestyle is no more than a means of coping better with what they already have. The techniques that have allowed us to live without a salary have been just as useful to others — in altering their economic lives so they can afford to buy a home, go back to school, travel a bit, or just quit worrying about lay-offs. This book is for them.

For the conserver household, costs are more important than earnings.

• • • • • • • • • • • •

Businesspeople, farmers, rock stars and others who have forsaken the forty-hour work week succeed or fail by their ability to apply a fairly standard set of techniques and rules for profitable enterprise. These include marketing a product, overhead, capital formation, cost controls and cash flow. The techniques and principles required for business success differ only in scale from the rules that should govern an ordinary household economy. For the conserver household, there is one more critical difference — costs are more important than earnings. Whether we speak of initial costs, maintenance costs, replacement costs, or whatever, there is nearly always more advantage in reducing costs than in increasing earnings. That is not always the case in modern business.

The corporate attitude to costs has a lot to do with the enormous scale and bureaucratization of business, with the separation between ownership and management. For the professional manager, size carries more prestige, and more salary, than any other index of performance. One of the more simplistic assumptions of economic analysis is that, in a capitalist economy, individual businesses will act to maximize the rate of return on investment (profit). In theory, controlling costs is just as important to that end as increasing sales. But ask a bottling executive if he would rather run the neighborhood soft-drink plant returning a healthy twenty percent, or be president of Coca-Cola with profits of ten percent, or even zero percent. I'll wager he would rather run Coca-Cola at a loss than manage a small-town plant at any level of profit, just as the aspiring rock star would rather be a bankrupt Beatle than work the beer halls for a steady $50,000 a year.

Of course modern business has an interest in profits, but the managers and bureaucrats who run them also have a stake in size and prestige that undercuts the profit motive and tends to make cost a less-than-equal partner in the planning equation. It amounts to keeping up with the Joneses on a giant scale. Like the suburbanite, proud of owning the most expensive car on the block, the modern businessperson has more at the bottom line than the rate of return on investment.

That's not to say that growth for its own sake is necessarily bad for business. It would be akin to arguing that minimalist art is superior to Flemish realism. It's really a matter of choice. No less so in the household economy. Whether you want the biggest car on the block, the most efficient car, or the most efficient way of getting from A to B (even if it means taking the bus), it's a matter of choice.

The point is that the conserver household can use techniques for decision making that are very similar to those used by business. The tools are no less valid if the motives and objectives are different. If the objective is to survive without a salary, or merely to put some fat back into the household budget, then the question of controlling costs is paramount. If the objective is growth, then the revenue side needs greater effort, and damn the costs.

The Joneses and the bureaucracies, government or corporate, have traditionally taken the "bigger is better" route, and damn the costs. Conservers look at what it costs to be bigger, what it costs to consume more, and even what it costs to make a bigger income.

Why make the distinction, though? Aren't income and outgo, costs and revenue, merely different sides of the very same coin? In the purest form of analysis, and if all costs are considered, income and expense are plus and minus of equal units. In theory. In practice it just ain't so.

A Penny Saved

I hate to argue with Ben Franklin, but in the twenty-first century a penny saved is not a penny earned. Sorry, Ben, but today, a penny saved is a heck of a lot *more* than a penny earned. Consider the simple example of a $1,000 purchase: a holiday, a little furniture, or a replacement for the worn-out fridge. Nothing unusual or extravagant, but it's more than the paycheck will cover. So put it on the credit card, right? And don't forget the sales tax of, say, seven percent, or whatever it is where you live. If you pay it off in a year, at a credit card interest rate of 15 percent, that new fridge will end up costing you $1,230. Now, if you are in, say, the 25 percent federal income tax bracket, you will have to earn $1,640 in order to buy that $1,000 item. If you also pay state or provincial taxes, the price goes up even further. We could also add the costs of earning the $1,640: a portion of commuting costs, payroll deductions, union dues, and so on, but let's keep it simple, this time, and call it $1,640.

Meanwhile, the cost-conscious conservers found a quality used fridge or a "no name" holiday resort for half the price the Joneses paid. They paid cash (which is one of the reasons they got a better deal, but more on that later) and, to be fair, we'll add the foregone interest they might have earned by charging the item and leaving their cash in a three percent interest account. So the fridge, or whatever, will cost the conservers $500 plus $35 sales tax, plus $15 in lost interest, for a total of $550. If they are in the same 25 percent tax bracket as the Joneses, they will have to earn $733 in order to buy that $500 item . . . while the Joneses had to earn $1,640 in order to buy the $1,000 model. A difference in earnings required of $907! So, in this case, $500 saved is the equivalent of $907 earned.

Moreover, if the conservers are really conscientious, they've either put those unused earnings to work in investments, or they've been able to cut back on their income from employment. If the unused earnings are invested, the difference between the conservers and the Joneses gets bigger by the rate of return on investment. If the conservers stick the savings in their infant's education fund, even at a lowly four percent the conservers will have doubled their advantage over the Joneses, with more than $1,800 by the time their child is ready for college. If they take the alternative route and cut back on earnings, rather than invest the unused earnings, they will drop into a lower tax bracket and will likely reduce at least some of the costs of working cited above. In either case, the difference in necessary earning will almost certainly be greater than the basic $907 calculated, and the difference will continue to grow over the years. And remember we started by saving only $500 on a very ordinary purchase.

What's the catch? There is none. There is only a change in emphasis. Having grown up in an era of cheap energy, stable prices and material expectations limited only by personal ambition, we of the post-depression generation were taught that the only route to satisfaction and success was to continually increase our earnings and consumption. The world has changed. Inflation, taxation, and some pretty basic arithmetic all tell us that today there is more to be gained, more easily, by reducing costs than by increasing income.

This book, then, is about two things: saving money and earning casual income. Of the two, saving money is by far the more important. In the first place, as we've seen, a penny saved is worth at least two or three earned. And secondly, North Americans — particularly those born here after the Second World War — know a great deal less about saving money than they do about earning it. It's part of the tradition. The only people who watched their pennies were those who had to. There's more pejorative venom in the word "cheap" than in the word "extravagant." A spendthrift can be admired, a miser cannot. We not only have a lot to learn about thrift, we must also be convinced that it's socially acceptable.

A Penny Earned

What about the other side though? If we're all so inept at spending money and so adept at earning it, why waste words on casual income? I'll elaborate later but let me admit, at this point, to a minor case of semantic chicanery: surviving without a salary is not the same as surviving without money. Life without a salary is possible, socially acceptable, and can be accomplished with a surprising degree of comfort and satisfaction. Living without money can be none of these. In the 1960s, there was a popular myth among the granola set that anyone could take a roll of plastic sheeting and a Swiss Army knife and go to live in the woods and cohabit with Mother Nature. Like the lilies of the field, they withered in the fall and ended up selling insurance in the suburbs. It takes very little money to live, but it does take some.

If there is any apology due for including a section on income, it's to those readers, probably a majority, who have no desire or intention of leaving their careers. Their interests, quite legitimately, lie in making better use of what they already earn: to buy a home, to travel, or just to cope with rising prices. For them, the making of casual income is probably superfluous. Their regular income, wisely spent, will likely stretch to cover all their needs.

For those who are serious about living well without a regular job, it is virtually impossible to escape the need for some regular source of cash. However, earning casual income is at once more difficult and simpler than most careerists imagine. The difficult part was described by Will Rogers when he said, "There's nothing dumber than an educated man, once you get him off the thing he's educated in." We've swallowed our own propaganda about specialization of skills to the point where many otherwise intelligent people doubt their ability to take on the simplest task without a degree, a night course, or a learned consultant to unveil the mumbo-jumbo and nonexistent mysteries. That's the difficult part — convincing highly trained people that they have other saleable skills and personal assets besides the thing they're educated in.

The easy part of generating casual income lies in the huge range of possibilities that exist for casual employment, part-time, self-employment, and simple fortuitous enterprise. There's a market for just about anything you feel like doing. But there is a catch: the more highly organized your enterprise gets, or more profitable, the faster the market contracts. There is wider scope for tiny business than for bigger business.

It's the casual nickel and dime stuff, the once-a-week-if-I-feel-like-it jobs that are easiest to start and stop, and that provide the freedom only dreamed about by desk-bound nine-to-fivers. You may never get rich being a dilettante in the marketplace, but most of the time it feels like being rich. If your needs are simple, it can be more than enough.

Can Anybody Do It?

How easy is it? Can anyone survive without a salary? When visitors ask me those questions, I assume they are really asking, "Could I do it?"

and I tailor the answer to the questioner. I used to think that just about everyone could, provided they were prepared to work hard and prepare themselves thoroughly. The human race, after all, is a good deal older than the forty-hour week and superannuated security. The humblest citizen of ancient Rome took far more holidays than the cushiest union contract in today's industrial world can provide, but then they didn't have automobiles and color TVs to support. Poor, hungry, illiterate peasants in the harshest parts of today's developing world build and occupy homes of their own, an impossible dream for many young middle-class families awash in North American affluence. But those peasant homes don't have the requisite plumbing and wall-to-wall carpets that dissatisfied North Americans expect.

It is, I have often thought, entirely a matter of making the choices. Conscious choices, deliberately calculated, like the economists' models we studied in school: so many guns or so much butter. Each of us could choose . . . two hours' leisure or the electric knife, a bigger car or another bedroom, a condominium in Florida or an earlier retirement in the backyard. Every choice, every wish, was theoretically possible as long as the equation balanced. If there could be a sacrifice of equivalent value in another part of our lives, any goal could be achieved, any dream come true.

My mother told me if I practiced hard enough and long enough I might someday play second base for the Cincinnati Reds. Being twelve, I chose to spend the requisite hours talking to girls instead, but, as far as I was concerned at the time, it was a deliberate and calculated choice. There were risks involved in either course; I might spend the hours practicing baseball and still not find the talent to get off the bench of the farm league duffers, but then there was an equal chance I could spend all that time with the girls and not get to second base with any of them either.

How real is that freedom, though? Can we still make choices about our lives or are there more illusions of freedom than practical opportunities?

I can't put the question any more graphically than the woman who told me that all she wanted out of life was a vegetable garden and the time to work at her pottery. She was a career administrator, stuck in a middle-aged rut.

"Is it all just a romantic dream?" she asked, with a poignant touch of quiet desperation.

For her, I'm sure, the will and resources to realize her dreams are there. The hardest part will be climbing out of the rut itself. She will probably find life on the "outside" surprisingly easy. The question, though, is central to everyone making such a decision: Is freedom from the nine-to-five just a romantic dream?

I answered the woman somewhat equivocally by saying that it depended mostly on her own attitudes and expectations. A bucolic life of crafts and gardening was remote from her own experience, and yet something she valued highly. In that sense it was romantic. But that didn't make it unattainable or unrealistic. If she had the skills and resources, or was willing to sacrifice more time to get them, then the dream was certainly obtainable.

The critical question was whether she could make the dream work in real life, and moreover, find the satisfaction in it that she was looking for. If the dream was all sunshine and flowers, would the rainy days and inevitable weeds spoil it for her? Could her amateur artist's ego stand up to a few initial rebuffs in the marketplace? Would her willpower and sense of humor be able to survive the compromises, disappointments and setbacks that distinguish real life from dreams? In the end we agreed that, yes, it was a romantic dream, but that didn't mean that — with a few warts and weeds — it couldn't also become a reality. It really depended what she was made of.

The ways in which dreams come true or crash on the rocky shoals of reality are as timeless as the dreams themselves.

In the wake of the 1970s back-to-the-land movement, *Harrowsmith* magazine ran a feature called "Why Homesteaders Fail." The case histories of unreal expectations, inevitable disappointments and occasional success made a remarkable parallel with the first homesteaders who settled Upper Canada 150 years earlier. Susanna Moodie and Catharine Parr Traill were sisters who settled an area north of Peterborough, Ontario, in the 1830s. Their backgrounds were the same: English gentility more or less forced by financial circumstances to try a new life in the colonies. They were neighbors in the new land. Both women faced similar hardships: bitter cold, unaccustomed labors, crude facilities and unfamiliar social mores. The list will be familiar to any twenty-first-century back-to-the-land type. Both sisters brought their dreams. They dreamed of land and vast estates and an escape from the strictures of an empty purse in a genteel hand. And there were warts such as dishonest land agents, uncooperative neighbors, sickness, and even a rebellion that drew the men into the militia and left the women to cope alone.

The problems and circumstances are well known to the most casual reader of history. Especially instructive in this case, however, are the attitudes of these two women and the effect that had on the success of each in adapting to her new circumstances.

Susanna Moodie pined away for English comforts. She was resourceful enough to make coffee from dandelions and hard-working enough when necessity demanded it, but the hardships engendered more bitterness than cheerful accommodation. In the end she wrote: "If these sketches should prove the means of deterring one family from sinking their property, and shipwrecking all their hopes, by going to reside in the backwoods of Canada, I shall consider myself amply repaid for revealing the secrets of the prison house, and feel that I have not toiled and suffered in the wilderness in vain."

Her younger sister, Mrs. Traill, faced the same hardships with a more cheerful determination. Obstacles, to her, were challenges instead of defeats. She adapted and thrived until she died at the age of ninety-seven, a mother of nine, a respected botanist and a widely published author. In her introduction to *The Canadian Settler's Guide,* she wrote:

> In Canada persevering energy and industry, with sobriety, will overcome all obstacles, and in time will place the very poorest family in a position of substantial comfort ... To the indolent or to the intemperate man Canada offers no such promise ... He has not the elements of success within him. Canada is not the land for the idle sensualist. He must forsake the error of his ways at once, or he will sink into ruin here as he would have done had he stayed in his old country.

The warning could have been aimed at her sister and it applies as well to today's refugees from urban pressure. Some will make it and some won't. And to bring this ramble back to the original question, it's not always a matter of choice. Some, in Mrs. Traill's words, just don't have the elements of success within them.

Nor is it always talent — spiritual or temporal — barring the way to personal choices. I, for example, am already too old to ever make it in the major leagues — even if I never talk to a girl again. And the only time I ever tried to chew tobacco, I threw up. It's a dream that I'm no longer free to choose. The fact is that there are many people who will never be able to survive without a salary.

Happily, there are many half-measures on the way to a conserver lifestyle that provide the advantages without the risks of actually telling the boss what you think of him. In other words, not everyone is able or willing to declare economic independence, but everyone can apply at least some of its lessons to get more out of the money they work so hard to earn.

Nor should city-dwellers feel that they have to move to the country to gain independence. Life in the country, indeed, has many advantages. Food, housing, heat and many other necessities can be obtained more cheaply or even for free in the countryside. But the urbanite has access to cheaper electricity, telephones, entertainment and cultural facilities. This is not a back-to-the-land book.

What does it really take, though, to go all the way to economic self-sufficiency? How difficult is it? It's pointless, of course, to talk about dollars and cents. It depends on how elaborate your needs are. If you're hooked on T-bones, Guccis, and Club Med holidays you may never be able to kiss your paycheck good-bye.

As a starting point, I suggest that most people who are serious about surviving sans salary should begin with the acceptance of four basic premises:

1. The key is to control expenditures.

2. No matter how low your cost of living, you will require some form of income.

3. Some time will be required to prepare yourself. Lifestyle changes don't happen overnight like a New Year's resolution.

4. Welfare, charity, or indulgent rich uncles may help some people survive without jobs but they are still forms of dependence. Some people need them, just as some people will always need careers. But this book is about independence and self-sufficiency, not swapping one form of servitude for another. Ask those who have to survive on welfare. Most would find more satisfaction in the meanest of jobs.

By now it should be clear that I don't have any magic formulae for retirement to easy street. If you're looking for miracles, buy a lottery ticket. Reality takes a lot more hard work and preparation. But it can be done. And it can be enormously satisfying. If you are prepared to work at it, and if you can manage some self-confidence, flexibility, patience and a touch of self-indulgence, then you're already equipped with most of what it takes to escape from any rut.

Hard Work

Leaving the drudgery of nine-to-five means less work and more leisure, right? Wrong! If you believe in the dynamics of capitalism, it won't take much to convince you that most people are already working at the most remunerative task they can do. Or, if you believe in the Peter Principle, you will know that most workers are already employed at the most highly paid job they *can't* do. In either case, be aware that the job you've been doing for the last ten or thirty years probably returns more dollars and cents per hour of your time than you'll be worth at just about anything else.

Let me illustrate with hypothetical neighbors, a plumber and a gardener. The plumber, who gets, say, $300 a day for his skills, decides that food is getting too expensive. So during a twenty-week growing season, he spends one day a week tending a big backyard garden. He keeps careful records and by October figures he has produced fruits and vegetables that would have cost $2,000 at the supermarket. He's thrilled . . . until his wife points out that if he had spent his days off plumbing instead of fooling around in the backyard, he could have earned $6,000! He would have to work three times as hard at gardening to come out even with plumbing on an hourly basis.

His neighbor is a gardener who makes $100 a day. When the gardener's plumbing springs a leak she panics at the potential expense and decides to do it herself. After three days of shopping for supplies, dismantling the pipes, consulting a do-it-yourself guide, and putting it back together twice, she proudly shows the finished work to her neighbor.

"That's a terrific job," says the professional plumber, "you probably saved yourself a $150 service call."

Of course, she could have made twice that much by spending the three days gardening.

Obviously the example is oversimplified. By the time the plumber paid taxes, union dues, transportation expenses, and wrote off a few unpaid bills, his $6,000 for plumbing on his days off would have shrunk considerably. And the next time the gardener's pipes begin to leak she'll doubtless know how to do it faster and with fewer mistakes.

Nor does this example explore the non-monetary considerations. The plumber's homegrown veggies will taste better to him than anything he could buy at the supermarket. When the gardener's toilet erupts some Sunday (like toothaches, these things never happen during office hours) she may rue the time and work involved, but if she can do it herself at least she won't lose a night's sleep over what the bill might be.

Finally, most humans are far too complex and clever to be satisfied with the exercise of a single task, a single skill, or a single career to the exclusion of everything else. Few plumbers could stand to spend every waking hour at the trade, no matter how much we offered to pay them. It's no less true for brain surgeons, civil servants or gardeners. Economists tell us that workers, like nations, can maximize their incomes by specializing in the things they do best, and buying or trading with other specialists to obtain their other needs. But common sense tells us that for sanity's sake, if not for profit, it behooves us to perform other, less highly paid tasks as well. Even economists shave themselves, drive their own cars, and some even mow their own lawns. In theory, they should hire others to perform these tasks and spend their time doing whatever it is that economists do.

In practice, everyone performs some unprofitable tasks. To the extent we spend our valuable time on work that someone else could do faster or cheaper, then we're earning less than our maximum income potential, or working harder than we must to obtain the same result. This is true for the economist who mows his lawn or the administrator who would rather make pottery. Those who are planning early retirement, a year or two off, or just cutting back on overtime will almost certainly have to spend less or work even harder at something else to maintain their regular income.

That's the bad news. The good news is that it doesn't have to feel like work. Spending that hour in the backyard garden can be a pleasure, even if it is an inefficient way for a plumber to spend his time. On the other hand, if he gets carried away and spends the entire week gardening, the forty-first hour amongst the veggies will almost certainly start to feel like work.

The good news is that many of us happily choose to work twice as hard at the things we enjoy rather than the things that might pay more. Paul Gauguin was a successful stockbroker in Paris. When he chucked it all to paint in Tahiti he took a drastic cut in the hourly returns for his time. From comfortable urban affluence, he was reduced to cadging credit from the local grocer. An economist might say that the painter chose the hard way to make his living. But Gauguin didn't seem to mind, and the world is certainly a richer place for his colors than it ever was for his stockbrokering.

Make no mistake about it, though, surviving outside the normal economic modes of a nine-to-five career takes a load of hard work. You may enjoy it more; you may consider it more worthwhile. But don't expect the world to make you richer for your greater efforts, and don't expect to have forty extra hours of free time on your hands.

Cincinnatus was plowing his fields when he was called to Rome to become dictator of all the empire. When the campaign was won he resigned his lofty post and happily went back to his plowing. His accountant was no doubt aghast at his folly, and we can only speculate on the entreaties of his advisors: "Just hang on one more year as dictator and you can buy the biggest farm in the Roman Empire; you've got a career ahead of you here, don't throw it all away on a whim; you're a good emperor, farmers are a dime a dozen; maybe it's just the male menopause, take a holiday and then decide." But Cincinnatus went back to the farm, the Senate found another Caesar, and the Romans honored him above other, more ambitious leaders. For all the honor and satisfaction, though, the fact remains that plowing is harder work for the money than being emperor.

Whatever your job, if your needs are as great as your paycheck, giving it up will likely mean working harder, not less.

Confidence

Alternative lifestyles, like everything else, are only possible if you *believe* they're possible. Surviving without a salary means a lot of doing without, doing it yourself, or doing something else for money. All that doing means that much of the time you'll be doing things you've never done before. At times, the only resource you'll have is yourself, and if you don't believe that's enough, it won't be.

It's here that modern Western people are at their greatest disadvantage. We've spent generations listening to economists preach specialization. In a sense, they were right. Western capitalist society is a showcase of material well-being. Our psyches may not be in such great shape, but we're up to our well-fed tushies in all the things that other people make for us. Most of us, in turn, have been trained to make or do just one thing for the rest of the economy. We do it extremely well, but by and large that's all we do.

It's the poor people from places where the goodies are not so abundant who have been led, by necessity, to learn and retain a wider variety of survival skills. Peasant farmers can build a house, repair a plow, butcher meat, make a cart, select and store seed, and so on. Our modern farmers pay specialists to do all of those things. Primitive families grow food, preserve it and prepare it. They deliver babies, make cloth, tan hides and pull teeth . . . without a degree in any of those skills. Highly organized Westerners can doubtless do all of those things to a higher standard. Perhaps we can do them more efficiently. But, individually, most of us would find more than a few of those simple everyday tasks overwhelming.

Don't believe me? Try making yourself a shirt from a cotton plant. Or try to convert a live animal into a meal. Walk into McDonald's with a live cow and a bushel of wheat and ask them to whip up some hamburgers. Every last kid behind the counter would know — in theory — that the flesh of the cow has to be cut and minced, and that the wheat must be ground, risen and baked, but I'll bet that not one of them would have the confidence to try it. That's why we have packing houses, butchers, millers and bakers. The processes are complex, skilled and highly regulated. Or is it just that we've organized the processes into such highly specialized tasks that we've lost touch with the real and basic simplicity of the thing?

I once corresponded with a highly educated man — a psychologist and an academic. He told me that he had a piece of property covered with beautiful stone and that he wanted to build a stone house. He enjoyed working with his hands, but wanted experts to build the house because he thought the skills were beyond his capacity. Design stress, load factors, bearing walls and whatchamacallits were highly technical engineering problems. He was a simple Ph.D. I advised him to try it anyway, just for fun and the pleasure of working with stone. I tried to assure him that stone walls stayed up because the law of gravity kept them there, not because a computer model pronounced them sound. He demurred and went to Mexico instead. He returned with his enthusiasm for stone renewed.

"Stone walls everywhere," he wrote. "Maybe it's simpler than I thought!"

The psychologist might have understood if I had reminded him that salesmen, seducers, and mothers of little children practiced psychology long before there was a word for it. His Ph.D. is merely for understanding what they have done intuitively, and perhaps for explaining it or practicing it in a slightly more sophisticated way. But that doesn't mean that the seducer needs a diploma to influence another's behavior; mothers don't need Ph.D.s to offer lollipops at the proper time; and psychologists don't need engineering tables to put one stone on top another and call the result a wall. Any peasant can build a wall. All the engineer can do is explain why it did, or did not, fall. I hope someday he finds the confidence to put one stone atop another and trust that it will stay there; or have the courage to try again if, by some mystery, it falls.

If confidence is essential for the do-it-yourselfer, it's downright critical when it comes to doing-it-for-money. Most of us are mildly conflicted about our skills. There are one or two things for which we have a license or a union card (our standard vocation), and then there are other things at which we may be equally skilled but have practiced only for our own amusement (our avocations). We charge as much as the market will bear for our vocational skills, and still feel underpaid. But we give away the product of our avocations almost apologetically. At our daughter's birthday party, a little friend arrived with a beautiful handmade present — an intricately braided belt. Her mother was embarrassed. "I'm terrible sorry," she explained, "but there just wasn't time to get to the store." Without reservation, I can say, it was the nicest present at the party.

I have often suggested to people that they could supplement their incomes by selling crafts or hobby skills. The usual reaction is modest demurral: "Oh, I'm not good enough for that" or "Anybody can do this . . . why would they pay for it?" or "I'm no good at selling things." And yet they may work at jobs that almost anybody could do, and sell their services there with great effectiveness. They believe in their jobs, but they don't accept their avocations with the same degree of confidence. It's too enjoyable to be work, and it (the hobby) is too easy to have value in the marketplace. But, most of all, is it good enough to be worth money to other people?

In many cases avocations may not be worth a whit in the market-place. But there is only one way to find out. Without the confidence to try . . . and try again . . . you'd better have an income that doesn't need to be supplemented.

Flexibility

If there is a single thread that runs through most efforts to reduce the need for cash, it is flexibility. An adaptable, inventive approach to life and its problems allows us to substitute cheaper resources for more expensive ones, and find simpler answers. It's the ability to solve problems, often in unconventional ways.

Our chickens had a problem one year with foxes. Predatory attacks on the flock were even more severe than those threatened by the lady of the house every time she found them pecking in the spinach patch. It became imperative to fence the chickens in, or fence the foxes and the mistress out. The universal solution is chicken wire. Fencing a yard thirty feet square takes a small fortune just for the mesh, however. Appalled at the expense, we began to look for alternatives. A board fence was functional, but the cheapest lumber around at the time was random, rough-sawn cedar picked up at the mill for thirty cents a board foot — or $180 for a fence five feet high. In the end, for a mere twenty dollars, the saw mill delivered an enormous load of slab waste. From it we selected the requisite 600 board feet of solid lumber (good on three sides, bark on the fourth) and cut the rest into three full cords of firewood. The fence is more durable than the mesh, at a fraction of the price, and the free firewood will boil maple sap for the next few years.

We boil sap in a large stainless-steel pan that a sharp-eyed friend salvaged from a company that saw the expensive pan only as a used "hot oil bath" and had thrown it out. The fire is built in an arch of discarded chimney brick, and the heavy pan slides neatly back and forth in a steel bed-frame that someone threw away.

More on such substitutions later. For now, I only want to illustrate that the most common solution to any problem is often the most expensive one as well. The commercial economy provides a ready answer to meet any need. The economy expects you to go out and buy the patented answers to your problems. You, on the other hand, have to be flexible enough to dodge through and around that network of ready-made solutions if you want to keep your money for more important things. A wise con-

The most common solution to any problem is often the most expensive.
● ● ● ● ● ● ● ● ● ● ● ●

sumer learns where he can buy the cheapest chicken wire or get the best deal on a syrup evaporator. The conserver goes one step further and learns to do without, adapt alternatives, or invent his own solutions.

Not that long ago, and even today in some parts of the country, mention of this kind of flexibility as a unique quality would have seemed redundant. It was a way of life. Stale bread became bird food and turkey stuffing. If you didn't have a cellar shelf, a packing crate would do as well. Our short, sweet taste of material abundance seems to have spoiled all that. Today, we throw the stale bread away and drive to the store for the commercial bird feed and prepackaged stuffing mix. When's the last time you saw a kid on a cart built from a crate and a mismatched set of lawnmower wheels?

The "good old days" weren't all that terrific, but people did have the personal qualities to cope with the difficulties. One of those qualities was a healthy skepticism toward the marketplace. Few of our grand-mothers could have been hoodwinked into believing that packaged breadcrumbs were any better than the ones from the bottom of the drawer. The idea of selling freezers in the Arctic used to be a joke. Now supermarkets sell prepackaged ice cubes in the depths of winter and it doesn't even raise a chuckle.

If the doomsayers are right and we do have hard times ahead again, we may all be forced by circumstance to forgo our extravagances. We may all have to revert to meeting needs with what we have around us instead of running to the marketplace to apply the balms that advertisers say we need. I hope that we can regain the flexibility that this requires.

Some of us, though, are choosing hard times now: tightening belts to buy a house, paint nudes in Tahiti, or just take a year off to write the novel. For us, choosing alternatives and adapting them to needs is not like the grim regimen of real poverty. It's a challenge, a game of Monopoly between us and the commercial lords of Boardwalk and Park Place. We're looking for shortcuts around the high-rent district for reasons of our own. In one sense that makes it harder. If we really were poor, we would not have any choice. We would be excluded from the fat and baubles of the marketplace automatically, without the option of dropping back in from time to time. Having the high-priced options all around us makes it even more difficult to find and adapt to cheaper alternatives. It's easier to think of the ready solutions dangled before us by advertisers and accepted so unquestioningly by our peers. It's harder to see choices that would be obvious to a poor person or a poor society.

We once had a small city garden that the neighborhood children treated as a roadway/shortcut from the alley on which it bordered to the busy street in front of the house. Nothing grew but the gum wrappers and litter of the junior parade. We tried everything: earnest pleas, threats of mayhem, lying in wait with the garden hose. We even tried partial surrender — a flagstone path so the little lemmings could keep the shortcut but stay off the blankety-blank plants. They trampled everything but the path. We put up a wire fence — they climbed it. We put up a board fence — they vaulted it. Fellow sufferers across the alley escalated their defenses to a high, chain-link fence with steel posts set in concrete. That seemed to work, and I was almost tempted to raid the savings and buy the deluxe solution myself.

With that in mind, we renewed our interest in the garden and brought in a big juicy truckload of rotten, wet manure. We took it right up the alley and dumped it over the board fence in a long, waist-high pile at the edge of the would-be garden. Bright and early in the morning, the thunder of little sneakers came pounding up the alley, vaulted the fence, and planted themselves knee-deep in what only they could describe so colorfully . . . at full volume. By the end of the summer, the expensive fence across the alley was breached once more, and our fertile little patch was still untrodden. That was a cheap alternative that we stumbled onto, so to speak, rather than chose. Nevertheless, it taught me a lesson about inventive solutions that neither I nor those kids will ever forget.

We don't often see the corporate world being that flexible, but one classic example comes to mind. My first year as an undergraduate saw the completion of an extensive campus rebuilding program. After several years of mud and disruption, the college finished in grand style with a lavish icing of outdoor lights, lush sod, and winding concrete paths. Within a year there were muddy ruts and impromptu paths all over the sod, and the concrete walks were hardly touched. The landscapers tore up the useless paving, resodded the entire area, and waited.

Two months later they came back. This time, they paved only the functional paths the students were making across the lawns from building to building. Planning is important, but being flexible enough to recognize and accept shortcuts pays as much in the long run.

Patience

Not everybody can live without a regular paycheck. Even fewer can afford to walk away from a job when the mood first strikes them. Unless you're the only heir of an ailing granny, there's comfort in knowing your lifestyle is pretty well self-sufficient before you ask the boss where she keeps her brains. Patience. Self-sufficiency takes some preparation.

Patience is also a virtue when it comes to the somewhat erratic shopping habits that are part of living on less. As you'll see in chapter 3, regular weekly shopping — buying as the need arises — is the working man's way to spend his pay. Rich folks and conservers buy things only when the price is right. You can buy in bulk, ahead of time, or at sales, in anticipation of a need. More often, the need arises first. Then you put it off and put it off until the whatsits are being sold at half-price for clearance, or you happen to find one on the rummage table. My wife accuses me of elevating lowly procrastination to economic theory, but from whatever vice it springs, biding your time is the essential part of bargain hunting.

A Touch of Self-Indulgence

Having listed hard work, confidence, flexibility and patience as the essential personal qualities it takes to survive sans salary, I've already scared off the vicarious daydreaming Walter Mittys of the would-be drop-out set. Lest serious readers start to worry that this is becoming the Dale Carnegie course for abstemious lifestyles and voluntary under-achievers, let me add that luxury, too, has an important place in the conserver household.

Real poverty is not a laughing matter. It's destructive, depressing and self-perpetuating. It's an economic state but it's also a state of mind. It's not the same as living cheaply.

Our little family has lived quite happily and comfortably on a great deal less cash than the same-sized family might get on welfare. We aren't poor. We don't feel poor and don't live poorly. We have few of the material things that really poor people around us take for granted. No cable TV, instant foods, or fashionable clothes. Even if we wanted to, we couldn't afford to smoke. On the other hand, we enjoy drinking wine with meals, eat the finest of foods, and travel abroad more frequently than most. These are modest indulgences, but in our lifestyle they are vital.

The problem is that penny-pinching gets to be a habit. Fortunately, we enjoy the simple life and have never felt deprived for want of snow-mobiles, fitted carpets and expensive toys. There are times, though, when I must admit that we are sorely tempted to blow the budget. There are times when the rusty old lawnmower balks and we think how nice it would be to put it out with the trash and buy a zippy new rid-ing model with an electric starter. There are times when winter begins to drag and we feel a little envy for folks who can book the first avail-able flight for Nassau and to hell with waiting for the charter deal. Oh yes, there are times. But almost always the old habits prevail, and we keep our spending to careful limits.

It's times like that when we need a pressure valve. Without some release, the constant discipline on money matters would begin to feel rigid and mean — more like a dreary trap than a means of freedom and independence. In a word, we would feel *poor*.

That's when we throw another log on the grate, open a bottle of the best wild grape, and sit down to a juicy roast of loin or brace of squab. Candlelight, a little music and a crackling fire. By the end of the evening we're back to feeling grateful that the clunky old mower can be patched again and there's at least another week of skiing left before the sap begins to run. By the end of such an evening we can feel richer than any Vanderbilt cruising Bermuda in the Bentley.

It seemed to work with the children, too. My daughter always wanted the brand-name jeans her classmates wore, but knew that most of them could not afford the trips to Europe and the Caribbean that she enjoyed. My son coveted the pro-quality skates that seemed to be de rigueur on the hockey rink, but visiting friends envied his tree house and handy swimming hole. As long as they had a few juvenile "luxuries" to compensate for the sacrifices, they didn't have to feel poor. Of course, if families were really democratic, I'd be voted back to work until they finally had all the things they thought they wanted. And that could take a very long time.

I would not advise that anybody blow the budget on the whim of luxury. Our own little indulgences are, after all, mostly free. Giving yourself the afternoon off to sit in the shade with a glass of wine, tended only by Pan, is hardly going to break the bank. But it feels so damned good that you can't possibly miss the double-breasted suit and three-martini lunch that you can no longer afford.

Choices

What, then, is the catch? The qualities I've described above could be a prescription for success in any endeavor. There is no catch. It's as straightforward as becoming Minister of Finance, president of Coca-Cola, or the best darn second baseman in Cincinnati. There's no easy formula for "the good life" outside the confines of regular employment — just as there's no easy formula for success within that world. It boils down to what's within you, and what choices you make: how much money you spend and how and where you earn it.

I suspect that the reason a life like ours arouses incredulity is that many people are so accustomed to letting society and advertisers make the important choices for them that they no longer see them as choices. The greatest joy I find in teaching people how to retire is the dawning of awareness on ordinary faces as they begin to see choices that they never realized were theirs — even if the choices are little ones, mundane ones, nickels and dimes. A young man marveled as he realized that being a one-car family instead of a two-car family would make them richer by at least $4,000 a year. He was an educated man. He had simply never added up the cost and made a conscious choice before. A woman who needed cutlery found it at a tiny fraction of what she otherwise would have paid at the department store. A tight household budget expanded before her eyes as she began to see the unadvertised alternatives. A hobbyist who spends hundreds every year on cameras and equipment chose to keep his interest up, but suddenly saw it as an investment that could bring profits as well as expenses. *Choices.* Choices that most of us have and few of us realize. Choices that not everyone would wish to make, but choices that should at least be consciously considered and not made simply because that's the way the Joneses do it.

Individuals have different needs, different assets, and different skills. If they behave in identical ways, it really is too bad. Thoreau said he was not out of step with other men, he simply heard the beat of a different drummer. I trust that those independent souls, sufficiently attuned to different drummers that they would contemplate breaking the nine-to-five norm, will understand when I say that the techniques and sources discussed in this book are not meant to be applied in every situation, like a recipe. It is, rather, a menu from which the reader might pick and choose ideas suitable for his own needs or useful to his own ambitions.

That's enough of generalizations for now, however. Surviving without a salary raises some practical problems that must be solved. The following chapters raise those problems and suggest some practical approaches to solving them. That's what we're here for, so let's begin . . .

~ 2 ~

Assessing Yourself (Making a Budget)

Surviving without a salary is by and large a financial endeavor. Oh, there are countless physical problems, aesthetic rewards, and maybe even some spiritual moments, but at the end of every month it's clear that the essence of the exercise — the foundation — is finance. You either have it or you don't, and the beauty of the sunset, for all its incalculable value, won't begin to pay the utility bills.

The starting point for every financial plan is a budget. The declaration of financial independence is no different. And ironically, making plans to live on less requires a more carefully wrought budget than the big-money plans of the rich. High finance can afford to be sloppy. The less you have, the more carefully you have to count it.

I have to admit right here that, essential or not, making a budget is a dreadful bore. It really isn't fair. One of the fundamental reasons we left careers was a yawning indifference to dollars. So this then is the drop-outs' Catch-22. Those who like money enough to spend their time earning it don't need to bother with budgets and the like. On the other hand, those of us so indifferent to money that we leave our jobs must spend a great deal more time planning our more minuscule financial affairs. *Boring!* But you can't have your dessert until you eat your spinach, so let's get budgets out of the way first and save the good stuff until later.

What's a Budget?

A budget is an estimate of income and expenses. A financial plan of what you'll have and what you'll need in the coming year. If you work at a regular job, the income side of the estimate will be a piece of cake. The expenditure side will take a little more effort. For most of us mortals, trying to remember where our money went last year is tough enough to do in any useful detail. To figure out where it's going *next year* means an evening of sweat and guess, and at least one spat with your mate. It's particularly hard on reformed smokers. Chew an eraser and persevere. Next year you'll be glad you did.

It's next year that the other role of budgeting comes to the fore. If a budget were only an estimate of what will happen to the family finances in the year to come, it would have no more value than any other type of forecast. Tarot cards or the bumps on your head might tell you as much about what the future holds. Knowing your economic future might cure a few sleepless nights (or create a few), but it won't help you do anything about it unless you also use the budget as a control mechanism.

Why Bother?

Most of the time I can assess my economic health by counting the change in my pocket, and I automatically know the answer to any question beginning with, "Do you think we can afford . . . ?" Yes, a budget is a big pain in the old wazoo, but it really is worth the effort — for three big reasons.

First of all, a budget helps to identify and solve problems before they happen. It's no guarantee against unexpected bills and other nasty surprises, but it does give you a way to make provision ahead of time for things that might go wrong. Even when things go right, most of us have times of the year when cash gets short and other times when it looks as if there's some fat in the wallet. If we're lucky, the fat and the lean balance out over the year and we come out even at the end. Without a budget, it gets harder to predict and recognize those times. One month we end up with a few extra bucks and feel flush enough to blow it on a big night out. Then next month the kids are due at the dentist and we wonder if we'll have to put the family jewel in hock. A budget can tell you ahead of time that the kids will be due at the dentist, the front tires are getting smooth, and the washing machine is ten years old and likely to start spitting out of unplanned orifices. If your budget is good enough to predict such problems, you'll still have surprises but more and more of them will be nice surprises, like "Gee, no cavities this time!" And when you've budgeted for the dentist's trip to Disneyland such announcements fall like a gift from heaven on your ears. Or, "Gee, Junior put his bubble gum in the wash and now the machine doesn't leak anymore!"

Secondly, a good budget is a valuable tool in making specific decisions or choices. Any dunce can look at the balance in his checkbook and decide whether or not he can afford a new suit. That simple approach, however doesn't tell him that having a suit means not having the ski weekend or the extra insulation in the attic he was hoping to have "when he could afford it." Viewed one at a time, such choices are evaluated only on their own merits and the day-to-day state of the pocketbook. A budget exercise sets up a whole year's array of choices in a single shopping list. Decisions are then made with all the alternatives in mind at once.

Once the budget is done for the year, subsequent decisions are easy. "Can we afford it?" isn't guesswork anymore. The extra money is there (and it shows) or it isn't, and some other specific expense has to be cut to make room for the new need.

Finally, a budget is important for the sense of security it provides. It's easy to get depressed these days. What with faltering economies, **A budget provides a sense of security.** runaway deficits, dwindling oil reserves, sassy kids and cancer, nothing is as safe as it used to be. There are people who make a living telling us how terrible things are, for God's sake. When the price of gas goes up for the third time in a week, when you can't remember which kind of 'illions the newscaster used to describe the national debt or Exxon's profits, when sucking your thumb seems like the most rational response to more bad news, then there's some comfort in pulling out the family budget and convincing yourself that, yes, you really can make it through another year. It might not be getting any easier, but knowing what's ahead, in dollars and cents, is more comforting than wondering and waiting for the worst. It's not the answer to the world's problems, but it beats the heck out of sucking your thumb.

Getting Started

If you've never done a budget before, the place to start is in last year's records. Pull out all the check stubs, credit card receipts, tax forms or other records that you can find. Then get a long piece of paper, and down the left-hand side list all the things you spent your money on. Group them, where possible, in broader categories. Across the top write: *Week - Month - Year - Special - Total.* The result will look something like the format of the sample expense record (Figure 1).

The categories for your expenses will have to be tailor-made. If, for example, you live in an apartment, "housing" might include only rent, utilities, and cleaning supplies.

Now, start adding up the receipts and bits of paper you've saved. Check the dates to get some idea of how complete they are, and then do some guessing to fill in the gaps. For example, if you usually gas up the car once a week but have only forty receipts instead of fifty-two, figure out how much the average fill-up cost, and multiply that by the fifty-two weeks:

1. 40 receipts total $1,000

2. Average fill-up was $25 ($1,000 ÷ 40)

3. Total gas expense for year is $1,300 ($25 × 52)

The idea is to come as close as possible to what was actually spent. If you've saved every receipt from every expenditure then it's a simple job of adding up all the numbers. But if you're that fastidious then you are probably an accountant and you can skip this chapter. We mortals will have some gaps to fill in.

The biggest gaps will be from the smallest expenditures, the day-to-day cash from the pocket outlays. Each of these pocket-money expenses is too small to bother recording, but the overall total can be a surprisingly large hunk of money. To get a handle on it, try carrying a pocket notebook for a week. Jot down the small change as you spend it. Bus fare, coffee break, newspaper, lunch, a haircut, parking meters, and so on. A week's sample times fifty-two will give you a good idea of what goes in a year. Be fair though! For accuracy's sake, don't cut back just because you're keeping track.

Filling in the Numbers

As you arrive at reliable totals in each category, put them on the chart. Record the usual weekly or monthly amount in the columns, and an annual total on the right.

The "special" column is for expenses that you don't expect to have on a regular basis: an addition to the house, another car, that broken tooth or the furnace that finally had to be replaced. If it's not something that happens every year, stick it into "special." That's for last year's expenses. Forecasting special expenses for next year's budget gets a little stickier, but last year you *know* what was spent. Put it in.

The usual procedure is to enter the total for any purchase. Many items are not paid for in the same year they're bought, however. Cars are often bought on time payment. Houses almost always are. How you record such payment is largely a matter of what's convenient and comprehensible to you. For instance, it usually makes more sense to record monthly mortgage payments than to carry a "special" $200,000 purchase of a house over twenty-five years of annual budgets. If you bought a car last year, you may find it convenient to enter the down payment in the "special" column, and the installments in the "month" column.

Do it in a way that's easy for you, but be aware of two common mistakes. First, don't double count. If you enter the full purchase price of an item, don't then keep entering monthly payments as well. Second, don't lose track of *what* you're buying by burying a lot of big or regular items in a general category like "credit card account" or "bank loan payments." One woman I know was not concerned that her credit card ran over $6,000 a year. In doing her very first budget exercise, she was horrified to learn that nearly all of that was spent on clothes. She decided to take up sewing. Be specific!

Check

Now that you're satisfied you have accounted for last year's expenses, and that you have recorded them in reasonable order, here is a crude but simple way to check:

1. Add up all the expenses actually paid last year (that's the bottom of the right-hand column).

2. Add anything you might have saved (the amount by which bank accounts

increased over the year — if the balance is smaller than it was a year ago, you have a negative savings so subtract the difference).

3. Add all the income taxes, pension plans, unemployment and other payroll deductions that did not appear as expenses on your chart (you'll find these listed on your tax form).

4. Compare the total of the three above with your total income (also shown on the tax form).

If the two totals match, you're either an accountant or you cheated. Skip the rest of the chapter.

If income is smaller than savings and expenses, then you've probably made a mistake. Check your figures. You may have double-counted a credit purchase, or listed the full value of something for which you've only made partial payment.

Chances are, however, that the total income figure will be larger than the grand total of all expenses and savings. That almost certainly means you've overlooked some expenses. Not to worry. That's why accountants invented the word *miscellaneous*. Call the discrepancy "Miscellaneous Expenses" and enter it on your chart. Obviously, the smaller the amount in the "Miscellaneous" line the more accurate are your accounts. For most of us, though, budgets are guides — not obsessions. Close is good enough.

Figure 1: Sample Expense Record

Item	Week	Month	Year	Special	Total
Food:					
groceries	100				5,200
office lunches		25			1,250
coffee breaks	10				500
eating out		100			1,200
freezer beef			300		300
				Total Food:	**$8,450**
Housing:					
mortgage		600			7,200
property tax			3,000		3,000
repairs			500		500
heat			1,000		1,000

Item	Week	Month	Year	Special	Total
(Housing cont'd)					
electricity		30			360
water			65		65
insurance			900		900
maintenance			45		540
other				750	750
				Total Housing:	**$14,315**
Transportation:					
gas	20				1,040
car down payment			2,000	2,000	
4 car payments (Oct-Dec)	260		1,040		
insurance			900		900
maintenance			360		360
new tire				90	90
plane fare				260	260
bus pass (Sept-May)	60				540
				Total Transportation:	**$6,235**
Clothing:					
mother			575		575
father			425		425
child			360		360
child			340		340
				Total Clothing:	**$1,700**
Health:					
insurance			1,800	1,800	
drugs			18		216
dental checks			360	360	
broken tooth				200	200
				Total Health:	**$2,576**
Other:					
telephone		32			384
cable TV		21			252
furniture			575		575
new fridge				1,000	1,000

Item	Week	Month	Year	Special	Total
(Other cont'd)					
charity			200		200
movies		35			420
birthday party			100		100
wine	10				520
subscriptions			48		48
life insurance			500		500
retirement plan		100			1,200
gifts			800		800

Total Other: **$5,999**

Preliminary Total: **$39,270**

Miscellaneous Expenses (see "Check" below)   ????

Check

Actual earnings

full-time salary	36,500
part-time salary	17,000

Combined gross earnings: $53,500

Preliminary total of expenses (from above)	39,270
Add payroll deductions:	
income tax withheld	9,100
unemployment insurance	620
recreation fund	120
company pension plan	900
government pension plan	1,150
Add income tax paid on filing (subtract if a refund)	–(126)
Add savings during the year (subtract if balance dropped)	+370

Total expenses identified: $51,404

Difference (enter above as "Miscellaneous Expenses")	2,096

Now look again at the sample expense record (Figure 1). If it seems extravagant to you, that's because I've tried to include as many different circumstances as possible. The method is more important than the numbers, however. Notice, in particular, the quick check at the end and the calculation of miscellaneous expenses.

At this point, many first-time budget makers go into a swoon as they see just how much cash is slipping away in dribs and drabs. The big items, like rent or mortgage or the grocery bill are familiar enough. The surprise comes with realizing how fast the less visible expenses can add up to big ones: the car, clothes, or bits and pieces for the house. That is the main reason it's so useful to break the records down into as much detail as possible. You might have more to learn by looking at your little expenses than at the big ones.

When you're satisfied that the chart you've developed is reasonably accurate and organized in a way that will be easy enough to maintain, then you're ready to tackle the *real* budget — the estimate of next year's expenses.

The Year Ahead

Using the same categories developed for the record of last year's expenses, estimate what will happen to each item in the coming year. Account for any changes in circumstances. If the mortgage is up for renewal, recalculate it (or ask the bank to recalculate it) at current interest rates. If you plan to have the car or another debt paid off during the coming year, don't multiply payments by the full twelve months to get the total — extend it only until it would be paid off. If you're planning a holiday, put it in. If you've sworn off booze, take it out of the budget.

The "special" expenses warrant some special mention here. The problem is that they don't always fit so neatly into a one-year budget. There are several ways to account for them. The choice is yours. For guidance, consider three basic alternatives for budgeting a common purchase, like a car:

Method 1. This is for people who save their money until they have the cash to buy big items. The purchase can be budgeted as a one-shot expense in the year they plan the purchase. That's simple enough to enter in the budget, but difficulties can arise with major items. The problem is that expenses coast along at a steady level, and then in one year they zoom up to cover the big purchase. That's fine if the bank balance is big enough to handle it, but if it's a strain on the reserves, this lump-sum approach has to be planned for or spread out a little.

Method 2. Another way to plan for the replacement of high-cost items like the car is to link a savings plan to the depreciation or "wearing out" of the old one. Cars depreciate at different rates depending on the model, your driving habits, and other factors. You can get an idea of how the value of your own car is depreciating by asking the dealer to quote used prices for your vehicle at different ages (these are sometimes called *blue book* values). Let's assume the value of your car is dropping at an average of thirty percent per year. You've just paid $16,000 for it, so after the first year it's worth only $11,200 as a used car. It has lost thirty percent or $4,800 of its value. So the transportation budget includes an expense of $4,800 for "car depreciation." The $4,800 isn't spent, though; it's put in the bank or in an investment to await the day you'll eventually need it to replace the car. The next year the car depreciates another thirty percent, and the budget includes a depreciation expense of $3,360 under transportation ($11,200 x 30 percent = $3,360).

After five years, you're ready to trade in the old heap. Your depreciation table has marked its residual value down to $2,689 and you've put $13,311 away in the bank to replace it. The dealer consults his blue book and offers a trade-in of $2,600. Actually he offers $1,300, but he'll settle for $2,600 if that's what the book says it's worth. The trade-in value, plus the saved "depreciation expenses," gives you the $16,000 you need to replace the old clunker with a new clunker. Yes, yes, I know — I forgot inflation. The old clunkers might have cost $16,000, but the new ones cost several thousand more. True, but meanwhile your replacement fund has been building up over the last five years in investments that pay interest. So the replacement fund has been inflating too, as has the resale value of the used clunker. Although depreciated to $2,689 on the books, inflation will have increased its dollar value, too. With a bit of luck you'll come out even.

Method 3. In principle, from a budgeting point of view, borrowing to pay for expensive items is very similar to saving for them, as in Method 2. The cost is spread out over several years. The major difference, of course, is that the bank does it for you and you're paying interest rather than earning it. You've borrowed the money to buy the clunker and are paying it off in installments. Each payment provides the bank its interest and a little something to reduce the balance owed until the whole thing is paid. Your transportation budget will include all the monthly payments for the year. Rather than showing a single lump-sum purchase, the budget will show the expense of being spread out evenly over the life of the loan.

How you record these expenses in the family budget is up to you. You'll likely have a mixture of several different methods, depending on the nature of the item and your resources at the time. The cost of your house may appear as a regular debt (mortgage payments), the car as a replacement fund, and that big holiday as a lump sum "special" expense. Mostly you'll want to avoid losing sight of the big costs that may be creeping up without notice in the budget. You may, for example, be cruising along on $4,000 a year for transportation. The budget balances with plenty left over, so you decide to raid the savings and buy a bigger house. Then the following year the car needs replacing and suddenly the transportation expenses jump to $16,000 to include a new car — more than the resources can stand. A budget like that isn't of much use for planning. Pick the budgeting method that's most convenient, but don't double-count and don't lose sight of the big expenses that might not happen every year.

Making Guesses

When you've accounted for all the things that you *know* will happen in the coming year, make some guesses as to what other changes are *likely* to occur. It's a pretty safe bet, for instance, that prices will be going up. Take a stab at predicting price increases by category. If, for example, the cost of living has been bumping up at a steady two percent per year, that can be a general guide. But everything doesn't go up at the average rate. The mortgage payments are usually fixed for a period of time and may not be due to go up at all for the next few budgets. Gas and heating oil may be going up at a faster rate than the average cost-of-living increase. Food and clothing may move up more slowly.

But don't worry about being too scientific; this is the place for some common-sense guessing. Economists try to be scientific about such predictions and they are about as accurate as the weather report. Don't waste your time being fussy . . . you're going to be wrong regardless. Close is good enough.

Figure 2: Sample Budget

Item	Week	Month	Year	Special	Total
Food:					
groceries	105				5,460
office lunches	26				1,300
coffee breaks	10				520
eating out		110			1,320
freezer beef (eliminate)					xxx
cheap freezer cuts					175
				Total Food:	**$8,755**
Housing:					
mortgage		600			7,200
property tax			3,060		3,060
repairs				510	510
heat			1,030		1,030
electricity		30			360
water			65		65
insurance			920		920
maintenance		50			600
				Total Housing:	**$13,745**
Transportation:					
gas	21				1,092
car payments		260			3,120
insurance			920		920
maintenance			368		368
new battery				75	75
Florida vacation (Feb)				1,800	1,800
bus pass (Sept-May)		60			540
				Total Transportation:	**$7,915**
Clothing:					
mother			585		585
father			435		435
child			370		370
child			365		365
				Total Clothing:	**$1,755**

Item	Week	Month	Year	Special	Total
Health:					
insurance			1,850		1,850
drugs		18			216
dental checks			370		370
				Total Health:	**$2,436**
Other:					
telephone		32			384
cable TV		22			264
new carpet				950	950
furniture (eliminate)					xxx
charity			200		200
movies		35			420
birthday party			100		100
wine	10				520
subscriptions			48		48
life insurance			500		500
retirement plan		100			1,200
gifts			800		800
				Total Other:	**$5,386**

Miscellaneous Expenses ($2096 last year, plus 2% inflation)	2,138

Expenses withheld from pay:

income tax	9,100
unemployment	620
recreation	120
company pension	900
government pension	1150
Total Withheld:	**$11,890**
Savings:	**$680**

Total Expenses: $54,700

Income:

full-time salary	36,500
part-time salary	17,000
sell boat (May)	1,200

Total Family Income: $54,700

The initial arithmetic showed expenses exceeding income by $155. Rather than borrow to cover the deficit, our sample family amended the budget by eliminating any new furniture purchases for next year, and by replacing the freezer beef with cheaper cuts. Those two steps would reduce planned expenses by $875, or $680 more than they needed. They then decided to put the $680 into savings, just in case another unforeseen expense (like last year's broken tooth) happens. Now the budget "balances" at $54,700.

You will be able to correct your guess work at the end of the year. After living with a budget for a year, compare the amounts actually spent with those you predicted. Were the differences due to inflation? Changed circumstances — your mother-in-law moved in? Decreased needs — you grew a garden? Increased needs — you took up smoking? After a few years of trial and error, estimating gets a lot more accurate.

The Income Side

When all the costs are more or less projected, amended, and inflated for the year ahead, it's almost time to sneak a peek at the balance. Unless you're a politician hooked on deficit spending, you'll want to see if the income will cover the outgo.

The budget, of course, is concerned with *next* year's income, so start with your basic salary. Add any upcoming raises, bonuses, or overtime pay that you can confidently predict.

Income can be expressed in either gross or net terms, whichever may be more useful for you. Net income, or take-home pay, is easier. The comparison between household expenses and take-home pay is useful and direct. The net income approach does, however, ignore all of those big payroll deductions that really should be seen as "expenses." Deductions for the pension plan, unemployment, medical insurance and even income taxes can sometimes be changed for your benefit. But you might have to take the initiative. It may be easier to take control of those decisions by thinking of them as "expenses" and putting them in the budget. If you want to look at *all* your expenses in the budget, use the gross income figure, and list taxes and other deductions as expenses.

If you do it right, the result will be the same for either the gross or net approach. What you gain by putting in the larger figure for gross income, you must also lose by counting payroll deductions as expenses. It sounds like a shell game with algebra — now you see it, now you don't. But seeing the extra income and expense, however fleeting, is a useful part of making money decisions, and that, after all, is what budgets are all about. This, in fact, is what led our own family to early retirement. By budgeting with the gross income method, we saw that our biggest expense was income tax. It was clear then and there that the most effective way to cut the cost of living was to cut down on our taxable incomes!

So What If It Doesn't Balance?

Now compare the income figure with the total of estimated expenses. Remember to include the "miscellaneous" figure in the expense estimates. If income equals expenses, *you've been cheating*. That comes later. At this point there's bound to be a difference. Let's start with the good news and assume that the difference is positive — that income will be greater than expenses. We'll call the difference *savings*, knowing very well that it may not end up in the bank or mattress. It's an advantage that exists only on paper.

This is at once the most difficult and most enjoyable part of budgeting. So far the expenses are mostly straight projections of last year's performance. The savings give you some extra choices. Now's the time to make a list of all those things you've talked about doing *if and when*. It's time to make choices. The choices have to have costs attached, and if you're normal, the "wish list" will cost a great deal more in total than the size of the savings will allow.

Budget balancing is a matter of deciding what is most important to you. You may even decide that the best thing to do with the savings is to save them. Whether it's another expense, true savings, or investment of another sort, when the decisions have been made on disposal of the surplus, list the new costs on the chart. Now it should "balance." That is, the total expenses plus savings should equal the income.

Balancing the budget isn't quite as much fun when the difference is negative. That is, when the first summing-up shows that expenses projected for the coming year will be greater than the estimated income. The process, however, is the same. Expenses have to be reviewed and decisions have to be made about the relative importance of each expense — what can be eliminated or reduced — until you cut down to match the total income.

Obviously some expenses, the mortgage payments for instance, cannot be arbitrarily reduced. Others can be eliminated only by increasing other expenses. Cutting out the freezer beef, for example, will likely mean the grocery bill will go up. It might not go up by the same amount, particularly if you switch to cheaper cuts or substitute more vegetables for meat, but you must recognize that some reductions will have offsetting costs in other areas.

When expenses have been trimmed to match the income figure, then the budget is said to be in balance. It should resemble, in form at least, the sample budget (Figure 2). Notice the differences between the "budget" format and the "sample expense record" in Figure 1. The "special" items have all changed. Most of the regular expenses have been inflated. The important difference, however, is in what happens to the total. When we recorded actual expenses, the difference between income and outgo was used to calculate "miscellaneous expenses." In contrast, the budget exercise (Figure 2) already has a figure for "miscellaneous." Now the gap between income and expenses has to be accommodated by changing the estimates. In the example, freezer beef and furniture were eliminated, while cheaper meat and some savings were added so that the amended total expenses would match the total family income of $54,700.

Now What?

Now that you've got a budget, what the heck do you do with the thing? Actually, the most important purpose has probably already been served. If you've worked your way right through the exercise, you now at least know where all that money goes. It's amazing how many people haven't the vaguest notion how it disappears so quickly.

The budget is a marvelous means of self-assessment. Knowing exactly where the money goes is the most graphic way to determine whether your spending choices have been good ones, where and by how much your needs can be trimmed to meet your means and whether, at this rate, you can survive on your salary. Can you *hope* to survive without your salary?

The budget is also a planning tool. By setting out what you'll need and what you'll have ahead of time, there is time to make the adjustments, think out problems and look for the best solutions — not necessarily the quickest ones. A large part of this planning function is what businesspeople refer to as *cash flow* considerations. In a nutshell, that means it's not enough to have the cash, you must have it when you need it. Look at the sample budget again. The Joneses' funds are in balance for the year. But that holiday trip in February is going to take $1,800 that they won't have to spare until they sell the boat in May. They have a cash flow problem. Better to plan around that now than to realize it in February when it's too late to get the deposit back or switch to a summer holiday.

If you were setting up a business budget you would probably want a more careful cash-flow plan, dating expenses and receipts and plotting them over the year to see that there was always enough to cover the bills. For most family budgets, though, it is enough to check the big items or special expenses and see *when* they will occur. Christmas gifts, for example, are in November and December. By then you will have set aside the required amount automatically from paychecks through the year — not by joining a club or opening a special account but by showing it in the budget, spending only what you've budgeted for, and leaving any surplus to accumulate. That surplus has been budgeted for gifts. By the end of the year the entire amount will have accumulated in your account.

Budgets Have Their Drawbacks Too

For those of us who get squinty-eyed and cranky at the very thought of spending an evening with pages of little numbers, a budget isn't something we do unless we have to. Let's face it, budgeting is right down there with income tax and thank-you letters on the long list of things we would rather put off until tomorrow. That's why I hesitate to even whisper the fact that budgets do have some shortcomings. If the fact that they are boring is reason enough to put them off, will genuine drawbacks, however small, drop them off the end of your priority list along with losing weight and writing to Great-Aunt Bessie? If that's the case, please keep in mind all the positive things that budgets do before you read — and then forget about — the shortcomings.

A budget is a deliberate, self-imposed constraint. To the extent that it limits our frivolous or more negative impulses it serves us well. Being human, though, we do have the occasional positive impulse as well. Constructive urges may not strike as often, but it would be a pity if we let a budget, or any other arbitrary discipline, constrain us from virtue as well as from vice.

How, for example, would a tight conserver budget accommodate some fantastic bargain on the whatsits that the family won't need for another year or two? *Opportunity buying* for future needs is a legitimate long-term money saver for any smart shopper. So, what gets violated — good sense or this year's budget? Obviously, good sense should prevail. The question is how to break the news to the budget. There are really only two ways: make room in this year's budget by chopping something else, or extend the budget over a longer period. If you were going to buy the whatsits next year anyway, a two-year budget would include the cost. Looking at these upper limits over the longer period may show that there will be an overall saving by taking advantage of the bargain now. Do, however, keep the potential cash flow problems in mind. Spending income before you've earned it, bargain or no bargain, is a shortcut to trouble.

Finally, a budget is a poor respecter of good intentions. Like harsh medicine, it won't do you any good if you can't keep it down. The budget is the place for predictions, not for resolutions. Save those for New Year's Eve, and stick with accuracy rather than good intentions for this exercise. If you do manage to cut down on expenses during the year, that's terrific. You'll have a surplus at the end of the year. Invest it or blow it — it's your reward. Then change *next* year's budget to reflect your new, inexpensive lifestyle.

~ 3 ~

Needs

There's a story, supposedly true, that the wife of one wealthy credit card executive proudly does her bit for conservation by ordering her servants to turn off the self-cleaning ovens during the evening period of peak energy demand. It's nice to know that we're all in this together, and the world is certainly a better place for Milady's restraint. But the thoughtful matron also does us a favor by underlining, in more graphic terms than I could ever have imagined, the major premise of this chapter: *need is very much a relative concept.*

Needs Are Relative

Take my relatives for example. The cost of cleaning an oven with electricity rather than elbow grease would have been daunting to say the least. And servants — though it was rumored that we once knew people who knew people who had them — were somewhere in the Cinderella class. A servant with a self-cleaning oven would seem as absurd as a farmer buying food, or a credit card mogul paying cash. If servants didn't clean ovens, what on earth did they do?

We used to be shocked, even embarrassed at times, when the annual "poverty line" was drawn by some all-knowing, and no doubt highly paid, bureaucrat who would pronounce via unquestioning press that "it now costs umpteen thousand dollars for a family of four to live in this country." We never knew whether to feel lucky or poor to realize that we were incapable of existing on our meager incomes, much less of enjoying the comforts and happiness we have. Now we're merely amused. Our needs are simply different from the bureaucrat's. Our needs are different from the poor. Our needs are only what we decide they will be.

The problem is that so few of us bother to define our needs. We accept them, ready-made, from television, peers and advertisers. Letting others determine our needs might be acceptable in a stable, traditional society. It is quite another thing in a dynamic society like ours whose economy is based on obsolescence and growth. North American economists abhor a stable Gross National Product (GNP). Not only must the economy expand continuously, but it must expand rapidly lest we hear wails of *stagnation* and *recession* from industrial leaders. Common sense, the Club of Rome and the second law of thermodynamics all tell us that such continuous expansion is impossible in the long run, but here and now we seem to be stuck with it as a political necessity. Commerce must either continually create new customers, through population growth, for example, or it must persuade each of us to consume more and more each year, whether we need it or not. If we let ourselves be persuaded without resistance, if we don't bother to define our own needs but let society do it for us, then the constant inflation of needs and consumption is inevitable.

There's nothing inherently wrong with progress, with improving our material lives. Increasing consumption may get more difficult as we exhaust cheap energy resources or face demands from the developing world for a fairer sharing — but condemning it is not the purpose of this book. I won't presume to quibble with those who find that more is better. May Ms. Credit Card's servants continue to enjoy clean ovens the easy way, if that's what they really want. But right there lies the real tragedy of the consumer society: the gulf between what so many of us may really want and what we've been persuaded we ought to have.

Not all North Americans aspire to jet-set luxuries, but our aspirations — our material expectations — certainly aren't what they used to be. How many young couples have you known who expected to begin married life where their parents left off? A fully furnished house, a car, and all the trappings that their parents took a lifetime to acquire are seen by the newlyweds as normal, a starting point, something on which to build. High housing prices, job uncertainty, and roller-coaster interest rates put a crimp in that little illusion of birthright, but sadly, the imposition of such realities does not seem to lead as readily as it should to a closer examination of needs and resources. It seems to be leading instead to a new middle-class militancy seething with frustration from what it has been denied. How much healthier would it be if that energy were turned to the question of what we have earned, and what we *really* need?

Experience Tells Us What We Need

Needs are relative to each person's experience and tastes, to time and place. Experience — each individual's material history and environment — is the most obvious arbiter of need. If you were to ask a street urchin in Dacca, or a refugee from African famine about needs, the answer would almost surely be centered on food. Housing of any kind, or decent health care, might be considered as optional comforts. But *need*, to someone facing imminent starvation, is food and water — physical survival. The notion of a North American poverty line — high enough to include plumbing, cable TV and telephone as basic needs — would seem like a cruel joke to someone facing starvation. Self-cleaning ovens wouldn't even be credible.

> **Needs are relative to our experience and tastes, to time and place.**

If your experience has been one of hard work and few comforts then the needs relative to that experience might be more elaborate than mere survival, but still more basic than what most of us take for granted. For over a century, North Americans have felt alternately amused and threatened by the spectacle of new immigrants arriving from poorer countries and — through working at the most poorly paid jobs — quickly amassing capital to buy houses, sponsor relatives and send their kids to college. They seem to succeed so much faster than the natives. In our conceit we too often attribute such success to the superiority of this society. It may, however, have more to do with needs. The immigrant is consuming according to needs established in the old country. Consumption catches up with earnings; and by the next generation they're slogging along with the rest of us, trying to meet the mortgage payments, keeping up with the Visa account, and wondering how the newest wave of immigrants manages to get ahead so fast.

Another of our pioneer diarists, Anne Langton, observed how much better prepared were the workers than the gentry for success on New World homesteads. Those with upper-class experience felt they *needed* carpets, pianos and servants, and wore themselves out trying to lug around and support those encumbrances. Their hard-working servant class, unaccustomed to such frills, got on with clearing the land and succeeded where their "betters," trying to satisfy more complex needs, went broke.

Taste and Circumstance

Needs are also relative to individual tastes and circumstance. Obviously families with children have greater, more complex needs than childless couples. Some people need music in their lives. Others have essential attachments to pets. Illness may demand drugs. And some people are as hooked on space and privacy as others are on neighbors. Any assessment of needs must account for these differences.

Time is also a determinant of needs. Some needs such as food are immediate. Others, like health care, may be equally vital but can be deferred. Warm winter clothing is a periodic need, shelter a constant need. Not every need must be met as soon as it is felt. It is worth money to the conserver to understand the time demands of his needs.

Needs, finally, are relative to place. Living in the country may create a need for a car, but in the city public transport may suffice. U.S. residents may need private hospital or medical insurance that would be provided through the public plan in Canada. Northerners need to heat their homes in winter, while southerners don't.

Looking at the nature of needs is not just an academic exercise; it's a vital process to the conserver. It could help anyone who has to sit down with a budget and decide what they can and cannot afford next year. It doesn't have to be a conscious process. The cartoon character who staggers parched and ragged from the desert may need clothing, food, a ride to town, or a hundred other things. He may not examine the character of his needs, set priorities, and budget his resources, but he knows enough to get a drink before worrying about any of those other things. By knowing the nature of our needs, it's possible to set priorities, budget for them and, most important, decide whether the need can be eliminated more easily than it can be satisfied.

It's an old story, but it still says a great deal about the nature of needs. It's the busy executive from the city who spent two precious weeks each year fishing in one particular northern lake. Each year, he fished with the same local guide, and after twenty years or so of this he was emboldened enough to ask the guide how much he earned. Shocked at the pitiful amount, the businessman offered to find the guide a job in the city paying twice as much. The guide refused. The executive was confounded.

"Why don't you want to better yourself?" he asked.

The guide asked the executive how much he earned.

"And what's the most expensive, most satisfying thing you can buy with all that?" the guide asked.

"My annual fishing trip," was the answer.

"Well, you see, I don't need that much money," the guide replied, happily casting his line across the water.

There is no standard or absolute when it comes to needs. They're related to a whole array of other determinants. That's why it's so ridiculous to talk about a poverty line. Can you imagine creating a corresponding *wealthy line*?

". . . and, finally, the wealthy line has gone up again this year. It now costs $147,241 a year to support the average rich family in North America. The Chamber of Commerce has called for a federal investigation into the cost of being rich, and the Rockefellers have demanded an immediate increase in oil depletion allowances . . ."

Why is that little scenario any more absurd than a poverty line? An amount like $147,241 might seem like poverty to the parents of university students, or to anyone who needs a lawyer and an orthodontist in the same year. On the other hand, working people win that much in lotteries and are driven to drink and nervous breakdowns by such overwhelming wealth.

Incestuous Needs

If needs are determined by all sorts of relevant individual circumstances, then the most relevant determinant of all is *other needs*. Needs themselves are interrelated to a remarkable extent. If there is any law of family spending, it would have to be that meeting any need is bound to create at least three more needs. This concept will be obvious to any parent who has ever bought a battery-operated toy. Other examples abound.

Most North American households, for instance, now feel they need nuclear-powered clothes dryers, hooked into giant utilities and metered for their consumption. But the cost of having a dryer is a great deal more than the cost of the appliance itself and the power to keep it running. The dryer creates other needs. It needs

Meeting any need creates at least three other needs.
••••••••••••

special wiring, extra space, another hole in the wall for venting, special (and expensive) additives to cope with "static cling," fabric softeners and sprays to make the clothes "as fresh as all outdoors." Our poor ancestors managed to get their clothes as fresh as all outdoors by hanging them outdoors, using solar-powered dryers for nothing. Static cling was something you got on the radio. We solved one problem — rainy days — and created half a dozen more that need to be solved with hard-earned cash.

A number of years ago we decided to join the modern world by discarding our old hand pump in favor of pipes and an electric pump to bring water on demand. In the first month of modern living the labor-saver pump spent three days in the repair shop while we hauled water from town (plumbing was to save us from hauling it from the well by the back door). Then lightning storms and errant cars knocked out the wires that power the pump on what seemed like a daily basis — and always at bath time. Leaky pipes, balky taps, and threats of underground freezing all left us wondering if it was the unmixed blessing we welcomed so uncritically. We decided to resurrect the old hand pump. It, at least, was reliable enough to deliver water no matter what the weather, and the only mechanical failure was a broken handle — solved with the help of a nearby locust limb in ten minutes flat. There is nothing wrong with indoor plumbing; 360 days a year it's terrific. But we do know now that it takes more to have indoor plumbing than a pump and some pipes. The labor-saver has appetites and demands of its own.

For most of us, there's no going back to the simple life where needs are basic and easily met. It's an idyll and perhaps an ideal, but modern comforts, once known, are not that easy to discard. Even Thoreau, whose *Walden* is synonymous with simple needs, moved back to town after two years at the pond. "Simplify, simplify," was Thoreau's motto. But, in the long run, there wasn't enough at Walden Pond to satisfy his more complex needs.

If it is neither possible nor particularly desirable to stem all of our expensive modern appetites, it is at least worthwhile to work at controlling them. And the key to that process is to recognize the difference between the needs we accept for ourselves and the needs that are created by the things we accumulate around us. We might need clean, dry clothing, for example. It's the electric dryer that needs anti-static agents, a forty-dollar-an-hour repairperson, and a nuclear reactor to keep it going.

If spending money is a matter of making choices, it's axiomatic that we can make better choices if we're more consciously aware of how our needs arise and whose needs they really are.

Examining Needs

Whenever we set out to spend money to satisfy some need or another, we go through a fairly rigorous examination of just what we're doing and why. It's not a formal process, and it isn't exactly the same for every purchase. Much of the process is automatic and internalized. We ask the questions without thinking about them. It is, for us, simply the way we behave as consumers. If I describe the process of examining needs in some detail, it's not because the process is complex. It's the individual needs and situations themselves that are complex. The process of examination may take some time at first, especially if you're not already a natural skeptic of commercial blandishments. You may have to consciously reach for reasons to keep your wallet unopened, but once the habit is formed, you'll find that saying NO to the salesperson isn't really that difficult or time-consuming. The process of examining needs is based on six simple questions:

1. What's the problem?

2. Who needs it?

3. What would change the need?

4. How long will it last?

5. What are the alternatives?

6. What are the costs?

1. What's the Problem?

The usual consumer response to a problem is not to look at the problem, but to look at the solution — the normal, expensive, commercial solution. Consumers say, "We need a new car," when they ought to be saying, "We need a means of getting to work, getting out of town on weekends and to the in-laws at Christmas." The answer may well turn out to be a new car, but if you're going to start with the solution instead of the problem you'll never find out if there might be other, less expensive answers. One young couple I know asked themselves that very question, and by examining the true nature of the need, realized that they didn't need a car at all. Now they take the bus to work, take taxis for evenings out, and rent a car for weekends out of town. They're dollars ahead and no longer have to worry about parking spaces, repair bills, and having "one for the road" at parties. That's not everybody's solution, but it suits them. More important, it's a solution that never would have occurred to them if they had accepted the obvious solution and bought a car like everyone else.

The process begins with asking, "What is the problem? What objective must be accomplished? What function has to be performed?" What you need to buy (the solution) is the end of the examination, not the beginning. *We begin by asking what needs to be done.*

My long-suffering mate, having brought one baby through the diaper years with no more than an outdoor pump and a clothesline, finally raised the question of an automatic dryer. I was surprised, mostly because she, herself, had always resisted the notion of a dryer. The high temperatures were hard on the clothes; moreover, she preferred the smell and feel of clothes dried in the fresh air and sunshine.

"The problem," she said, "is the winter. The wash takes two or three days to dry outside when the weather is cold and damp. The kids are running out of clean clothes for school. I still prefer the clothesline, but — in winter we need a dryer."

We stopped right there and backed up one step. "Do we need a dryer or do we need dry clothes?" I asked.

"Dry clothes," she agreed, "but they have to dry faster."

"Would they have to dry faster if we had more clothes? Is there anything wrong with leaving the wash on the line for two to three days in bad weather — as long as nobody runs out of clothes?"

As the one who balances the checkbook, she hit me with the standard family line, "Can we afford all those extra clothes?" And so we took an inventory. It turned out that with less than $100 worth of extra clothing, nobody would run out of anything if the washing took a few more days to freeze itself dry in a snowstorm. By looking at the problem instead of accepting the usual solution, we saved hundreds of dollars and made everybody happy. *We examined the need in terms of the objective, not the solution.*

Examine the need in terms of the objective, not the solution.
• • • • • • • • • • • •

I should warn you though, that this approach drives salespeople frantic. I have a lot of respect for the poor retailer, and really hate to ruin anyone's day, but it often comes to that when a conserver shopper meets a high-pressure salesperson. There was, for instance, the day we bought the mattress. We found the one we wanted, tried it out, and were down to discussing the price.

"The price is $X for the mattress and the box spring."

"We like a hard bed."

"Of course," said the salesman, "it's much better for the back. We have a box spring that's so firm, you'd think you had a piece of plywood under the mattress. Just the thing for health-conscious people like yourselves."

"We'll take the piece of plywood."

"Ha. Ha. Ha."

"We're serious."

"You need a box spring."

"No, we don't. We need to support the mattress firmly."

"That's what a box spring does," he argued, still smiling but with a telltale flush of red creeping up his neck.

"So does a piece of plywood."

"What's the difference?"

"Two hundred bucks."

We finished our shopping at the lumber yard. It wasn't the solution the salesman wanted, but it fulfilled the functional need.

Not long ago I was listening to a gardening expert field questions on a radio phone-in show. The caller had a stump that she wanted to get rid of. "What can I *buy*," she asked the expert, "that will dissolve the stump?" Following her cue, he responded by suggesting several ready-made commercial solutions (with appropriate warnings about keeping kids and pets away from the treated stump). If the woman had asked, "What will make a stump disappear?" instead of, "What can I buy?" he might have thought to tell her that stumps, made of wood, will rot all by themselves, and that they will rot away even faster if surrounded by moisture, air, and helpful bacteria that come free from the earth and from other rotting vegetation. Knowing this, our early pioneers, surrounded by the stumps left from clearing land, heaped leaves and other organic "garbage" over the stumps and planted squash in the rotting molds. Here in the midst of dead elm country we have the same problem as the woman who asked, "What can I buy . . . ?" We, however, have followed the lead of unlettered homesteaders instead of professional gardening experts, and get rid of our stumps by growing pumpkins on them — worth $1 apiece at Halloween — rather than buying ready-made solutions. It has a lot to do with how you ask the question. "What will perform the function?" leads to more interesting, and cheaper, answers than, "What do I *need to buy*?"

2. Who Needs It?

The process of examining needs gets downright introspective at times. When you begin to ask why you *need* to buy a particular thing, or better still, ask why you *want* to buy a particular thing, the answers can reveal more about yourself than about the state of the economy or the cost of living.

It's just possible that some of us, some of the time, are influenced in what we think we need by those around us whom we respect, admire, or wish to emulate. There's nothing profound in that observation. That's why advertisers use movie stars and athletes to shill their goods. The fashion industry lives by that urge to emulate. They count on us wanting to emulate not only the beautiful people but also each other. Now advertisers have twigged to the idea that it's not even necessary to tell us that Mr. and Mrs. Rich-and-Famous use Acme soap, drive an Acme car or drink Acme beer. It's sufficient to tell us that Mr. and Mrs. Average Jones down the street are doing it: "For five years now, Average and the boys have been getting together to shine their Acme cars and quaff a few Acme ales."

There's nothing inherently wrong with emulation. Self-improvement is a fairly healthy urge. And maybe the Joneses really are the most tasteful people on the block and the neighborhood would be a better place if everyone dressed, looked, and acted just like them. Maybe. But then maybe the Joneses' ostentatious lifestyle has brought them to the verge of bankruptcy and they're waving good-bye to their repossessed Acme car and wishing they were solvent like everyone else on the block. Maybe. The point is that in spite of industrial America's urge to have us all keeping up with the biggest spenders on the block, some of us are not yet convinced that the Joneses have all the answers.

Children are perhaps the most gullible conformists. Perhaps it's because they're so busy learning everything else by emulation that they conform to our superficial tastes and habits as well. Our six-year-old, for instance, loved dessert. You could get him to do just about anything but clean his room by promising to give or withhold dessert. It was the ultimate weapon — until he figured out that, in fact, he didn't really like dessert at all. When it was awarded, he never finished it. It was greeted with frantic applause and giggling, and then it sat there virtually untasted while he went off to more interesting things. In fact, it was his big sister who loved dessert, and what he really wanted was to be just like her. She set the fashion.

Fashion is a neutral term, though. There are good fashions and bad fashions, just as there are traits in others we could very well emulate. What then, does fashion mean to the conserver? It means two things really: *obsolescence and the creation of artificial needs.* Obsolescence, planned and programmed, is a fact of our commercial lives. I needn't belabor you with tales of light bulbs that are designed to burn out, cars that are built to disintegrate, and children's snowsuits that are fiendishly made to last just slightly less than one winter. Not only are they predestined never to become hand-me-downs, but the intent is also obviously to ensure that each child needs *two* to get through the winter. This sort of structural obsolescence is well-known to every frustrated consumer and is well documented in most consumer guides. What is

Fashion means obsolescence and the creation of artificial needs.
• • • • • • • • • • • •

not so well-understood, however, is the link between obsolescence and fashion.

Fashion is obsolescence through changing tastes and preferences, persuading us to buy replacements, not because the old ones wore out, but because they're no longer in vogue. Skirts get shorter and longer, ties get wider and narrower, and woe betide anyone caught in last year's model. Did you ever notice, though, that those things that don't change by the dictate of fashion never seem to wear out? It seems easy enough to build durability into those goods that changing fashions will render obsolete. It's only where fashion doesn't apply that structural obsolescence is required to ensure that we have to buy some more.

If light bulbs could be made to change their shape and size each season, and we had to replace them to be socially acceptable, then they might be made to last for years. And who would spend an extra eighty bucks to get a fashionable snowsuit for junior? You just need something to keep him dry, right? Snowsuit fashions couldn't be sold to most parents, so they have to be made with structural obsolescence built in.

Cars used to be made to last. Sturdy frames, wrinkle-free bumpers, and panels that took a decade to rust. But then they had fins and chrome and stylish features that had to be changed each year for fashion's sake. When buyers began to ignore the fashionable style changes, the makers had to ensure that if fashion wouldn't bring them back to the showrooms then rust would have to do the trick. Structural obsolescence seems to have replaced car fashions.

Look again, however, at the goods that fashion does change. They are the ones that don't need to have structural obsolescence built in. They last forever. When is the last time you wore out a necktie? And a Nehru suit, like a diamond, is forever.

Real conservers are impervious to the dictates of fashion, but are victims, nevertheless, of planned obsolescence. They may not change their ties to match the current width, but their light bulbs will burn out like everyone else's. Knowing, however, that fashionable goods are discarded because of style rather than wear, they can often find the best value by deliberately seeking out-of-fashion bargains.

Conservers, examining their needs or reaching for their wallet, ask themselves: "Whose need is it — mine or the Joneses?" By ignoring artificial needs created by fashion and emulations, conservers concentrate their money on the things that are really important to them — not on the straw men set up by the electronic snake oil peddlers. From the day my son understood this simple concept, he was never again suckered into anything with the promise of dessert.

Some years ago, Grandmother was cleaning out her ragbag, cutting up wool for a rug she was making. She pulled out a heavy camel hair coat gleaned from a rich and distant cousin's discards. There was absolutely nothing wrong with the coat, except that camel hair and narrow lapels were just a year passé. Over protests, I salvaged the intended rug and wore it simply because it was delightfully warm. I wore it for thirty years. It was indestructible. And, in at least two years out of those thirty, my coat was back in fashion! At least I presumed it was back in fashion; those were the years when acquaintances would admire and marvel that I could afford such a wonderful coat. In the other twenty-eight years, I got sympathy and was treated to coffee a lot. All that mattered to me, though, is that for thirty years the coat fulfilled my need perfectly. It didn't always meet others' criteria of what a coat should be, but distinguishing clearly between their needs and mine saved the cost of thirty years of topcoats.

3. What Would Change the Need?

Conservers are self-directed people. As such, they never accept that things must remain as they are. They can arrange and rearrange their lives in ways that make sense to them. Needs, then, are never wholly given; they are set in response to other variables. In other words, a conserver examining needs looks not only at the need itself, but also questions whether the need would be the same under other circumstances.

The need for warm winter clothing, for example, is not an absolute, but might disappear if the conserver decided to move far enough south. A conserver who needs a lawnmower also calculates that if he dug up the grass and grew vegetables instead, the need for the lawnmower would change. A heating bill can be lowered not only by shopping for the cheapest source of fuel, but also by insulating and caulking, issuing sweaters and living at cooler temperatures, closing off little-used parts of the house, and so on.

Changing technology plays a role. Mail, for example, used to be the mainstay of family and business communication. But the need was communication, not mail. When the telephone company wanted $3,000 to hook us up to a party line, we declined and lived without a phone. Seven years later, when the price had dropped to $300, we took the hook-up but still used mail in preference to expensive long-distance calls. When the price of a stamp rose to forty-three cents and late-night long distance fell to thirty-four cents, we switched to the newer, cheaper alternative. Now that modems have become cheaper than voice or fax transmission, we've gone back to typing our messages in e-mail. We don't really need a stamp, a telephone or a modem. What we do need is an efficient means of communicating. And technology will continue to change the answer to that need.

4. How Long Will It Last?

Needs change with time. When we examine needs we not only have to ask *what* is needed, but also *when* and for *how long*. Will time make the need more acute, or will delay allow the need to abate?

Asking *when* a need must be satisfied is an essential part of planning purchases, as we have seen in the budget chapter. The purpose is not only to plan expenditures for when money is available, but to plan them for times when the price is right. End-of-season clearances, annual sales, and just plain lucky finds, all make waiting worthwhile (more on seasonal buys in chapter 9). Waiting makes any new technology less expensive. And waiting leaves more time for comparison shopping. Considering the time frame of any need is another way of asking yourself, "How long can we put this off?"

Some needs disappear whether you satisfy them or not. Knowing for how long you may require something does occasionally provide an excuse to let procrastination do it for you. Most young families, for instance, feel the need for extra space — room to relax without sitting on sticky toys. At that stage, I know it seems improbable, but the day does come when the house is empty and parents are trying to talk the youngsters into staying home for a change. The house eventually gets more spacious whether you added the extra room or not. I'm not suggesting that such needs are less important than the ones that don't go away, but knowing that the difficulties are only temporary can affect what you decide to do about it. It's a little bit like a snowstorm in March. Shoveling out the driveway becomes a lower priority when you know it's going to melt soon anyway.

Checking the time frame is especially important for those needs that arise from your nonhuman dependents: the car, the house, the TV set, and so on. Unlike we immortals, those things have finite lives and we have to judge their needs against some measure of their remaining usefulness. Consider, for example, the driver of an eight-year-old car on the day her friendly neighborhood mechanic tells her that her clunker needs a new battery. Now anybody driving an eight-year-old car is part conserver to start with. As such, she might have expected her clunker to live another two years. Everybody in such a pickle winces at the thought of parting with a hundred bucks for a brand-new battery. But the conserver does more than wince or give up on the clunker in disgust. The conserver will likely need a battery for only two more years. She knows she doesn't need a new battery — she needs a quarter of a battery. Even the cheapest new battery is made to last longer than the clunker. So the conserver gets a used battery from a wreck, from the junkyard, or from a less careful consumer who has just worn out another clunker with a perfectly good battery in it.

We're unlikely to ever be so calculating with human needs, but when our *things* need things, it's useful to number their days before deciding on the best way to meet the need.

5. What Are the Alternatives?

By this point, anybody who has subjected a need to such rigorous examination can't help but have an obvious solution or two in mind. The marketplace makes it so easy to think of things that will meet our needs that it takes some effort now to blank out the obvious solutions and spend a little time trying to think of less obvious ways to meet the objective or fulfill the function.

It's a mini version of brainstorming, if you like. The faster the ideas come, the better. If they get a little absurd, don't worry, you can weed out the nonsense later. The important thing is to keep the initial problem in mind, and not waste time trying to think of things that are substitutes for the standard commercial solution.

We use a wood stove in a place where, for safety's sake, the wall must be shielded from the heat. It's a common problem and most wood stove dealers also sell heat shields. Most are simply a sheet of noncombustible material (usually metal or ceramic) mounted on insulated fasteners an inch or so from the wall. Decent ones cost eighty dollars and up. Even the ugly ones were beyond our resources, and so we had a closer look at the need. As long as we were thinking of heat shields, all that came to mind were variations of what we had seen in the shops, and so we went back to the functions that had to be fulfilled. What we needed — functionally — was a sheet of non-combustible material and some insulated mountings. The mountings were easy. A little brainstorming came up with the ten-cent ceramic insulators used for electric fencing. And since we were then down to looking merely for a sheet of non-combustible material (preferably attractive), the answer came soon enough. Within a week I'd found a pile of antique ceiling tin at an auction. We only needed a couple of pieces, but had to buy the whole pile for two dollars. The total cost of the heat shield was $2.40. The leftover tin will eventually make more heat shields for presents or profit.

Finding alternative solutions brings out the inventor in people. It's one of the things that makes surviving a challenge. It means that we're constantly involved in examining processes, functions, and the way things around us work. It's no accident that the best survivor in my acquaintance is in fact a scientist, a freelance scientist no less. He and his wife live and work in a van, traveling about the continent from contract to contract, consulting, building, fixing, lecturing, and yes, inventing. At last report they had gleaned and stored a year's supply of food in the van. It meant that they stopped for a summer to grow a pig and a garden on borrowed land, and spent some time during the rest of the year gathering wild foods. They practically lived off the fat of the land for that year. In other years, when he lived alone (sort of) in a smaller van, our inventor friend would stop occasionally on his way through town and ask if we were using the shower. Then he'd bring in his soap and towel and lather up — his alternative to plumbing.

The amateur inventor is bound, of course to make mistakes. Since the object is to avoid the pains of commerce, the mistakes are usually cheap ones; they can, however, be more serious at times. There was, for instance, the summer I decided that the most efficient way to shower was to take a cake of soap out into the rain. It was cheaper than plumbing and a whole lot easier than trying to squeeze my bony frame into the old-fashioned, round tin tub. Waiting for the rain was a great alternative, and all went well until the day my soapy aria was interrupted by a crescendo of thunder overhead. I froze, one foot raised like a stalking heron and peeked, one-eyed, through a lather of hair, at the distance between me and the back door. And then — with a crash — there appeared a thick white line, arcing from the nearest puddle to the end of my upraised toe. I broke the world's record for the one-legged fifty-yard dash for naked men with soap in their eyes. The reek of smoking toe and ozone turned the air as blue as my oaths, swearing I was through with crazy ideas.

The next crazy idea was to put a fifty-gallon barrel of water on the roof where the sun could warm it. A garden hose from the barrel gave us hot running water in an outdoor shower. Being solar-powered, it didn't work so well on cloudy days, of course. But then, it was a long, long time before I could bring myself to remove my boots on cloudy days, anyway.

Not all of our crazy ideas and money-saving inventions are that out-landish, and certainly not all of them work. Enough of them have worked, however, that a pause to consider alternative solutions is an automatic part of any purchasing decision.

6. What Are the Costs?

By now, you should have some alternatives in mind, as well as an obvious commercial solution or two. The next step is to compare the cost of each of the several ways of meeting the need. Establishing cost goes beyond the initial price, however. For most material purchases, there is also the useful life to consider (how long is this thing going to last?). In effect, then, you are looking at the *annual* cost of a dryer compared to a clothesline, the annual cost of a home encyclopedia (remember they get out of date) compared to the cost of hooking up to the Internet or taking X-number of trips to the library per year, or the annual cost of one good pair of shoes compared to several cheaper ones that wear out faster. The initial price, divided by the expected life, gives an annual cost that makes it easier to compare apples to oranges — easier to compare the obvious commercial solution to the crazy alternative you just dreamed up.

On big items, you might want to make the comparison even more realistic by including the possible resale value. Comparing the cost of a car, for instance, with the cost of taking buses and cabs, would mean starting with the initial cost of the car, deciding how long you plan to keep it — let's say, five years — subtracting the resale value of a five-year-old car from the initial price, then dividing that *net* cost by five to arrive at the annual cost of owning the car.

If you plan to actually drive the car, you'll also have to add operating costs such as gas, oil, insurance, repairs, parking, tolls, and so on. These operating costs are so often overlooked that it's little wonder consumers have so many unpleasant surprises at the end of the month. And it isn't just cars either. Nearly everything we own consumes *something*. It's a pity all price tags aren't required to list operating costs along with ingredients. Some appliances are now sold with ratings on energy consumption so we can tell, for example, that the frost-free refrigerator consumes up to fifty percent more electricity than the ordinary model. Even the furniture consumes cleaning materials. It's part of the cost of owning something. And, no, this is not being picayune.

Consider something as innocent as a pet. Unless you want a pedigree, pets are free. In fact, if you're not careful, your neighbors will leave their unwanted kittens on your doorstep. But they do come with certain "operating" costs: shots, de-worming pills, flea collars, and (unless you want to be the doorstep depositor) neutering. Then there's food, grooming, kennel fees (in case you want to go away), and obedience training or claw clipping so they don't tear the house to shreds. Or the cost of separate accommodation if obedience training won't keep them off the couch. With the operating costs added in, there are few things more expensive than a "free" puppy.

There's one more cost that is harder to put a number on. That's your own time — the time it takes to cope with all the new problems the solution brings. If a car is the answer to your transportation problems, consider the time you spend waiting in the garage while they fix the faulty whatsit, the time you spend washing it, the time you spend stuck in traffic jams, and the cold winter mornings when you can't get the damned thing started. All the maintenance, extra problems, aggravations and frustration that are part of owning *anything* should be considered as part of the cost.

With all of these costs in mind, we can at last make some reasoned judgment as to which alternative solution may best meet the need. In fact, one of the most useful results of such a thorough examination of needs is that finding out the *real* cost of all the solutions often shocks us into asking what would be the cost of *not* meeting the need. Would life with this unfulfilled need be any more difficult or unpleasant than it would be with the extra problems brought on by the solution?

My favorite fishing partner decided one summer that paddling the canoe was altogether too much like work. So he got a motor, and all the tools, gas cans, mountings, and other paraphernalia to make it go. The motor had to be cleaned, tuned, tested, hauled around, and stored. And, instead of pausing only to dig a can of worms, fishing trips had to be planned and started earlier. Packing the motor and all of its needs was only slightly less pleasant than humping all the mechanical gear through the bushes and over the bank to the lake. Then it had to be mounted, hooked up, and started — and usually restarted halfway across the lake. We were working harder at the solution than we ever were at the problem. When I suggested that we switch to river fishing and let the current move us along, he readily agreed — and I haven't seen the motor since.

Thoreau, who exhorted us all to "simplify," was at his best when scorning the human urge to own things:

> I see young men, my townsmen, whose misfortune it is to have inherited farms, houses, barns, cattle, and farming tools; for these are more easily acquired than got rid of ... They have got to live a man's life, pushing all these things before them, and get on as well as they can. How many a poor immortal soul have I met well-nigh crushed and smothered under its load, creeping down the road of life, pushing before it a barn 75 feet by 40, its Augean stables never cleansed, and 100 hundred acres of land, tillage, mowing, pasture, and wood-lot.

The examination of needs, then, ends not with the question of, "Do I really *need* it?" but with a more introspective note: "Given all the aggravation, do I really *want* it?"

There's bit of consumer in all of us, though, and we regularly decide that, yes, there are things we need and want and, yes, we are going to pay the costs. The best things in life may be free, but we do need some of the other things, too. What then?

Procrastinate

What then? Nothing. We do nothing. Not for a while anyway. Mind you, there's some discord on this point, and my excuse about the stores being closed or pressing business elsewhere aren't always received with good grace and understanding. My wife says I'm just a plain old procrastinator. When pressed for action, I will often go so far as to put it on the list: "Things We Need." The next time the matter is raised I can be goaded into transferring it to another list: "Things We Need Right Away!" Rarely do we go right out and buy whatever it is we've decided we need.

Procrastination has several effects, all of them profitable. The most common is that eventually we decide we don't really need it after all. Or we forget about it (losing lists periodically helps), which is simply a less conscious way of deciding we didn't really need it after all. Some needs, however, are even more enduring than my capacity to put them off. They survive for months on lists. Sooner or later, we see just what we were looking for on sale, or at an auction, or in somebody else's castoffs. The longer we can put it off, the more likely we are to get it for less than we had planned on.

Procrastination has several effects, all of them profitable.
• • • • • • • • • • • •

Anybody who bought a pocket calculator, personal computer, VCR, cam-corder, compact disc player or DVD player in the first years these became popular will know from painful experience that they soon became much cheaper. Being the first to have any new product is a costly competition. If it's new technology, let the Joneses buy the first one and pay the most. The first model on the market is not only the most expensive, but is often plagued with the most problems. Procrastinators wait until the price comes down and the bugs are worked out.

It doesn't even have to be high tech. One room in our house has a flagstone floor. In it was a gaping hole that led to a cellar cum pit, wherein resided the pump, a few pipes and a frog or two. Unfortunately, the hole lay right in the path to the coat rack. Since the floor was of stone, the standard wooden door on hinges would be difficult to fit. The junk yards had nothing that would do. Custom-made iron work was much too expensive. We put it on the list of things we need and forgot about it. So did several assorted guests, who disappeared — with some discomfort — down into the frog pit. When a couple of children took the plunge, we moved the trap door onto the list of "Things We Need Right Away," and promptly put it off again. Months later, at a party, someone was describing the horrors of renovating old houses and happened to mention a large iron grate he'd had to rip out of his living room floor. Pressed for details, he remembered hauling it to a dump some five years previous. He even remembered just about where he'd dumped it, which was just about where we found it. It's a perfect fit, a perfect solution, and didn't cost a penny — thanks to procrastination.

Reviewing Needs

No matter how careful we are with the initial decisions on whether and where to spend our money, there are certain expenses that continue on a regular basis. The problem is that circumstances change, and the wisest choices may become money wasters as time goes on. It pays to take up the checkbook occasionally — budget time is a handy occasion — and review the regular expenses that are usually kept up without the close attention they might have received initially.

Insurance is a good example. Cars depreciate quite rapidly, and yet many drivers continue paying "collision" premiums, only to discover that even a minor fender-bender can't be fixed on an older car for less than the "write off" value. Time alone will leave a car over-insured, and leave you paying the bills. On the other hand (though I hesitate to ever advise spending more) remember that household insurance may have to be raised periodically to cover the inflated replacement value of your property.

I once had a student, a single woman in a professional job, who had done well enough that she was on the verge of taking an early retirement in order to travel. She handed in a budget as part of a class assignment, and — to my amazement — she was still spending hundreds of dollars to insure herself against income loss should she become too ill or injured to work. The decision might have been sound when she had family responsibilities and needed the income to survive, but she had failed to review her needs as her other circumstances changed.

The point of this somewhat tortuous examination of needs is neither as difficult nor as academic as it might appear. Not spending money may begin as a difficult exercise, but after a while it gets to be a habit. It becomes as ingrained and natural as smoking cigarettes, reaching for the credit card, or any other habit. At first, you have to think about it. It may even hurt a little, but in time it becomes easier not to spend than it is to spend. Thinking of needs as problems to be solved rather than solutions to be bought leads naturally to alternatives, and to time and cost considerations. It often leads away from the marketplace to a greater use of your own resources. Alternatives usually include the prospect of doing it yourself, doing it for less, or doing without. With a little practice, your own skills and resources — whatever they may be — will become as familiar as the brand-name resources of the marketplace.

Most possessions cause more problems than they solve.
•••••••••••

The critical point is passed when consumers begin to realize that most possessions cause more problems than they solve, that *convenience* is often a nuisance. It was no accident that the flower children of the '60s, the last great wave of anti-material sentiment, were the progeny of the affluent upper-middle class. They had learned from experience that material possessions didn't solve their problems. Flowers and grass didn't solve their problems either, but that's another story.

Most consumers — those of us with kids of our own to raise and grass that only gets high when the lawnmower is broken — have to learn the hard way that what we choose to buy, consume, and own are precisely that: choices! We can learn to say NO as easily as we've learned to say yes. Our needs can be what we say they are. If we need the time to make pottery, grow gardens, or write a novel, that need can be just as valid as the electric knife or the talking-bass-on-a-plaque we might otherwise be tempted to buy with our time. *It's a matter of choice.*

There was a time when we accepted that what we owned defined us. Our stature rose with the grandeur of our possessions. When we discovered that those things didn't always bring us joy, we began to ask ourselves just what we needed — and learned that life can be simpler than we thought.

~ 4 ~

Getting Ready

Just about everybody has days at work when it doesn't seem to be worth the effort, days when you begin to wonder if that's really what you want to do for the rest of your life. My weak moments were always in spring — those first warm days when the sun made a suit too sweaty and prickly for comfort, when I began to plan the garden on the backs of unread memos.

Those were the days for dreaming. And when dreaming was no longer enough, they became days of planning and preparation. Those were the days that made surviving without a salary possible. Thorough preparation is essential to a self-sufficient life. The years of idle afternoons and coffee breaks that we devoted to *getting ready* have paid more dividends than any amount of good luck or meager talent we could muster.

Economic independence, happily, is one of those great leaps that can be made with tiny steps. It takes longer that way than winning the lottery or being born into the proper family, but working at it slowly, over the years, is the only way most of us can make it. Getting ready — mentally, physically, and financially — is the practical way to begin a new lifestyle. It happens gradually, step by tiny step, until finally, one day, the pieces are all put together and you know you can make it on your own.

The alternative, of course, is to move when the impulse strikes. Tell the boss exactly what he's doing wrong, and hope to goodness you can find another way to meet the mortgage payment before the end of the month. There's a lot of visceral satisfaction in following urges spontaneously, but being prepared is easier on the nerves.

Increasingly, "independence" is being imposed from above, with staff reductions, belt-tightening or plant closure. If it hasn't happened yet, the fear that it will happen in the future can be just as chilling. Being prepared to survive without a salary means putting the family finances in order now. Those preparatory steps work just as well for a lay-off as they do for an early retirement. Being laid off isn't as much fun as quitting, but the financial steps to getting ready are the same.

Debts

The biggest obstacle, naturally, is money. And the easiest way around that hurdle is not to make more, but to spend less. The last chapter dealt with reducing needs to minimum levels. That's the most important step, and one that anybody can begin to practice now, but it's certainly not the only step.

Those of us raised with the standard array of middle-class North American appetites usually end up with a raft of financial entanglements that must be rearranged to make self-sufficiency possible. The chief villain here is debt.

Good Debts

It's time to be fair. I don't like it, but I do have to admit that debt sometimes does have advantages. If you're clever, or lucky, or both, it's one way to beat inflation. The principle is really quite simple: *borrow to buy resaleable things whose value is inflating faster than the rate of interest on the debt.* That turns inflation to the borrower's advantage. For example, anybody who borrowed money to buy gold when it was $200 an ounce might have paid 15 percent interest on the debt, but a year later gold was selling for around $400 an ounce. Over that period, it cost the borrower $30 in interest to earn $200 in inflation.

Of course, in the long run, interest rates will never be lower than overall inflation rates. The gnomes of Zurich, or whoever sets the interest rates, will see to that. But, from time to time, certain commodities do inflate faster than interest rates. The housing market has periodically boomed faster than the bankers could raise the mortgage rates. Most people who have bought homes in the right place at the right time have seen their property values rise fast enough to match the interest on the mortgage.

When interest rates are fluctuating, borrowers should do some comparison shopping before deciding what to pay off and when. Take a simple mortgage for instance, locked into a fixed interest rate for several years. During those years, other rates might have changed significantly.

Example: When the Joneses renewed their mortgage four years ago, the rate was five percent, fixed for a five-year term. By now they've whittled the balance down to $60,000. In the meantime, Jones has managed to save $60,000 and is tempted to pay off the mortgage one year early. He checks the alternatives:

1. He can pay off the mortgage now, saving $3,000 in interest payments this year. If the penalty is equal to three months' interest ($750), his net savings will be reduced to $2,250.

2. He can put his $60,000 into a one-year term investment with a 3.5 percent return. This would earn $2,100.

3. He can buy a five-year term investment at five percent, earning $3,000 a year.

On the surface, it appears that he should keep the mortgage debt and invest his money at five percent instead. Both time and the tax collector may change the conclusion, however.

First, taxes. The investment earnings would be taxed, the savings would not. If Jones is in a 25 percent tax bracket, his after-tax earning on the five percent investment is really only $2,250 for the year — the same as paying off the mortgage (to save $2,250). Since he would have to wait five years to get that amount through the term investment, he might be better off paying his mortgage.

However, determining this is more complicated in those places where mortgage interest is deductible. In Jones's bracket the deduction on a $3,000 mortgage interest payment would amount to $750. The loss of that deduction, combined with the penalty for early payment ($750), means that he actually saves only $1,500 by paying off the mortgage early. For the Joneses, the term investment is a better deal — this year. Next year, when the mortgage is up for renewal, the early payment penalty does not apply. If mortgage rates remain at five percent, the Joneses would save $3,000 in mortgage interest and lose a deduction worth $750, for a net saving of $2,250. Next year, without the penalty, they would be further ahead by paying off the mortgage — so they may wish to put their savings into a one-year term investment now, and pay off the mortgage when it comes due.

No, it's not simple. And there are many more investment alternatives than one- and five-year investment certificates. That's why it's important to do the calculations, and re-do them every time interest rates shift. When the cost of a debt is lower than the return on alternative investments, debt is not only defensible, it makes good business sense. But do remember that the comparison must include the effect of taxes, deductions, and penalties.

Leverage

You don't have to be a stock market whiz to make money with investments. Everybody who spends is constantly making investments. The problem is that so few expenditures return much profit. Nevertheless, we do find a good investment from time to time: a bargain used car that can be sold for more than you paid, a house whose value is rising, a spare room that can be rented out, a profitable hobby. All of those things can be good investments, and a good investment can be made even better with a little *leverage*.

A lever is a simple thing that lets us use a little muscle to move a lot of weight, and financial leverage is much the same — using a little money to return a lot of profit. The financial lever is debt — using someone else's money to invest.

Some years ago the Smiths set out to buy their first house. They had $40,000 saved for a down payment. They weren't particularly fussy about looks, or cupboards, or color schemes, but they were determined to buy into an area where property values were sure to rise. The house was to be an investment as well as a place to live, and as such, it was to be judged on investment criteria. Consequently, most of their house shopping involved foot-slogging research to find the area that might next become "trendy" — where property values could be expected to rise the fastest. When they finally found the neighborhood, they were confident that any house on the street would increase in value by ten percent a year or more — and that proved to be on the conservative side. Only picking out a house remained.

At the time, a $100,000 house would have been more than adequate for the Smiths. If values rose by ten percent, a $100,000 house would increase in value by $10,000. With $40,000 down, they would borrow the remaining $60,000 from a credit co-op at eight percent. Interest on the mortgage would come to $4,800. The increase in value ($10,000) minus the cost of the mortgage ($4,800) would give them a gross return of $5,200 on their $40,000 investment, or thirteen percent.

But the Smiths knew they had an advantage as long as real estate was inflating faster than the mortgage rate. A $200,000 house would require a $160,000 mortgage, which would increase the interest costs to $12,800 a year. But a $200,000 house, inflating at ten percent, could be worth $20,000 more after one year. The gross return on the more expensive house would be $7,200, compared to $5,200 on the cheaper house. The debt would be bigger, but the returns would be bigger still. The *leverage* would allow them to earn eighteen percent on their down payment, rather than the thirteen percent they would earn on the house that was merely adequate.

For the Smiths, buying the more expensive property was justified by the interest rates alone, but I should complete the story by adding that the Smiths were not the type to rattle around in a house that was twice as big as they needed. They rented out the excess space and paid all the mortgage, tax, and maintenance costs with the rent money. They had "free" housing for themselves, a healthy return on the $40,000 invested, and a very hefty capital gain when they sold out three years later.

The key to the Smiths' success, however, was that real estate was appreciating at a higher rate than the cost of borrowing money. Real estate values aren't always that predictable. In fact, in some cities, the 1990s and 2000s have been most unkind to real estate values. Leverage only works to advantage if prices go up. When prices fall, or rise at a lower rate than mortgage interest, the Smiths had better be in a small house, with a minimum level of debt.

The classic example of leverage is in the stock market. Speculators, buying on margin (on the cuff if you like), can use a small amount of their own money to obtain credit to order much greater values of stock. If the stock increases in value, the speculators profit on their credit as well as on their own capital invested.

The trick, of course, is to pick only those stocks — or any other investment — that return profits larger than the cost of the debt. Leverage allows the investor to profit on someone else's capital, but it works the other way too! If the investment turns sour, the speculator must cover the entire loss — including the credit portion. That's what put all those ambitious young men out on the window ledges of Wall Street in 1929. As long as the market was rising they could make large paper profits by operating on margins, but when the market started to drop, and they had to pay off the credit extended by their stockbrokers, the result was financial ruin.

Risk

Using debt is a perfectly acceptable way to make money, but there are always risks involved. For the investor who can accept the risks, understand the investment thoroughly, and still have confidence that the investment will make money, debt and leverage can build up capital far faster than only investing personal assets could do.

For a family living without the security of a salary, the element of risk takes on a whole new character. A speculator hit with a bad investment presumably has the means to cover the loss with salary or income from other investments. Without a salary, the capacity to recover from financial loss is greatly limited. When those losses are multiplied by debt and leverage, the unsalaried person of little means is doubly vulnerable.

Bad Debts

Some debts are risky but worthwhile. Others have all the risk with no possibility whatsoever of earning a profit, and so have no redeeming features at all. These are consumer debts: money borrowed not to make money but to consume. When borrowing money to invest, the very worst that can happen is that you will have to repay the loan from your own resources rather than from profits on the investment. Consumer debt, where you don't expect to recover costs, much less make any kind of profit, is a deal that's guaranteed to be at least as bad as the worst investment.

"Buy now, pay later" is an insidious form of bondage. The deal amounts to trading a part of your future life for immediate gratification. Signing away future earnings to borrow for today's consumption guarantees that you'll need that job. You won't be free to give it up. And you'll worry all the more that someone will take it away.

"Buy now, pay later" is an insidious form of bondage.
• • • • • • • • • • • •

How bad is it? According to the Federal Reserve Board, 43 percent of U.S. families spend more than their income; only 30 percent manage to save. And the outstanding consumer debt is over $3,000 per person!

The cost is enormous. Credit cards, which can usually be paid off within thirty days with no interest charges, are not wisely used. Only a little over half of card holders pay up within thirty days. The rest carry an average balance of $1,000, and pay 15 percent interest (or more) on that. Department store cards cost the consumer up to 28 percent interest.

The distinction between good debt and bad debt has little to do with how much you borrow or from whom. The distinction centers on what you intend to do with the thing you've bought. If you're going to use it up, like a new suit, a stereo, or a holiday, then it's clearly a case of consumption. If it can later be sold, at a profit if possible, then the expense is not consumed, it's invested.

Investment debt is always risky, but it can bring rewards. Consumer debt is one hundred percent risk. It's absolutely certain from the beginning that you'll have to pay the whole thing back, and then some, from future earnings.

There's one more reason to distinguish between consumer and investment debt. The cost of investment debt (money spent to make more money) can be deducted from income for tax purposes. So a $1,000 investment loan at six percent actually costs $60. But a $1,000 consumer loan, for someone paying taxes at a marginal rate of, say, forty percent, costs $100. The consumer has to earn $100 to have $60 left after taxes to pay the interest on the loan. The investor pays six percent to borrow while the consumer pays ten percent — six percent to the bank and the rest to the government. So, if you want to buy a car and some bonds when your savings won't cover both, borrow to buy the bonds and use savings for the car.

If you ever hope to walk away from a salary, make a clear distinction between investment debt and consumer debt. Judge the former on its merits and your skills as an investor. Avoid the latter like the plague.

Breaking the Credit Card Habit

It's no accident that one of the costliest forms of consumer credit is also one of the slickest and easiest. If it weren't so darned easy to whip out the card, the costs would deter any would-be borrower.

The costs are more than the interest on the account. Paying the credit card bill within thirty days or using a direct debit card instead of a credit card helps, but there is a hidden cost as well — you don't count plastic money in quite the same way as the real stuff. When you have to pull out the actual cash and count it into the seller's hand, there's a tug of pain at the parting. At that point it *matters* that the same thing is on sale cheaper around the corner. It *matters* that you're having to give something up, something real, to buy this whatchamacallit. The plastic money isn't real. It doesn't seem to matter if the whatchamacallits cost more here. *The process is too painless.* The casual ease of it puts us to sleep and makes us less discriminating, less careful consumers. The convenience is costly. Paying should be as inconvenient as possible.

The theory of inconvenience even seems to work with cash. That's why I always try to carry small bills when shopping. When I have a twenty-dollar bill to throw on the counter, I'm hardly aware of whether the widgets are six dollars each or two for $12.99. When I have to count out a handful of bills, the price seems to matter more. The theory of inconvenience likewise tells me to take only big bills to the fair or the ball game, where one is surrounded by easy temptation to shell out a buck here and a fiver there for snacks and tidbits. These petty tricks for self-manipulation may only work for fanatic non-spenders like me, but giving up the convenience cards can save a lot of consumers a lot of money.

Don't believe me? Try this little test. Put away the plastic money and go back to cash — cold turkey — for a month. Make a note of all the expenses that you normally would have paid by card. At the end of the month compare the cash total with the normal credit card bill or even your debit card statement (remember to take note of the service charges for these transactions). If the cash method has saved you money, you can cut up the card and flush it down the toilet. That's the easiest way I know to stay out of debt.

Cutting the Cost of Debt

If you really must borrow money, remember it's a business deal, not a favor. Don't fall into the arms of the first friendly financier who kindly offers to help you out. You pay a price to borrow money, and, like any other expense, it pays to shop around.

A mortgage is usually the largest debt for home-owners, and the interest can be one of the most expensive items in the family budget. Interest varies from source to source.

◆ Credit unions and cooperatives often have cheaper mortgages than profit institutions like banks.

◆ Bank mortgages are usually cheaper than finance companies and other "near banks" that specialize in riskier loans.

◆ Assuming an older, existing mortgage may give you a break in interest if rates have been rising.

◆ Private mortgages, held by the seller or another individual, may be less costly than an institutional loan.

◆ Mortgage rates vary widely over time. If rates are high and expected to go down, you might save a bundle by waiting to buy when rates are better.

Some borrowers take low-interest loans from their life insurance policies. We'll look at insurance more closely in chapter 10. Suffice it to say here that the rates are low because you are borrowing your own money.

For small amounts of money, cheap (sometimes free) loans can be obtained by deferring payment on other bills. Most of the people who receive your monthly checks charge penalties for late payments. These penalties are the same as interest paid on a loan. Credit card companies, willing to "lend" free for thirty days, have taken late payment the final step by slapping on an 18 percent interest penalty and implicitly encouraging the practice with higher limits. In many cases, however, the penalties charged by other creditors are cheaper than the interest on regular commercial loans. Check the penalty clauses on your accounts and compare them to commercial rates. Do, however, keep track of changes. Back when banks were getting fifteen percent for their loans, the U.S. Government charged only eleven percent for late payment and

Canada twelve percent. Consumers who "borrowed" by deferring tax payments and governments learned a lesson. Now tax interest rates change in step with bank rates, and penalties are tacked on top. Late tax payment is no longer a bargain.

If it seems slightly underhanded to borrow money by deferring bills, consider that institutions are constantly borrowing from you, the consumer, by soliciting and accepting advance payments. "Lay-away" plans, where you pay now and pick up later, are a form of interest-free loan from the consumer to the department store. Many utility companies now send "interim bills" before the meter is read — their way of borrowing from you for nothing. And taxpayers give the government interest-free loans by overpaying income taxes and getting a refund at the end of the year. Some taxpayers even feel so good about getting a refund that it seems mean to remind them that they've given away the interest.

The Psychological Cost of Debt

A debt, even a cheap one, is a burden on the person who has to pay it. It's not so much the money as the obligation — the future commitment and the loss of freedom that it entails. Debt is a millstone around your neck in the present, and a limit on what you can choose in the future.

This is doubly true for those who are preparing themselves to live without salaries. Debts require a future income to pay them off. Giving up future income (of the predictable, salaried kind) means giving up debt. Even if the bankers would trust anyone crazy enough to give up a steady paycheck, debt is too hard on the nerves if you haven't got a predictable means of repayment. For people like us, there is always the horrifying thought that we might have to go back to a regular job to pay the damned thing off. That alone is enough to keep us away from borrowed money.

The surest measure of the psychological cost of debt can't be known until the debts are paid. The joy of being out of debt — of not owing a penny anywhere — tells us what we really paid to borrow money. That kind of freedom, which many harried consumers have forgotten, is one pleasure that can't be bought on any of the plastic cards.

Getting Out

The first and most important task, then, in preparing for life without a salary, is getting out of debt. Destroying the credit card and swearing off consumer debt forever is a great first step.

The second step is a long, hard look at investment debt. Some of it, a mortgage on rental property for instance, may be self-supporting. In other words, the income from the property will cover the mortgage payments whether you have a salary or not. Other investments may be equally profitable, but without the capacity to carry a debt on their own, like a mortgage on an owner-occupied home. The house may be appreciating rapidly — a great investment. But you can't profit from that increase until the house is sold, and the mortgage is due for payment every month.

When there's a regular salary coming in, any kind of investment debt that promises to make an eventual profit is open for consideration. When the salary stops, the investor should be more discriminating. Investment debts, at that stage, should be self-supporting. They should be able to pay themselves off.

For the peace of mind it brings, that's not a bad approach for people still on salary too. Do without rather than get into consumer debts; pay off non-income investment debts like a mortgage as rapidly as possible; set up income-producing investment debts to pay themselves off with or without your salary. Any family that can put itself into such a position is well on the way to economic self-sufficiency.

The prospect of paying off debts, as incomes or interest rates change, is reason enough to insist that mortgages (or any contracted debts) include a clause allowing early payment without penalty. If you have a mortgage with a penalty for early payment, wait until the new mortgage rates are higher than the rate on your own mortgage. Then ask the lender if the penalty clause can be renegotiated or deleted. Eager to reloan his money at the new, higher rate, the lender may be quite willing to encourage early payment by dropping penalties.

Savings

No matter how carefully you've laid out your retirement plans, something is bound to go wrong. It's the very same logic that ensures a slice of bread will always fall butter-side down, and that a three-year-old will always get his boots on the wrong feet (the laws of probability notwithstanding).

So, there's great security in having some money set aside just in case the purple Tahitian nudes don't sell, or the kids need an orthodontist as well as the dewy meadows and homegrown veggies. Having a mistake fund set aside separates the realistic planner from the romantic dreamer. It might not convince your in-laws that you're sane, but it will help your insomnia on the night before you resign.

The motive for setting something aside may be security, but that's not to say that savings can't also have some more active function. Like earning their keep for instance.

As a security blanket, your nest egg only needs to be accessible, and to earn at least enough income to keep pace with inflation. Those criteria are met in varying degrees by these common forms of savings:

Bank Savings are perhaps the most familiar repository. They are safe and easily accessible should the need arise, but they rarely pay enough to cover losses to inflation. They are a good place for emergency funds, but hardly the most profitable investment around.

Term Investment Certificates, offered by banks and other institutions, pay higher interest than demand deposits. They protect the capital, through deposit insurance, but commit the investor to leaving his money in for one- to five-year periods. You can sometimes have access to the money before the term is up, but there are penalties. A better investment than bank savings, but not an adequate emergency fund.

Bonds are like loans to governments or corporations. The interest rate is fixed, as is the term. But bonds, unlike term deposits, are traded on the market. This means you can sell a bond (i.e., withdraw your money) whenever you like, but the price depends on the interest rate. If you're holding an eight percent bond when current interest rates are nine percent, you won't be able to sell the bond for as much as you put into it, unless you hold it to maturity. The other element of risk is that companies and governments are sometimes unable to repay their loans and their bonds, uninsured, become worthless. Because there is more risk, bonds usually offer more interest than term deposits. Corporate bonds offer more than government bonds, and high-risk companies offer more than low-risk companies.

Stocks, which constitute a share in the ownership of a company, have the potential of earning much more than bank investments. Investors gain when company profits are distributed as "dividends." More important, the price of the stock goes up and down depending on the market's perception of profitability, long-range outlook, interest rates or astrology. In the short term especially, stock prices seem to depend more on psychology than on substance. Clever (or lucky) investors can profit from the price swings.

Funds are accessible, since stocks can be readily sold, but stock prices fall as well as rise and the unwary can get burned. Without a very reliable advisor, the "market" is not the place for the casual investor. To make the most of these investments, you must know the market well and follow it carefully.

Mutual Funds vary widely, but are usually invested in some particular sector of the stock market. There are growth funds, bond funds, blue chip funds, small company funds, global funds, metals funds, green funds, and everything-in-between funds. Experts handle the buy-and-sell decisions and investors share in their success or failure. For the amateur investor, mutual funds provide a slightly less worrisome way into the stock market, if only because the funds usually have more diversity and more expertise than the individual. They do the thinking for you, but they can't eliminate the risk.

Returns vary widely depending on the fund and its attitude to risk. The safer the approach, the smaller the profits. And don't forget that fund managers, and those who sell them, take a cut for their trouble. Even so-called "no-load" funds will have a built-in management fee of up to two percent. You'll have access to your mutual fund investments, but withdrawal could be expensive, depending on how the "load" is structured.

Real Estate can be a profitable and reasonably safe place for savings. Since it is a major component of the cost of living, the value of housing usually appreciates at least as fast as the general rate of inflation. Rental property may provide a tidy income as well, especially for the investor who can spend some time looking after it. Land speculation, with no rental income to cover the costs, is a more professional game. Residential property is easy to finance and not too complicated for the amateur who is willing to spend some time researching the market.

Location is paramount. House prices rarely rise in areas where the population is falling. Look for future growth areas, and consider what kind of house will be in demand (as families shrink and the population ages, the four-bedroom suburban detached, for example, might not be as popular as it once was).

Although returns can be high in real estate, and (unless you're very rash) it's usually one of the safest investments outside of a bank, the money invested is not easily accessible. Not a place for emergency funds.

Mortgage Investments can be as simple as using surplus funds to pay off your own mortgage faster, or as complex as lending your money to another home buyer. Current rates compared to alternative investments will determine the advantage of paying off your own mortgage. Lending mortgage funds to someone else is a safe investment, but only if you can be tough enough to foreclose should the need arise. No mortgage investment is easily accessible if you need the money in a hurry.

Rarities such as stamps, art, or even comic books have been money-makers for experts, but it is essential to know what you're buying, and even then the markets for rarities are volatile. Not an amateur sport.

Commodities such as gold, silver, or soybeans are another sphere best left to the pros. In the last gold boom, hordes of eager buyers lined up outside banks to put their life savings into a few thin wafers of metal. A few people made a lot of money. The ones in the lines got burned.

Retirement Savings Plans are particularly attractive for the working person who plans on being without a salary in the near future. RRSPs in Canada are 100 percent tax deductible. That is, up to a limit, any money saved under a registered plan is exempt from income tax, as is the compounding return on that money. You don't pay tax until you withdraw it — usually after retirement when you're in a lower tax bracket anyway. Investors can choose from a range of RRSP investments, from safe, low-interest bank deposits to high-risk mutual funds. Even in low-interest accounts, the tax advantage can be very lucrative (see chapter 10). In the United States, the Keogh SEP and IRA plans are more restrictive than the Canadian RRSP, but if you can qualify, the tax advantages are the same.

Depending on what you want your savings to do, no one plan may meet all of your needs. Some families find it practical to divide their funds into three separate plans: an emergency fund at the bank, a less accessible but more profitable investment for income purposes (bonds, term certificates, etc.), and a risk fund with speculative potential. The emergency fund is there whenever it's needed. The income investment may be the largest reserve. And the risk fund is just that — something they can afford to lose.

Some families like to set priorities on savings. For example:

1. concentrate on paying off all consumer debt first;

2. then contribute the maximum to a tax-sheltered investment like an RRSP;

3. top up the emergency fund to a level that will see you through a one- or two-month lay-off;

4. pay down the mortgage to cut future expenses;

5. invest in a dividend fund or a term deposit to pad future income;

6. finally, take a flyer on something more speculative, like a growth stock or a lottery ticket. The lottery ticket, as the least likely to pay off, should be the last priority in the budget, not the first.

The management of savings will certainly affect other kinds of financial decisions. A healthy emergency fund, for example, may eliminate the need for certain kinds of insurance. Maximizing tax-sheltered savings like RRSPs will lower your tax bill and should send you to the payroll office to ask that your withholding tax be lowered to the minimum.

Likewise, other circumstances will determine the type of savings plan best suited to each family. Your own skills and interests will guide investment plans to areas you know best. Current interest rate comparisons will help to determine whether it makes more sense to pay down the mortgage or invest in a term deposit. The family's health, number of children, nearness to pensionable age — all these things and more will shape decisions on how much money is enough and where it should be kept.

How to Save: The Material Fast

A savings plan, like a diet, is one of those simple and reasonable things that's easier to describe than to do. Savers put quarters into big glass jars, have regular amounts deducted from paychecks, save whatever happens to be left between paychecks, moonlight and put all of the extra pay away. There are as many approaches to saving as there are diets — and for much the same reason. Dieting and saving both involve a degree of personal sacrifice: curbing appetites. And just as all dieters have a choice between the cheesecake and a slimmer figure, all consumers have a choice between buying everything they think they need and having money in the bank. It's a matter of overcoming appetites.

All would-be savers know their own psyche best, and how they can trick themselves into curbing the material appetite. My favorite, however, is *the material fast* — buying nothing but essentials during a pre-determined interlude of Spartan discipline.

Saving in little bits and pieces never worked very well for us. Skimping here and there forever was just too unappealing. In the face of eternal deprivation, however slight, the temptation to cheat was ever present. Worse yet, the money never added up fast enough to make the sacrifice seem worthwhile. Like the thought of never eating another pastry — forever and ever — with the object of losing a pound a month, the short-term result never seemed to justify the permanent sacrifice. Crash savings, like crash diets, were more our style. We could give up anything if we knew we could have it back some day.

Crash savings require a specific objective, a specific time period, and a mutual willingness to sacrifice every expense for that period. The plan is carefully laid out at the beginning. A bare-bones budget is set that includes nothing but the simplest food, housing and essential bills. Nothing is sacred. Rent can be lowered by moving (who cares if it's too small, it's only for a year). You can give up the car (we'll walk for a year), clothing (everything that wears out will be mended, and we'll buy clothes next year). Once the budget is set, it's inviolable. Even rational exceptions are put off until after the fast. Every other penny of income is saved. It's a radical change in lifestyle. But it works. And it doesn't seem so bad as long as there is an end in sight.

Sue and Mark started married life with brand new jobs at the bottom of the ladder, where visions of the future are supposed to compensate for the meager pay. They had nothing else — no savings, no car, no TV, no stereo, not a stick of furniture to their names. They decided to continue the material fast for six Spartan months, putting most of the two paychecks into the bank. Six months later they left on a three-month, round-the-world tour, traveling in comfort and paying cash. Six months of famine followed by a three-month feast. A matter of choice.

Because you know it's going to end, the material fast is never as grim as is sounds. It's different. Like traveling in an unknown land, you may even find that it's better in some ways than what you left behind. Not surprisingly, many families who submit themselves to radical saving binges find their lifestyles permanently altered. Some find that walking feels better than driving, that evenings spent in conversation do more for a marriage than a television does, that old shoes are more comfortable than new ones. The material fast can actually start to become an attractive way of life in itself. The sense that less might actually be more is the beginning of becoming a conserver.

A Toe in the Water

Getting ready to live without your regular job can be more than idle dreaming and saving your loot for a sunny day.

Outside the silver spoon set, most of us who contemplate leaving jobs also have to contemplate other means of earning a living. Of all the people I've met who've realized there must be more to life than what they're doing, most already have something else in mind — something else they would rather do instead of what they're doing now. The usual problem is making it pay, or finding something else to do for money that doesn't dominate your life the way a regular job can.

The sense that less might be more is the beginning of becoming a conserver.

More than half the battle can be won by simplifying needs. But there tends to remain a stubborn residue of bills that just won't go away. Sooner or later you are going to need some cash. Not much, mind you, but enough to know you must improvise some casual source of income.

Income schemes centered on hobbies, crafts, scaled-down versions of your present job, or freelance anything are a major part of getting ready. This is the time to find out if your schemes will really pay, if you can really do it, if you can really enjoy doing it.

Putting a toe in the water simply means testing those alternative income schemes to make certain they work — before you kiss your seniority good-bye. This is the time to

Test your skills — making sure you have the talent to paint or pot or farm or whatever it is that draws you.

Test the market — making sure your paintings or pots or whatever will sell.

Test your confidence — knowing you can do it makes all the rest (budgeting, saving, and so on) a whole lot easier to endure. On the other hand, knowing that you can't do it, or finding it's not everything you thought it would be, may help you reconsider.

One old pal of mine, a PR man at the time, decided at a particularly stressful period in his career that a simple life in the country appealed to him more. He bought an old farm and a new straw hat, and resolved to grow cucumbers for the pickle factory. The romance went out of cucumbers as soon as he saw you had to bend down to pick them — somehow, he had envisaged trees. Louis, the walking pork chop, refused to die at butchering time; the septic tank backed up, and the house burned down. He's back in the city now, and refuses to grow so much as a petunia. Trying a new lifestyle before you buy it is just plain good planning.

Gathering What You'll Need

Ironically, a simpler lifestyle can often involve more complex needs. Growing your own food is about as basic as you can get, but it requires land, tools, fences, materials, and then all the gear needed to freeze or preserve it. Wood heat is making a regional comeback as an alternative to oil and gas, but to keep the old potbelly going takes tools for cutting, hauling and splitting, a storage shed and a woodlot. It's simpler than drilling your own oil well, but there's still a lot of work and expense between you and the cozy glow.

Getting ready is the time to start acquiring all the tools and resources the new lifestyle will require. That's not to say you should rush out and buy everything you think you'll need. It's enough to start with making lists: what you are going to need, where it can be found, costs and alternatives.

Planning the acquisition of such resources ahead of time permits the luxury of spending slowly and biding your time until the bargains and special opportunities come to you.

When we planned our own move to the country, one of the first and biggest items on the list was a tractor. I rushed around gathering specs and prices and catalogs. That was more than thirty years ago. In the meantime we've found a dozen different ways to do without a tractor for the small-scale jobs we had in mind. The tractor was still on the list somewhere, but gradually found its way to the bottom.

Moving to the country, or changing your lifestyle in any direction, is a little like an expedition. Knowing what you'll need ahead of time solves problems, but you don't have to take it all with you.

Budget (Again)

Cheaper lifestyles are fundamental to surviving without a salary. Spending less is the only way most of us can afford to live outside the forty-hour work week. It's clear, then, that the post-job budget could, or should, differ sharply from the budget of a working family.

Budgeting for a new lifestyle takes the same form as the budgets discussed in chapter 2. The numbers and the categories, however, should change significantly. Regardless of where you may be going, or what you may be doing, certain needs will disappear. Without a job, you may not need a house in town, a new suit every year or a second car, for example.

This preparatory period is the time to estimate just what the financial situation will be in your new circumstances. In other words, *make a budget.*

During the years that it can take to prepare for financial independence there is one overriding question that is asked more than any other: *How much money does it take to be independent?* And secondly, *how long will it take to get there?* The answers, of course, depend entirely upon your needs and your capacity to earn casual income. It depends even more on how secure you like to feel. Everybody's answer is unique, but for what it's worth, our own financial goals (at the getting-ready stage) were to hang onto salaries until we

1. were out of debt;

2. owned a house in a low-tax area;

3. were set up to raise most of our own food and fuel; and

4. had enough in the bank to cover several years of (minimal) expenses.

By virtually eliminating the cost of food and housing, and by knowing we could do without much of the rest, it didn't take much to make us feel secure. Less self-sufficient lifestyles would doubtless need more cash reserve. Smaller families might require less.

Whatever your own needs might be, an evening spent making up a "what if I didn't go to work?" budget will help you to answer the big questions in terms of clear financial goals.

Weaning

Regular paychecks can be addictive. Regardless of what the job is like, leaving a paycheck behind is an awesome thought. To cushion the shock, some folks prefer to wean themselves gradually rather than go "cold turkey." The gradual approach also leaves an escape route back to security for those who aren't quite sure about the merits of a brand new lifestyle. Like my friend the would-be pickle farmer, some find that idylls aren't all they're cracked up to be. He kept his city job and commuted for a while just to keep a foot in both camps until he was sure it would work. It didn't.

Some firms offer employees a Leave of Absence (LOA) for educational or other purposes. How about for lifestyle changes? LOA is usually without pay, but it does leave open the option of going back to the old grind if the new grind doesn't work out. The biggest hurdle to giving up a salary is often the grim prospect of giving up long-term security. If you can gather the wherewithal to live for a year (or whatever term the LOA policy offers), your security lies in being able to go back to work when the leave is over. If being your own boss suits you, and if you can still balance to budget after a year, you may not want to go back. LOA is sort of a year's free trial.

Some jobs, in sales for instance, are less structured than others and would-be retirees can wean themselves by gradually cutting back on their time — fewer calls, fewer hours. The paycheck drops accordingly, but the prospect of going back full tilt remains until you actually give up and go back, or drop the apron strings altogether.

In other jobs, employers can be persuaded to allow a switch from salaried to contract work. You continue to do the same work but are paid as an independent supplier rather than an employee. There is less security with such an arrangement, but the money is often better and you can control your working life more independently. Employers are often willing to pay more for contractors than for employees because the overhead (pensions, holiday pay, and so on) is lower and because it's easier to drop a contractor than an employee if business gets bad.

It is precisely that shift from permanent staff to outside contracting that worries many unions and individuals in today's leaner, meaner work force. Whether you like it or not, trading a job for a contract is not only a viable survival strategy, it can be a half-way measure in preparing yourself for real independence.

The Upside of Downsizing

Increasingly, early retirement is the company's idea, not the worker's. Whether you're laid off, re-engineered, downsized or dumped makes little difference to the fact that the paycheck is about to stop. The question is what to do about it.

Even if you hate the job, being pushed hurts more than taking the leap yourself. If you can, turn push into jump. Some companies start the downsizing process with buy-out offers for early retirement. The amount of dickering room you have will depend on your place in the hierarchy and how long you've been there. But there is usually dickering room. A buy-out offer is just that: an offer. Make a counter offer. Try to maximize pension and benefit entitlements rather than lump-sum payments, which may be fully taxable in the year you get them. In some cases, you will be allowed to transfer things like severance pay and accumulated sick leave into your sheltered pension fund, without tax penalty. But the rules are complicated and you may need some advice from the union, the tax department, or even a lawyer.

Try to extend the final departure date, especially if you want to look for another job; chances of landing another job are vastly better if you're not yet unemployed. When my friend Paul was headed for the chopping block, he had been with the company only a year — not long enough for a decent severance package. So he resigned, setting his departure date six months away. Six months to look for another job on full pay! The company decided that six months' pay would be cheaper than a pink slip and a possible suit for wrongful dismissal. And Paul found that "Looking for more challenge" made a better reason for being at a job interview than "I've been canned."

Preparing Yourself

Enough of financial preparations. What effect will life without a salary have on you? Is your psyche in shape for it? There are several differences between life on and off the job. Expect them and be prepared.

Self-Discipline

The greatest and most obvious change is discipline. Work goals, deadlines, the structuring of time, and objectives are imposed on most employees. When you are on your own, such discipline is up to you. You can structure your time to suit yourself. No surprise in that. That's one of the reasons for leaving jobs. The surprise comes when you realize just how quickly a totally unstructured day can disappear.

Jobs seem to consume such an enormous part of our lives that one tends to think that without the job there will be unlimited time to do all those things that are now crammed into weekends and evenings, plus time to do all those other projects that have been put off for "when there's time," plus all that extra leisure time to enjoy the freedom. Oh, if only it were so!

Granted, you can gain forty or so hours a week by leaving a job. But those precious forty hours don't last at home as long as they seem to last on the job. Only if you nurture them with a careful discipline will they serve all the ends you have in mind.

My own failing was leisure. Sitting behind a desk all week, I relished the chance to get outdoors on the weekend to dig the garden, chop wood, and hammer nails, anything. For a desk-bound paper-pusher, all that constructive physical activity was recreation. When we finally packed up our compost heap and moved to the country, we were suddenly free to do all those things we enjoyed most — like digging, chopping and hammering — plus all those things that *had* to be done, like finishing the house and digging, chopping and hammering. Six months later, we were physically exhausted and thoroughly fed up with digging, chopping and hammering. We had been playing "weekend" for six whole months, forgetting that our former recreation was now our work and that we needed time off from that, too. Waiting for the leisure to happen, or putting it off until the chores were done, just didn't work for us. We had to impose a discipline and set aside regular, inviolable family recreation time.

Thirty years later, our time discipline extends even to divisions within the work day: a certain portion for creative or mental work, and another part for the physical chores. There is still never enough time to finish all the goals we set ourselves. Indeed, we seem to be working harder at retirement than we ever did at jobs. But with the discipline to maintain a happy balance between mind work, muscle work and leisure, nothing gets too neglected and we can enjoy a little progress on every front.

Self-discipline is not at all in contradiction to the freedom of retirement. The discipline is merely one defense against the rush of time. And, unlike an employer's discipline, self-discipline can be arranged to suit you. The family day off, for instance. In the summer months, we kept a Tuesday Sabbath, simply because the parks, beaches, and museums were least crowded then. In the summer, when there is lots of physical work to be done, a cup of tea and a quiet read are *de rigueur* after lunch. In winter, when chores are more cerebral, the after-lunch break becomes skiing in the woods. When the children got to the stage of spicing dinner with spills, spats, and inane riddles, we invented a new tradition of adult dinner one night a week. They got packed off to bed early to read or play or do anything that couldn't be heard downstairs, and the grownups got candlelight and wine. You can structure time to suit yourself, but without the structure it soon degenerates into a morass of endless and undone chores.

Other families, infected with milder strains of Calvinist guilt, may need discipline to keep them working, but few of us are able to balance all the demands on time without some rules to keep us on track.

Administration

In the age of the paternal employer, much of the nitty-gritty paperwork of life is taken care of "at the office." Part of the result is the jigsaw of numbers, deductions, and indecipherable codes that make up the modern paycheck. Cutting the umbilicus means, among other things, becoming your own administrator.

Making budgets, keeping records, scheduling tasks, making sure the medical insurance is up to date and sorting out the tax and pension tangles aren't complicated jobs when you get right down to it. It's just that they are so easily put aside or forgotten when you are accustomed to leaving such headaches at "the office."

We're quite accustomed to shuffling our own papers now, but we use the office for other things . . . like complaints. All complaints are immediately referred to the office. All dumb questions like, "Do you think it will rain next Tuesday?" or, "Can I have a motorcycle when I'm twelve?"

are politely answered with a suggestion that they ask at the office. It's somewhere beyond the trees there. Very difficult to find . . . but keep looking.

The Rhythm of Life

Most jobs have a rhythm of their own: the pace of production, the end of the month, the fiscal year, or whatever; the work is geared to the ebb and flow according to some pattern of time. At the very least, most jobs force us into a cadence of weekend leisure, Monday blues, Friday's high, and regular checks. Our minds and bodies become so attuned to these rhythms that they disappear into our internal woodwork.

It comes as a shock, then, when we leave the workplace, to discover that other lives have other rhythms. If you are not prepared, adjustment can be hard.

Coming to the country, we had to adjust to the rhythm of the seasons. I expected to work hard, but my internal clock wanted to work and rest on a weekly pattern. For the farmer, planting, haying, and harvest seasons set the schedule of work, and "weekend" is the winter.

Changing lifestyles may mean changing life's rhythm as well. If you are not as young as you used to be, it may take your bones a while to catch up.

The Family Compact

Idylls are largely private things. Daydreams can be built into vivid and detailed shape in the recesses of one's own mind. The rose-covered cottage, the painting loft, the rigging on the schooner — we can privately design dreams down to the last nail and hue. That's a splendid way to plan the future if you are on your own.

When the future involves families of more than one, however, it helps to air those dreams with your partners from time to time. Better to find out ahead of time that the kids are allergic to roses, or Father can't stand drafty lofts, or Mother has her heart set on a yawl.

Parents are often ready to make sacrifices for themselves, but wonder whether they have the right to impose major lifestyle changes on the kids. There's no good answer to that one. You can ask them, but the reply will depend on their ages. For a while, they'll agree to anything, and later will agree to nothing. Ours loved having us home all day when they were young, and then felt the lack of privacy later. They loved the lake and the woods, and then hated being that far from the mall. In their rebellious years, they became unrepentant consumers; now I catch them making budgets and driving hard bargains for the things they buy. Perhaps no parent has the right to impose a lifestyle change on children. Certainly, we don't have the right to make them so different from their peers that they'll have trouble fitting in. The best we can do is prepare to amend any family plan as the children grow into individuals, just as we would amend it as the grown-ups evolve over the years.

Getting ready is the time for shaping and amending idyllic dreams into practical and affordable forms. If the planning isn't done with the full participation of the whole crew, then the dream may very well founder on a mutiny — and deservedly so.

What If It Doesn't Happen?

The biggest part of getting ready is organizing your financial life to spend less, get out of debt, and set aside some investments in reserve. For most of us, that's a slow, hard job. It is, however, a "can't lose" approach that takes the risk out of preparing for a crazy project like living without a regular job.

The worst that can happen is that the project fizzles to naught. You decide to stick it out at work and leave the Tahitian nudes or the trout farm or the polar photography until you're sixty-five. All that getting ready to survive without a salary was in vain, right? Wrong! All that getting ready should leave you out of debt with cash in the bank and a cheaper style of living. Not a bad sort of flop. Not a bad sort of cushion should the economy decide to retire you anyway.

~ 5 ~

Casual Income

It's one of nature's nastier laws that makes earning a living so much easier when you don't really need it: When money needs are reduced to simple maintenance — no debts or Joneses to keep up with — survivors learn that it's a whole lot simpler to earn small amounts of money than to find and keep a big-money job. Earning a small-scale living becomes, well, a casual affair.

It has something to do with changing the rules. A regular career is usually conducted with a tight little set of unwritten but immutable laws:

◆ Never take a job paying less than the last one!

◆ Never take a job with less status than the last one!

◆ Never take a temporary job if you can get a permanent one!

◆ Never take a job outside your own trade or profession!

The effect is to limit job prospects to that narrow range of openings on the next rung of your own occupational ladder. It's like going out for a walk and insisting that a real walk has to be uphill and in a straight line. No wonder the going gets tough.

Prospects change, however, when you throw out the rules. When earning a living is reduced from ego gratification to the simple matter of regularly obtaining small amounts of money, the possible sources of money expand like magic.

Whatever Happened to Ambition?

Is it merely weakness that leads some of us to leave careers that get too demanding? "When the going gets tough, the tough get going," and all that. Ambition is a fine and noble thing, and God forbid that anyone should abandon distant goals just because they're hard to reach. What is too often overlooked, however, is the simple idea that ambition and employment need not be synonymous. Ambition can exist outside the workplace.

Some of the world's most noted over-achievers have succeeded precisely because they abandoned careers to pursue other goals, and regarded money as a minor but necessary nuisance. If ambition and success were confined to regular jobs, Gauguin might never have painted and the Wright brothers would have stuck to fixing bicycles in Dayton.

Someone, somehow, has tricked us into believing that security and self-worth come only from what we are paid to do. We become our jobs and we're worth only what we're paid. What rubbish! Esteem ought to come from everything we do and not just what we're paid to do.

Deciding What To Do for Money

When ego has been removed from the minor but necessary nuisance of money, deciding what to do for income can have a whole new set of rules — or no rules at all. Being a structured type, I function better with lists and rules and don't mind sharing them here, but you make up your own as you like — it really doesn't matter in the least since the object of the new rules is to make paid work small and unobtrusive rather than large and self-enhancing.

1. The very best source of casual income is getting paid for things that you do because you like to do them. Getting paid for enjoying yourself. I write books because I like to write. If someone decides to buy them that's terrific, but the money has little to do with what, and whether, I decide to write. A sale is "found money," not the object of the exercise.

2. When that's not enough to pay the bills, casual income is generated as a by-product of work we would normally do for ourselves.

Growing food for instance. We never had the land, the skills or the capital to be real farmers, but we have enjoyed raising animals and vegetables for our own kitchen. One pig a year was plenty of pork for us, but it was no more trouble to look after five than to raise one or two. We would have been doing the work anyway, so a little salable excess was no extra trouble.

3. The most unobtrusive way to make money is with paper investments, and don't dismiss that option as the preserve of wealthy coupon-clippers. It may take some hard work to raise the capital in the first place, but once invested, it's the money's turn to work for you. We began by considering investments as an alternative to insurance, keeping our own emergency fund rather than buying corporate protection. Now we collect interest instead of paying insurance premiums. Personally, I find the investment field a total bore. So our rule is to pick safe investments that don't require our time or attention.

4. When these dribs and drabs of income still won't stretch to meet our limited needs, and we reach the point of having to devote real time to producing income, we look for projects that might prove interesting or projects that are easily started and stopped.

In general, if it's going to take time away from the things we would really rather be doing, casual income has to come from jobs that are interesting, or short-term, or both. Finally, it helps if the job can be related to some specific goal, like: "Three weeks of stone work will pay for the trip to Tortola." The goal makes the short-term drudgery more bearable, and the drudgery makes it easier to curb extravagant impulses.

Those are our rules. They suit us and still allow enough cash flowing in to keep us afloat. More important, earning a living is rarely allowed to interfere with living itself. Too often friends have said, "That's fine for you, but we haven't the skills to sell on a casual basis like that." Such false modesty is usually a whacking load of codswallop. It is *confidence,* not skill that is lacking. Nearly everyone who has spent some time in the work force has both material and personal resources that can be turned to profit.

Assessing Your Assets
No money to invest? Spent it all? On what? Unless you're an unlucky gambler or a hopeless gourmand it's difficult to get rid of all those pay-

checks over the years without having something to show for it. Equity in the house? Some land, a car, cameras, tools? You can't eat it all! Look around and do a quick assessment of your material resources. How much cash have you already invested in *things?* And they are investments. The problem is that you probably haven't been collecting the interest.

Space can be rented. The spare room, the garage, storage space in the basement. The basement's full? Of what? Stuff you don't use anymore? Sell it, and then rent the space to store somebody else's junk.

You have $1,000 worth of woodworking tools that you've used to make a $100 bed? Use the tools to make another bed, or something else that might sell. If you didn't enjoy woodworking you probably wouldn't have bought the tools in the first place.

You have $5,000 worth of PC hardware and software that so far has only played games and typed the odd letter? It's capable of much more if you want to put it to work.

You splurged on a big riding lawnmower that can cut the grass in half an hour? Spend another half hour and cut the neighbor's grass. If you don't have the extra half hour, rent the mower to the neighbor.

You have some country property for that retirement dream? What's it doing now? Good fields can be rented to farmers. Forested land needs regular thinning. That's firewood, and perhaps pulp or lumber to sell.

One friend owns some acres of scrub too far from town to serve as anything but an occasional retreat. He retreated once too often and has now become a proud and happy first-time father. The retreat hasn't changed; it's still a leaky cabin amongst the trees. Fatherhood, however, has changed the owner's perspective. Now he sees the young trees as an investment. Thinned and nurtured by neighbors who are happy to get the firewood, the timber will be mature enough to harvest in time to pay for the baby's college education — a neat little case of financial justice!

If you don't wish to sell or rent the things you own, at least consider using them yourself for money. It may double your value on the market. Your skill as a driver, for instance, may be worth only minimum wage. Using your own car, however, makes your services much more valuable. Part of the payment is for your time and the rest is a return on your investment in the car.

Putting your possessions to work pays a double dividend. Not only do you get some return on that investment, but also a share of the costs may be deductible at income-tax time. The basement workshop, the attic studio, the family car that does evening shifts delivering pizza, may all pay off in tax advantages. A friend of mine who does freelance TV interviews even deducts her hairdos.

What Are Your Personal Resources?

I was going to call this section "Skills," but that always makes people think of their jobs. It's really much broader than that. The inventory of resources should be expanded to include not only the things you already do for money, but also the things you do for yourself, the things you can learn to do, and most of all the things you're really interested in doing.

A woman once told me that she wanted to work her way around the world but had only one salable skill. With a little prodding she admitted that she could also drive, cook, shop efficiently, speak English and take quality photographs — all skills that can be profitably used by travelers. It's just that she had never *worked* at those things before and thus had not considered them as skills. The last I heard, she was halfway around the world, busily photographing the South Pacific. Another zero-budget traveler I know went from England to India *working* as a bicyclist; he asked and the bike-makers agreed that the ride would make a worthy testimonial for their ad campaign.

The most under-rated skill in modern society might be parenting. Some parents recognize their worth and expand into daycare. A father I know has turned his bed-time act into a successful series of children's books. Some mothers in Minnesota hire themselves out to the mall, keeping other parents' loitering teens in line.

Deciding what to do for money should be as much an assessment of interests as it is of your finances. Just don't make the assumption that because you enjoy it, someone else won't pay to have it done. Remember that just about everything you do for fun, someone somewhere gets paid to do.

Casual Employment

For some, the surest way to make a living — short of hanging on to a career — is to continue selling time or skills to employers, but on a part-time, temporary, or contractual basis.

For the worker, the trade-offs are obvious. You make less money, but spend less time doing it. You gain some control over where and when you work, but lose the sense of security that goes with a full-time job.

Some careerists have the false impression that casual employment is only possible in the less skilled jobs; the sort of thing that moonlighting cabdrivers, short-order cooks, and summer camp staffers do. The temporary hiring agencies do seem to specialize in unskilled placements, or easily transferable skills like typing. But casual workers abound in the professional world as well. They're harder to see simply because they often have more fanciful titles, like "supply teacher" or "sub-contractor" or the ubiquitous "consultant."

The range of casual jobs is almost endless. When I was eight or nine the neighborhood was blessed with an elderly couple who grandparented for all the kids around who flocked to their cherry tree and hammock. The old man suddenly died, and poor old Mrs. S., who had no other family, was all on her own. She asked if my brother and I would spend a few nights at her place, just to keep her company. She owned the only TV for miles around, so the treat was really ours. Nevertheless, she gave us each a quarter in the morning and sent us off to school. Naturally, the teacher picked that day to poll the class on the perennial classic, "What are you going to be when you grow up?" Still fingering my quarter, I allowed as how I would earn my living sleeping with widows. The reaction I provoked in those puritan Bible-belt days was enough to put me right off any thoughts of growing up.

Sleeping with widows may be on the outer limits of casual jobs, but just about anything else goes. One active young man worked his way through college as a deodorant tester. He had to go in to be sniffed every day, but most of the time was his own. I know people who've made their living as part-time preachers, evening teachers, truant officers (who only work when the weather's nice), and snow-plow operators (who only work when the weather's bad). I've also known seasonal sales clerks (who only worked at Christmas), and construction workers (who only work in the summer). A musician who does his work on Saturday nights livening up parties, and a hotel detective who's paid to make them quiet down again. I know a businessman who spends his vacations working as a cook/gofer on rafting expeditions, and a photographer who takes prospecting vacations. We once signed up as movie extras — the kids were thrilled to be making the same paltry wage as their parents, thrilled about costumes and make-up, thrilled about rubbing elbows with the stars; and three days later they were bored to tears, ready to go back to school and cured of glamour-envy for life.

Many of the casual jobs around are filled by "moonlighters" — full-time workers augmenting incomes with extra jobs in their spare time. Others, with smaller debts or simpler needs, manage to make a living on casual jobs alone.

Ray was a personnel officer in the civil service. He had a young family and a small salary — not a happy combination in a city where already sky-high housing costs were continuing to shoot up faster than his already inadequate salary. Ray decided the only way to make it was to start by working even harder. He went to the firms who were conducting weekend training seminars and hired on as a part-time trainer — the same sort of work he was doing full-time for the government. With the weekend job added to his regular salary, they soon had enough for the down payment on a run-down, ramshackle house in a more desirable part of the city. It was bigger than they needed for themselves, so the third floor was rented out to help with the mortgage payments and the cost of renovations. Evenings were devoted to plastering, patching, and painting. Ray was virtually working at three jobs. When the renovations were done, the house was worth almost twice what they paid for it. So they sold it and bought another cheapie. He did another year of the three-job schedules: a full-time civil servant, part-time trainer, and evening renovator. By the time they sold the second house, they could afford a third house all to themselves — without a mortgage! Life was getting cheaper. The last I heard, Ray and his family had settled in a permanent house of their own, he had left the civil service and was living happily on the income from the weekend training sessions, he was calling himself a "consultant," and — oh, yes — he had just reached his thirtieth birthday.

Finding Casual Jobs

Casual employment is a common practice partly because it has so many advantages for the employer. As the pace of business changes, it's easier and cheaper for the employer to add and subtract casual workers than it would be to hire and fire permanent staff. Regular employees must be paid whether business is booming or slack. An employer filling a permanent career position must be very careful with his hiring. Mistakes can be corrected and poor workers weeded out, but often at the cost of severance pay, union battles, and a lot of hard feelings on both sides. Getting a permanent job is, therefore, a long and drawn-out process. Because casual workers can be dropped more easily, they are usually hired with less fuss and bother too. The process is the same, it just doesn't take as long.

The shortest job hunt on record surely has to be the day I arrived on the island state of Tasmania. The ferry left me in the little town of Devonport, travel-weary, dressed in a T-shirt and shorts, and three days' wages away from the price of a ticket back to the mainland. Devonport didn't appear to offer very much: one long street of low-slung shops and pubs, wooden facades, and a sleepy afternoon heat. Hardly the makings of economic miracles.

At the far end of the street was a brick building, the only one in town — and it was two stories at that. If anybody along that drowsy street held the prospect of three days' wages it had to be the moneyed-looking place at the end. So I trudged through the dust and, still mystified (there wasn't even a sign outside), pushed through the big glass doors into a cool and spacious office lobby. The carpet was wool and deep. I could wiggle my toes in the thing. Across the center of the room was a long counter of dark, polished wood. Behind it were a dozen or so desks, the front ranks filled with young ladies typing earnestly and looking prim. Behind them were ranks of earnest young men in white shirts and ties. I wiped my hands on my T-shirt, hid my toes in the carpet and cleared my throat. The nearest typewriter stopped. There was quite a flutter of tics and squints across her face before she settled on a cool superior look that suggested I must be mistaken.

"Can I help you?"

Obviously not, but after walking all the way up the street I figured what the hell. "Yes, I'm looking for a job," says I.

Instantly, the necktie chap at the very back of the room jumped to his feet and blurted, "You're hired!"

I put my little finger in my ear to ream it out. He was halfway to the counter already.

"Can you start right away? I'll drive you to the job site . . ."

I was on my way to the mountains before I discovered I'd be laboring to build a hydroelectric dam. Christmas was approaching, and the regular gangs of casual laborers were drifting back to mainland families.

It's not always that easy. Getting a casual job usually follows the same rules as those that govern permanent jobs. The major difference is that letters and formal applications more often give way to the telephone and personal contacts. You still have to do the rounds, knocking on doors and making appointments until you find the places that have more work than workers. You still have to sell yourself and your abilities (though employers are usually more willing to take a chance with casuals). And you may have to work even harder as a casual than you would have as a permanent — remember that casuals are easier to fire, as well as easier to hire, than the career staff.

In certain occupations (secretarial, clerical, domestic, for instance) casual workers are commonly placed through agencies or labor pools. You'll find the agencies in the "help wanted" ads, or in the Yellow Pages of the phone book under "employment agencies." The agencies make the job hunt even easier, but they will also collect a healthy fee from the employer and thus pay you that much less. If you find job hunting distasteful, by all means try an agency, but do find out the size of the agency's fee and ask yourself if job hunting is really *that* distasteful.

It really is more profitable to decide what you want to do, what time you have available, then look for an employer whose needs might coincide with yours. Don't wait for the dream job to surface in the "help wanted" columns. The market for casual jobs moves faster than that. This is the place for knocking on doors and making your pitch.

One enterprising fellow in need of some extra cash was getting nowhere in his search for a part-time job. The problem was that he was only available for work on Thursdays. There were jobs around, but none seemed to fit his schedule. His final solution was artfully simple. On his next free Thursday, he did the rounds of the bars, striking up acquaintances, and asking them what they did for a living. When he struck an interesting answer, he asked his new-found friend what he was doing in the bar. "It's my day off," was the hoped-for answer. He paid for the drinks and made straight for the company mentioned, offering his services as a relief man to fill in when the regular staff was off. It turned out Thursdays suited the employer just fine.

When economies slump and jobs get scarce there is a natural desire to hang on to whatever threads of permanence one may have. Ironically, it's at just such times that casual workers become an even more attractive option to employers. Loathe to hire permanent staff in troubled times, employers are more likely to look upon labor needs as a possible short-term situation. If business does go sour, employers know they can cut casual workers more easily than full-time staff. Career personnel, however, are only marginally more secure. When business gets worse, the careerists go too.

The only real security workers have is in their hands and between their ears. The casual worker's position may be a little more precarious than that of regular staff, but in the long run, there's very little difference. Indeed, if casual workers are familiar with the temporary job market and accustomed to the mobility, they may be back on someone else's payroll before careerists have time to recover from the shock of a layoff.

The public service always seems to attract a particularly large swarm of camp followers: consultants, contractors, temporary and casual workers. Periodically (almost ritually) governments take new brooms in hand and vow to clear the deadwood out. Such reforms most often lead to even more scope for the camp followers. No bureaucrat would ever admit that the *work* of his department could be trimmed — that would make it seem unimportant. So, when staff controls come down from above, the "work" is shifted from the insiders, who can be controlled, to the outsiders, who can't be controlled so easily. There are no fewer memos, just fewer typists to type them. So, the typing agencies are called in to fill the gap. The press releases are pumped out by freelancers instead of information officers. As much or more money is spent to accomplish the same tasks, and everybody is happy, especially the casual workers.

If part-time bureaucracy appeals to you, avoid the regular civil-service route and offer yourself to the nearest, overworked department head — one who controls the department's budget.

Buying and Selling

If Western culture ever organizes economic alternatives into castes, working for others would still be somewhere near the bottom. The elite, the aristocrats of unemployment, the prima donnas of casual income, would always be the ad hoc entrepreneurs, sellers of anything that comes to hand. Such people were once affectionately known as "horse traders." They were more than survivors — they were *artistes*. Horses may have left the roads long before the Edsel, but the knack of buying and selling as the opportunity arises survives.

The rattly old pickup was dribbling ice water into the dust beside the forsaken country road.

"How far ya goin'?" I shouted over the clangor of errant pistons.

"Next pub . . . maybe farther," the driver roared back.

There hadn't been another car all morning and it was hot, dry walking. So I found a narrow perch amongst the litter and junk in the cab, carefully adjusting the springs that snaked through tears in the seat.

Conversation was impossible over the din, so I slumped at the window and took what I could of the breeze coming by. The forward progress was barely enough to keep up a breeze, but it seemed to be all the lopsided, jolting, shimmying hulk could manage.

Mercifully, he killed the motor as he turned off the road and coasted over the thirty yards of gravel to the front of the country pub, peeling in the white of the sun. Even after we stopped, it took a while for the heaving squeaks and wheezes to finish their codas and fade away. The final sound was the steady rivulet of water trickling over the battered tailgate.

My companion walked exactly like his truck — a noisy, rolling waddle wherein forward progress was less than half the total motion. Filling the doorway, he snapped his suspenders.

"Two beers!" he shouted.

The publican looked twice at the fat, old codger in the doorway before he saw me trying to squeeze in from behind. He seemed to be only half grateful for the company.

The old man put the glass to his mouth and sucked half a pint of foamy lager off the top.

He belched. "Gawd it's 'ot!"

The publican mopped the puddles off the bar with a towel, then wiped his face and draped the towel around his neck.

"Wot's for lunch, mate?" the old man asked.

"Pies," said the publican, turning towards the kitchen.

"No bloody fish?" roared my driver, full of indignant surprise.

"No fish around here." The publican paused, his hand on the swinging kitchen door. He sounded tired. "Ya wanna pie or doncha?"

"How come there's no bloody fish?" The fat man winked at me as he finished his question with a swig of beer.

"It's too bloody hot and we're too bloody far from bloody Sydney, ya silly bastard." The publican was getting a mite cross.

The old man relaxed and smiled at him in a genial, conciliatory way.

"Come on out 'ere mate, I got summit for ya," he said.

The publican had to think about it for a minute, and he still looked dubious as he followed us out to the rusty blue hulk disintegrating in front of the pub. The sun was merciless.

The three of us peered over the side of the truck at the homemade plywood box. It sat soaking in those few puddles that hadn't found the tailgate or a rust hole yet. The fat man reached inside the box and drew out a long, dripping knife. The publican knotted his jaw.

"How much can you use?" he asked the publican, raising the lid higher with his other hand so that we could at last see the enormous carcass of a single grouper awash in the remnants of ice.

The publican finally smiled. In fact, the smile got downright grinny as the old man hacked off an armload of cold, wet fish. It might have had something to do with the cool and delicious wash of air that rose from the box as we leaned in to admire the fish.

The publican gave us a couple more beers and the old man got a tenner for the fish. "Where'd the fish come from?" I asked him as we squeezed back into the rattletrap truck.

"Some dumb tourist at the coast gave 'im to me three days ago. Said he just liked spearin' em, not eatin' em."

Ten miles farther on, we stopped for gas, and the manager let the old man take a half-dozen discarded tires from the heap at the back of the station. By evening, most of the fish and all of the ice was gone. The back of the truck, however, was loaded to the gunnels with tires. The tire center in the next town took them all to be retreaded. The old man counted his roll as he squeezed back in behind the wheel again. He peeled off a couple of bills and handed them to me.

"What's that for?" I asked.

"Helpin'." He ground the motor into its usual cacophony and we rattled off to find the best steak dinner in town. We were both more or less headed for Melbourne. Me more and him less, however. After three days and barely 150 miles of net forward motion, I had to leave the old man to catch a faster ride, but I never found a more instructive one. It was slow progress, but we ate and slept in first-class places, had a beer in every pub along the way, and parted company with more cash than when we'd met. For all I know he's still on his way to Melbourne, selling everything along the way.

On our last night together, we split the day's profits and headed for an evening at the local.

"Take one beer and sip it all night," he muttered as we ambled into the bar.

Not my choice, but I knew enough by then to trust him. He stopped in the doorway, snapped his suspenders, and offered a round of beer for all. The dozen or so workmen propped against the bar responded in kind and within a few hours it was the most jovial and ... well ... relaxed bunch of good old boys in town. All except me. I slumped in the corner feeling a little left out until the old man, with more slurring of words than I knew was really in him, neatly turned the mostly incomprehensible talk to the subject of arm wrestling.

Amid the bantering and stumbling, the old man roared, "Ahhh, you puny lot of poofters couldn't even beat the likes of him!" and he pointed his glass at me, then drained it with a sly wink in my direction.

"That skinny bloke in the corner? Put up or shut up you silly old bastard!" and other words to that effect filtered out of the uproar.

A table was cleared, bets were laid, and (suitably handicapped) most of the aspirants were hardly capable of taking a grip, much less deciding in which direction they should pull. We left shortly after — by separate doors of course — and split the take in the truck. The master salesman strikes again.

I never managed to catch the old man's flair for drama or his sure touch at timing the "pitch," but I did learn that you can sell just about anything to anybody if you screw up the nerve to try, and try again if it doesn't work the first time. It can even be fun.

Understanding the Market
Few of us are really cut out to be itinerant, ad hoc salesmen. It's hard on the liver as well as the nerves. There remains, however, a great deal

of scope for casual, penny-ante buying and selling for profit. The key is to keep it on the smallest scale (so it doesn't take too much time from more important things), and to thoroughly understand what you are selling and the market for it.

That approach coincides exactly with the best way to shop for home consumption: understanding the goods and the market. Consequently, buying and selling for profit doesn't require a lot of extra effort; it's simply an extension of careful shopping. We rarely make major spending decisions until we're satisfied that it's the very best deal obtainable anywhere. When we're that sure, it doesn't take any more effort to invest in a little excess. If it's a bargain for us, it will be a bargain for others too.

Take building materials for instance. One year, we needed an inside door. We shopped around and learned that solid-pine inside doors were in the neighborhood of $100 new, and half to two-thirds that price used. Weeks later, at a country auction, a whole pile of discarded doors was on the block, and at the bottom of the pile were three that looked as if they might be suitable. The bidding was slow and the price was right, so I took the whole pile for six dollars. I knew it was a bargain for the door we wanted, so it must be a bargain on the excess too.

We broke even the next day by selling one of the extras to a neighbor who was building a garage. He got a six-dollar door and was thrilled. Another was traded for eight pine shutters, two are serving as shelves, four have been joined for a chicken pen, and the rest are still in the barn; every once in a while someone comes by and asks if we have any old doors around . . .

Urban conservers are even better suited to profit from casual buying and selling: quite simply, there are a lot more customers. The process is exactly the same — shopping carefully for family consumption and buying excess when the bargains are best. When Bradley and his wife got married, they couldn't afford to furnish their home from department stores. So they spent their Saturdays prowling around garage sales, picking up bits and pieces here and there. When the house was full, they were still finding pieces they liked at bargain prices. Brad kept buying. They made room in the house by selling extra pieces to friends (at a reasonable mark-up). When friends couldn't keep up with his bargains, Brad and his wife held garage sales of their own. Now they have a house full of valuable antiques and a profitable part-time hobby.

Others have done the same sort of thing with bicycles, stereos, TVs and cars. The advent of eBay and other online garage sales has made buying and selling even easier and more lucrative for many people. But I suppose somebody, somewhere is still trading horses in the classic fashion.

As a callow youth, I spent a horrible two weeks peddling pots and pans from door to door. The spiel was phony, the price too high, the pots shoddy and the sound of slamming doors memorably haunting, even now. I'll never have what it takes to make a career of selling. But when somebody pulls in the lane and asks if we have any extra eggs, some corn to sell, or any old doors lying around . . . well, it's easier somehow. When the neighbor says she needs a TV and you've got an extra one in the basement, or when the garden produces a load of perfect pumpkins for Halloween, making a sale can be a downright pleasant experience. It's the difference between filling someone else's need and trying to create one.

Cottage Industry

There was a time, in the British Isles, when crofters and "small holders" processed goods for the market right in the family home. Weavers kept a loom in the house, crofters spun, smiths and cobblers and all manner of small-scale artisans worked in their homes or cottages. This activity, in contrast to the centralized wage labor of factories, was referred to as "cottage industry."

The Industrial Revolution killed many of the old-fashioned cottage industries. Now the Technology Revolution has spawned a renaissance. At the heart is a whole new generation of cheap communications: cell phones, laptops, e-mail and web sites. The technology is affordable and portable. There is no longer the old need to have everybody in the same room to do business. It has become easier to work at home, in the car, or at the cottage. The technology of work-at-home, in combination with that other revolution in today's economy — contracting out — has led to a boom in new cottage industries. Self-employed people are now a significant part of the economy.

It isn't all computers. Stay-at-home entrepreneurs still sew, type, paint, write, weave baskets, string snowshoes, start seedlings, fix cars, make jewelry, and — yes — some still spin and weave. The cottage itself is an industry for those who offer "bed and breakfast" accommodation.

My favorite stay-at-home, however, was the young, bearded hitchhiker I picked up on my way to the city one day. In spite of his scruffy appearance, he wafted into the car smelling like grandmother's kitchen. His bulging rucksack was loaded to overflowing with carob rolls and peanut butter cookies. He was, he said, a baker, making his living from his kitchen stove and wholesaling the goodies to city cafes. The delivery system was a little unorthodox, but a small price to pay for the pleasures of working at home.

His approach was unusual, but the traveling baker had all the elements of a typical cottage industry: home-based, no paid employees, and labor intensive. Working at home with the immediate family involved is a familiar model. "Labor intensive" is a term that might require some explanation.

Simply put, goods are produced with three classes of input: the raw material, labor, and capital. The capital is whatever is invested in the tools, machinery, buildings, and so forth, that is used to produce the goods for sale. To a certain extent, capital and labor may be substituted, one for the other. Workers can be replaced by machines, and vice versa. The cookie man, for instance, took all morning to fill his pack with goodies. He put three hours of labor into that load, but the capital investment was negligible: a few pots and pans, a rucksack, and a fraction of the kitchen stove (most of it being used for family meals rather than salable production). Virtually all of the revenue goes to him for his labor. His approach was "labor intensive." On the other hand, he could have invested in automatic mixers and a big industrial oven to mix and bake all his cookies in a single batch. He might have cut his labor down to half an hour or so, but the capital input would have been a great deal higher. That approach would have been "capital intensive."

There's no law that says a cottage industry can't be capital intensive, but in most cases it just isn't practical. The cookie man couldn't afford to leave that big expensive machinery sitting idle for most of the week. He would have to keep it working to pay for itself. That means more cookies than he could carry in his rucksack. So, he would have to buy a truck and hire a driver, or pay another baker to stay home and keep the cookie machines going while he went out on deliveries. He would need somebody else to sell all that extra production and somebody else to keep track of the wages and receipts and the payments on the cookie machines and the truck and . . . and before he knows it, he's got a cookie factory instead of a cottage industry. The operation has certainly outgrown his little farmhouse kitchen, so he has to move the business to a larger building and the payments on that mean even more cookies have to be sold. The cookie man may get rich — or go broke. He may retire to Florida, or spend seven days a week at the cookie factory making ulcers. The capital-intensive approach may have any or all of those results, but it won't result in a cottage industry.

Cottage industry that hires outside employees, or builds up its capital plant to the point where it moves out of the home and acquires a life of its own, simply becomes another small business. Though the differences are mostly ones of degree, the changes in character between cottage industry and a "real" business are of fundamental importance to readers interested in the quality of life.

A small business has a life and momentum of its own. It must support not only its owner but also its employees, the building, inventory, the capital debt, accounts receivable, and so on. The larger a business becomes the harder it is to stop and start, to close it down for the summer, or to exercise fully independent control.

A central part in the life of most small businesses is debt. The risks involved in borrowed capital are high enough that new businesses go bankrupt with alarming regularity. Potential rewards for success may be high, but so is the risk of failure. It's that high level of risk that keeps so many would-be entrepreneurs from taking the plunge. No one with a good idea should be discouraged from launching a full-scale business venture, but it is a pity that so many who are discouraged by the risk believe staying with a salaried job is the only alternative. If the venture can be started at home, with you as the only employee, using labor rather than capital, the risk can be virtually nil. That's the attraction of cottage industry: Less risk — and greater independence.

The Hard Part: Deciding What to Do

There are two approaches to picking a cottage industry. The most obvious is to start with something you already know well: your job, past training, a hobby, or a craft. The other approach is to find a gap in the market that the big guys haven't filled very well — a specialty item or new procedure that may be too small or too new to have attracted organized commerce yet. These are easier to find than most people imagine.

How often have you gone shopping for something and not been able to find what you were looking for?

"Sorry, they don't make those anymore."

"Sorry, this is all we have."

"Sorry, you can only get those in . . . [someplace 80 miles away]."

You have just identified a gap in the market. Faced with such obstacles, enterprising conservers go home to see if they can build it, fix it, or adapt something else to the purpose. The usual outcome is finding out *why* the big guys aren't interested in selling the whatsit you had set out to buy. You discover it really is too expensive, or too difficult, or doesn't work the way you thought it might. Every once in a while, though, basement dabblers discover that they *can* do it better or cheaper than anything else on the market. That's a gap in the market ready-made for home industry.

Setting out to buy something and ending up providing it is just what got us into making heat shields. It sparked a frustrated connoisseur into setting up his own wine-importing business. And it turned one student veterinarian into a kitchen table surgeon. The poor chap couldn't afford to get his own cats spayed at professional rates, so he did it himself. The story spread and soon he was providing a much needed neighborhood service. He eventually got his license, an office, and a lucrative practice at professional rates. The old neighborhood, I expect, is overrun with cats again.

Ironically, opportunities for home industry seem to be growing rather than shrinking. One would think that over time all the gaps in all the markets would be filled, that all the profitable ideas would be taken. Seems logical — except for the fact that markets are dominated by the big guys, who continue to get bigger and bigger and more and more standardized. They're too big to be bothered with any items for which demand would be small, or specialized, or regional, or . . . . This is just the sort of thing a cottage industry is suited for. The big guys want to supply the world. If you want to make whatchamacallits for your neighbors, or elbow patches for one-armed poker players, or anything else where the demand is just about big enough to keep your basement in full production, chances are you may get some competition from your neighbors or from other one-armed poker players, but not from General Motors. The big guys only want big gaps in the market. The cottage industrialist is happy with little gaps.

Setting Up

The details of starting any particular venture as a cottage industry will vary too widely to generalize here. There are three points, however, that ought to be stressed:

1. Test the market for price and saleability. No matter how sure you are of your product, it pays to actually build a few prototypes first and see how well they sell. It's easier to change the design or the color or whatever *before* you get all geared up with a load of materials for full production.

2. Minimize capital costs. Any small-scale business goes through innumerable changes in the first few years as you learn more about the market and find shortcuts or improvements in the process. Such changes are easier to make if you haven't committed yourself at the beginning to a shop full of expensive tools and materials. In the beginning it pays to keep these capital costs as close to zero as possible. Borrow equipment, rent it, substitute more labor-intensive methods, but start on the smallest shoestring you can. It's easier to make the inevitable changes and there's less at risk.

3. Find out what licenses, permits, and zoning changes you would need to operate legally. Zoning regulations vary from city to city. The object is to control development and to keep you from becoming a nuisance to your neighbors. Government bodies require licenses in many specialized areas: cat spaying, brain surgery, and the handling of food, for instance. The object is to protect your customers. Most jurisdictions require a vendor's permit or business license to identify your commercial character. The object is to know where to send the tax bill. For details, check at city hall.

Selling Your Wares

For many otherwise clever and forceful people the actual selling of what they do is the hardest part of independence. It's not surprising. We are, after all, taught from childhood about the virtues of being modest, humble, and self-effacing. Then, to survive, we find it necessary to tout our skills or wares as the very best there are. Even if we believe it, it's hard sometimes to say it to others. It feels so . . . pushy.

Don't despair, modest reader. There's a way to be business-like without losing that virtue. It's called a *sample*. Samples of your work, shown to prospective buyers, can sell themselves. Whether you are planning to make planters or photos or latkes, have some samples ready and let the buyer judge the quality. If your income scheme is based on a service rather than a product (house-sitting, garden design or tax consultation for instance) the sample can take the form of a written description of the services offered, prices, photos if possible, and — best of all — testimonials from previous customers. If the quality of your work can speak for itself, all that remains is to find the buyers and set the price.

There is some advantage, not entirely psychological, in starting with smaller prospective customers. Chances are the big guys are already supplied by the other big guys. Those little gaps in the market that you are looking for are at the other end of the scale. So, don't go waltzing into Sears with your first two widgets hoping that they'll put them on a shelf for you. They may like them and ask for a thousand a week, when you're only geared up for two. Build if you will, but do start small.

Wherever you go for those first few sales, set the objective in advance. "This week I'm going to call on these five (or seven or forty) prospects." The objective is set on the basis of how many tries you will make, not on the number of sales. The only purpose is to ward off discouragement from the first few refusals, to keep you plugging away in the face of apparent defeat. Think of those first attempts as practice sessions, trial runs to get your knees to stop shaking and to find out what questions prospective customers want answered.

How Much?

The first question customers ask is usually, "How much?" The answer, of course, depends on whether you're selling retail, wholesale, or on consignment (where the retailer accepts your product for display and pays you a fixed percentage of the retail price after the goods are sold). The price depends on what the competition charges, what the product costs you to produce, and how many you wish to sell. In short, there is no one right price. You're your own boss and it's entirely up to you. You may wish to ask yourself a few pertinent questions, though.

What's fair? You know your costs of production and what your own time ought to be worth. Covering those costs is the basis of a reasonable price. Someone else, however, may have found ways to do the same thing more cheaply. If your prices are higher than the competition's, your venture may be short-lived. You may have to charge less than a "fair" price until you have found ways to pare down the costs.

What will the market bear? That's an even more critical question than fairness. If your price is too high you could end up with a basement of widgets and no customers. If prices are too low, your widgets will be sold faster than you can make them, and you will spend a lot of time saying "sorry" to disappointed customers. Economists call that the law of demand (the cheaper they are the more you can sell).

If you're lucky, your *fair* price will attract just enough customers to keep you as busy as you want to be. Your supply will meet the customers' demand at a point where everybody is happy with the price and there are no unsold widgets or unfilled orders. If you are not so lucky, you may have to fiddle with the price.

Undercharging, or even giving away free samples, is one way to get things rolling — to convince prospective buyers to try your wares and, you hope, keep buying after the price goes up.

Overcharging (setting a price that's higher than what you have decided is fair return for your time and costs) is a simple way to control sales volume when it threatens to become a landslide. The idea is to scare off just enough customers to bring demand in line with the level you want to produce.

Finally, there are times when it becomes necessary to be absolutely outrageous with your price. Times when you would really rather not sell. One October, the kids and I cleaned out the garden and decided to take the leftover squash and pumpkins to the market. We found a spot amidst the other vendors and sorted the future jack-o'-lanterns into a lumpy pile, a good pile, and one absolutely perfect scaremonger that the kids wanted to carve for themselves. When "Please don't sell this one, Daddy" didn't work, they tried sitting on it so no one would see it.

The first question from the first customer was, of course, "How much are they?"

The kids looked at me and I looked at them.

"What do you think?" I asked the seven-year-old, who had already checked out the competition.

"Seventy-five cents for the lumpy ones and one dollar for the good ones," she answered.

"What about the one you're sitting on?" asked the woman.

"Ten dollars," said the miniature tycoon, deadpan. Outrageous, but she got to keep her pumpkin.

Think Small

Those who approach income as serious business (driven by greed, ambition, or debt) often succeed through sheer hard work. "Think big! Aim high!" and all those other inspirational catechisms of the capitalist religion hang in their heads if not on their office walls.

The survivor, though, keeps a different set of rules. When income is given only casual consideration — as a minor nuisance or a means rather than an end — the inevitable outcome is that less hard work may go into any one venture. More of the survivor's income schemes may fail or simply wither from neglect. Let's face it, if the hard-driving, big-money, ulcer-riddled ranks of the real moguls fail at such an impressive rate, what chance do the casual survivors have after spending most of their energy on the nonprofit side of life? They decrease their chance of failure by treating debt like the plague, but the casual approach is — without a doubt — a handicap to big financial success.

Survivors accept from the start that their casual income schemes are handicapped, that not everything will succeed. The strategy, then, is simply to keep a number of schemes in motion at any one time. This is what distinguishes you from the "real" businesspeople. They work hard at one thing, and either fail or get rich. Survivors work casually at a number of things.

Making a living doesn't have to take over living itself.
• • • • • • • • • • • •

Some succeed and some don't. Since all their ventures start small and are free of debt, the flops don't lead to bankruptcy and ruin, they just don't make any money. And the successes don't lead to fame and riches. They're little successes — just enough to meet your needs if your needs are simple enough.

"Think small" is not an apology for dropping out, or a credo for all of life's little wallflowers. It's no more than a reminder that making a living doesn't have to take over living itself. *It is a way of scaling down financial risks and financial expectations simultaneously.* Think small and diversify. Any income scheme that gets boring, doesn't pay, or interferes with more important things can be discarded, with no more effort than ignoring it.

Freelance Living

So far we've talked about casual approaches to relatively standard ways of making a living: employment, buying and selling, cottage industry. These are small, controlled attachments to the regular economy. Those attachments can become even more tenuous when the workers (independently) seek markets for what they do rather than doing what the market asks.

In the confusing days of medieval warfare, the freelancer was *literally* that: an unattached soldier, a mercenary, later called (less romantically) a hired gun. Those types are still around, but modern freelancers can also be writers, artists, photographers, broadcasters, teachers, or just about anything else. They sell their skills or creations to anyone. I know a freelance bookkeeper, a freelance scientist, a freelance stage designer and a freelance builder of parade floats. It's like a cottage industry where the owner is also the product. It's like casual employment, except that there are usually several customers instead of a single employer and the freelancer is always the boss.

Apart from the obvious attributes of maximum freedom and independence, to be a freelance anything is to enjoy the justice of a system where success is almost solely a function of talent and effort. Freelancers live outside the usual rules of paper credentials, seniority advancement, and office politics. Their work is judged on its merits.

Paradoxically, this makes it easier to enter any field and yet harder to get established. Entry is easier because the work provides its own credentials. To be employed as a salaried photographer, for example, may require professional experience, accredited training, or the crossing of a number of other barriers set up to separate the wheat from the chaff. But the barriers are based on the *person*. Talented beginners may find it tough to cross those barriers, in spite of the quality of their work. But as a freelancer, you are free to call yourself a photographer and let your work be accepted or rejected on the basis of whether it's any good or not. There are still barriers, but they are more about the work itself than the person. Getting established as a freelancer requires that your work be seen by a number of potential buyers. Being seen is the hard part. Most people with money to spend on freelancers are busy people. Persistence, patience, the shotgun approach, or all those tactics may be necessary to get your foot in the door. After a few successes, getting in the door is easier. One job leads to another. Those first few jobs, however, take some special effort. It might help to keep in mind the lessons applied to a cottage industry:

♦ Do sample work (or even free work) if it will help to have your product seen by potential buyers.

♦ Diversify, keeping several projects in the works at once, in the hope that one of them will catch on somewhere.

♦ Refuse to be discouraged by initial rebuffs.

One would-be writer started his freelance career by vowing to always keep at least three articles in the mail at any one time. The first few rejections might have ended his efforts, except that he could always hope the other two prospects might be positive. Every rejection slip had to be followed by another submission. No matter how bad the news in the mail, there was always hope that better news could follow. It did.

Casual Income: New Beginning or a Way of Life?

There are many independent types who spend their evenings setting up a basement industry or trying to peddle that first short story. Some are compelled by dreams of success in a more independent line — something riskier, more far-reaching, and more rewarding than what they do for a work-a-day wage. They are seeking new beginnings. Others are less concerned with reaching the stars than with simply generating a few bucks to support some other dream.

Whatever the motives, casual incomes are invariably easier to generate than most nine-to-fivers imagine. There are more ways to make a living than ever appear in job descriptions at the employment agency. There are certainly more ways than I ever dreamed of when that rusty blue truck pulled up, rattling and wheezing and dripping water into the dust.

~ 6 ~

The Secondhand Market

The catalog beside me shows a simple wooden table. A card table. Four legs and a top. Not even a drawer to hide the aces in. And it's used. Sotheby's, a prestigious auction house, estimates its value at $125,000! They, of course, don't refer to it as "used." Status-conscious consumers don't buy used furniture — they buy *antiques*.

Fancy euphemisms like "antique" furniture, "heritage" china and "previously owned" cars are all aimed at covering up the stigma of buying secondhand. The euphemisms, naturally, affect the price, hence the fabled sign in front of the country *shoppe*: "We Buy Old Junk and Sell Antiques."

Thank goodness, though, there are such stigmas. That's what makes it possible for the conserver crowd to maintain a happy standard of material living at a fraction of the cost of shopping in the shoppes. We stick to *shops*, and buy used stuff and junk. What a difference a name makes!

Unfortunately, more vendors seem to be catching on to the name game. More and more junk is being sold as "junque," and advertisements for antique cars with automatic transmission and power-steering make one wonder if the term hasn't already been stretched beyond usefulness. When I start seeing ads for "old" antiques, I'll know it's time to discard the word entirely.

If you can stay ahead of the name-changers, however, and don't mind being seen in the low-rent district where junk is spelled with a "k," the secondhand market is still a bonanza for cheap living. Buying secondhand is not the same as retail shopping. The rules are different. If you like the convenience of the big plazas and department stores, you've probably also fallen into the habit of accepting prices on the basis of the store's reputation. One chain is known for cheap imports and bargain basement prices; others are known to carry medium quality at medium prices. And every town has at least one store whose prices have more to do with snob appeal than quality. When you want something cheap to wear in the garden, you don't shop around for price; you go to the store with the cheapest reputation and trust that the lowest price there will be the lowest in town. It's not that easy in the secondhand market.

The successful secondhand shopper has to judge price and quality independently — for each item — with less regard for the reputation of the seller. I have seen the most upright and honest of country auctioneers selling used household goods for more than the same item would cost new at the hardware store down the street. I have also found occasional bargains at the snootiest antique shoppes. In the secondhand market, there's just no way of recognizing a bargain unless you know ahead of time what you want, and what it's worth.

What You Want and What It's Worth

Secondhand shopping begins at home. Unlike retail shopping, the value of the thing you're after is not the same as what the store is charging. You have to decide fair value for yourself. The best place to start is with consumer guides, catalogs, websites and that enormous free library of price information: the junk mail circular.

The consumer guides (by subscription, or free at the public library) provide a wealth of comparative data on products — how they last, which ones work and which ones need loopholes in the warranties, which are safe, and what the average retail price will be. Exhaustive tests and brand-by-brand comparisons provide an encyclopedic review of all the things the ads won't tell you. For most common products, consumer guides will, at the very least, help to weed out some brands or products that will *not* suit your needs.

Of particular interest to the secondhand buyer is information on durability and potential problems. If the Brand X widget is prone to wear out in the left rear whatsit, that's the first thing to check when you find a used one. Faults in used products are easier to spot if you know what to look for ahead of time.

The least useful information in consumer guides is the prices. The national averages listed may be irrelevant in your own locale, and price information is rapidly outdated. Check current prices, local sales, and store-by-store price comparisons in the chain store catalogs and flyers that come with the mail in a daily stream.

Collecting such information need not be a major research job where you precede every shopping trip with charts and studies and a trip to the library. With me it's more like a habitual tic. I turn to the classified ads the way other newspaper readers turn first to the sports or comics. Knowing what we need to buy ahead of time, and then delaying the purchase as long as possible (remember procrastination) leaves a lot of time to register mental notes of prices. If I can't remember the current retail price of any item, it's easy enough to check the catalogs.

What's collecting in the head, though, are prices for new items — and remember we're going shopping for used. The new price is an absolute upper limit. There's nothing more embarrassing than buying a used anything, then finding it on sale, new, at a lower price. And I'm not being persnickety, because it happens all the time. Some time ago I was in a secondhand shop (which has since become a shoppe) and was surprised to see a modern wine bottle in the midst of a display of antique bottles. The modern bottle was familiar — an attractive earthenware imitation — but the price was a shocker at twenty dollars.

"You know," I said to the owner, "you can buy that bottle new at the liquor store for $9.85, and you get a liter of wine with the bottle."

"I know," he admitted, "but a lot of customers don't."

What's a Used One Worth?

If the new price provides a crude sort of upper limit on the worth of secondhand goods, it might save total embarrassment, but won't guarantee you any bargains. For a better idea of secondhand values, shoppers should consider the new price, reduced according to the age and condition of the used one. This approach will be familiar enough to used car buyers. The value of a year-old car in average condition is a given percentage of its new price.

The declining value from an initial new price is called *depreciation,* and most things that wear out can be given a value by depreciating them. It's not a precise calculation — more like organized guesswork — but it can be a more reliable guide to secondhand values than simply taking the seller's word for it. Here's how it works:

My favorite electrical repairman tells me that the small portable washing machine we want usually lasts only six or seven years. New ones are being advertised for around $630. That makes it worth about $105 a year ($630 ÷ 6 = $105).

After finding a used machine for sale, the first concern is to ensure that it is in good working order. That means turning it on, pumping water back and forth through all the cycles, looking for leaks, and listening for groans and rattles. The second step is to find out how old the thing is. The dates will be on the original warranty papers or bill of sale — ask for them! If the machine is three years old, we assume that it has used up half its life and is now worth a maximum of $315 ($105 per year × 3 years = $315).

That's a maximum and not an average because we know that the last three years of the machine's life are worth less than the first three years. In the last half of its life it will require more replacement parts and service calls. It may even die sooner than its allotted six or seven years. But we can set $315 as the upper limit, offer $100, and settle somewhere around $200. For that price we would expect to have at least two years of maintenance-free washing.

Appreciate What You Can't Depreciate

Not everything loses value with the passage of time. More durable items (like furniture, tools, building material, metal goods, and so on) must be valued more by their condition than by their age. Indeed, the older goods were often better made, of better material, than the newest models. Setting a fair value for such goods gets a little tricky. It helps to spend enough time at auctions and secondhand sales to get a rough idea of the market value of comparable items. Here, there is no good substitute for experience.

Take beds, for example. Old wooden bedsteads were more solidly and beautifully crafted than most of the stuff being manufactured today. It would be tempting then to say that an old bed is at least as valuable as any comparable new bed. The price of "antique" beds in the shoppes would seem to bear this out but, closer to the source, the price of used beds does funny things. Somehow, they seem to be a glut on the market. And it is not at all uncommon to see solid, old beds of maple and ash selling at auctions and farm sales for twenty dollars or less. No rule of thumb would tell you that, and an inexperienced buyer who finds herself a nice, old bed in an antique shoppe for a little less than the price of a new veneer one might think she had found a bargain. It would be a bargain, too — except that you can get it even cheaper elsewhere.

What's It Worth As Raw Material?

When experience, or depreciation from a new price, doesn't tell me whether a secondhand buy is a bargain or not, I often fall back on a basic rule of thumb: *what's the worth of the material in it?* Like semi-handy do-it-yourselfers everywhere, I make a lot of well-meant but worthless promises to build and fix things around the house "one of these days." Sometimes, I even get as far as drawing a plan or making a list of the materials needed for the shelves in the cellar or the kitchen table or whatever. At some point in my auction habit, it occurred to me that buying a table was often cheaper than buying the lumber to build one. If I didn't like the table on sale, I could take it apart and use the wood to build a better one. In fact, there are usable materials in a lot of bargains that might otherwise be ignored.

One of the more expensive items on our "one of these days" list was a greenhouse. Expensive because of the price of glass. So I kept "glass" on my permanent shopping list, and collected bargains here and there with an eventual greenhouse in mind. Then one summer, when our glass collection was about half what we needed, a nearby estate sale advertised a quantity of glass to be auctioned off. Obviously some others around here had the same idea, and bidding on the glass was brisk. The short guy in front, with the bald and well-tanned head, was getting most of the glass, and paying dearly for the privilege. I wasn't surprised, then, when late in the afternoon he bought a pile of storm windows, with two sheets of new glass on top of the pile. I was surprised, though, when he picked up only the smaller new sheets and started to take them away.

"I thought you were buying the storm windows," I said as he passed.

"No," said the bald man, with the sly grin of a successful bargain on his face. "I'm building a greenhouse, and all I want is the glass. Take the windows if you want them."

I loaded them quickly, certain he would realize at any moment that there was a lot more glass in the windows than he had in his hands.

We eventually finished the greenhouse with large, double-glazed windows from an office demolition. The demolition crew was happily smashing the three-foot by three-foot plate glass panes out of their aluminum frames. The boss had told them only to salvage the aluminum, then worth twenty cents a pound. We weighed a frame, figured it had three dollars worth of aluminum in it, and bought a truckload of the windows (with glass) for three dollars each.

When It Almost Works

Like the proverbial cup that's half-empty or half-full depending on your point of view, there are people who can see residual value in someone else's junk. A thing may be worthless if it doesn't work. But add the price of what it takes to make it whole again and you may have a valuable bargain.

An ax without a handle won't cut wood, and that's why ax heads are often thrown out or sold secondhand for pennies. The people who buy an ax head for pennies are the people who know that adding a ten-dollar handle will make it as good as a thirty-dollar ax.

There was the discarded freezer that wouldn't keep anything frozen. We added a five-dollar seal around the door and used it for eight years after it had been given up as worthless.

A common form of this talent is the guy on every block who can take someone else's junkyard car and add a whatsit, some bodywork, and end up with something as good as new. With cars, that talent is worth thousands.

It doesn't always take a special skill, however. Sometimes a different perspective is enough. Years ago, before my partner had learned to pound a nail, she saw the neighbor put out two broken chairs for the garbage. It was a matching pair: a rocker with a broken back and a straight chair with a broken seat. Liz went right over, pulled the broken back off the rocker and replaced it with the good back from the other chair. It's still in use today. The neighbor had seen two broken chairs where Liz had seen the makings of one.

If there is a secret to dealing in the secondhand market, it's buying on the basis of a thing's bad feature (the half-empty side) and using or selling it for its residual value (the half-full side).

Look At Function

Chapter 3 urges that needs be considered in terms of function. It's a simple change in perspective that has no other purpose than to open our minds to a broader range of possible substitutes, including the more unusual substitutes that may be considerably cheaper than the common commercial solutions to our needs.

The *function* approach is especially useful in the secondhand market, where prices and supply are so much more erratic than on the retail scene. The simple fact is that we often can't find what we feel we need, and have no choice but to look for substitutes.

I saw the lesson hit home with one woman who cleaned out her cupboards and brought her castoffs to the flea market rather than the dump. She had an old shower curtain in her discard pile.

"I don't know whether to put this thing on the counter or not," she mused. "I can't imagine anybody wanting *this* in their bath!" She finally shrugged and put it at the back of the sales table, hoping that for twenty-five cents some sucker would at least save her the trouble of taking it home again.

Later on, we munched a few of her bran muffins that she hadn't sold and the talk turned to fixing up houses. She was, she told me, in the midst of painting every wall in the house.

"And the hardest part is to keep from painting the furniture and floors at the same time. Good drop cloths are so expensive for what they are . . . my God!" she sputtered through a mouthful of muffin, scrambling to salvage her sturdy waterproof material from the sales table before someone else saw that it could function as something other than a dirty, old shower curtain.

One more example: Solar heat, the oil moguls tell us, is expensive and impractical. And if you go to the marketplace to buy solar panels — even small systems to heat water — their disdain appears to be justified. The darned things are expensive for what they are: basically a grid of tubing under glass or plastic. But, in the secondhand market, there are items that fill that function perfectly: large, elaborate grids of tubing, often copper, made for heat conduction. Most are already painted black, as solar panels are. They are so cheap that most people don't even bother trying to sell them. They're drained of Freon (a type of chlorofluorocarbon used in refrigerants) and dumped in landfills, or worse. The people throwing them out don't even know they're solar panels though. They call them broken refrigerators and never consider the function of all that stuff on the back! Just like the old storm windows —they have no value because they don't fit the new aluminum frames. Those people don't realize they're throwing out covers for solar panels and greenhouses.

A Good Seller Is Hard to Find

The thing that buyers must understand about sellers is that the source that's easiest to find is likely to be the most expensive. Take furniture for instance. Retail furniture stores are easily accessible, well-advertised and the most expensive source in the market. The buyer pays dearly for the convenience of knowing where to find furniture without looking. Secondhand stores aren't located in the big shopping plazas and don't blanket the area with full-color ads. They're harder to find and a little

The source that's easiest to find is usually the most expensive as well.
•••••••••••••

cheaper. Small-time sellers (who insert little classified ads in the paper to get rid of the old dining table) are usually cheaper still. In fact, that's where the secondhand dealers get a lot of their stock. The cheapest source of all is often the person who owns such things but never bothers to put them on the market. That's the guy who puts his old dining table in the basement and forgets about it until someone comes along and offers to take it off his hands. He places so little value on his discards that he takes no steps at all to make them accessible. That's one of the reasons there are so many enterprising souls in the want ads of any newspaper, offering themselves and their pick-up trucks to help clean up basements.

If you want to find the best deal on the secondhand market, the trick is to imagine who might be discarding the thing that you want but is too small or too busy or too something to bother being available to buyers. Readers who had to buy their own textbooks will remember that the rich kids bought them new at the biggest bookstore nearest campus. Students on a budget went to the secondhand bookstore that always seemed to be down an alley or in a basement. The real penny-pinchers, though, sought out the rich kids who had already taken the course and made them an offer for last year's texts.

Avoiding Fads

If accessibility makes secondhand buys more expensive, used items that are so popular and accessible that they become fads can cost more than the new version. There was a time not long ago when "barn board" was selling in the cities for a dollar a board foot (one square foot of one-inch board). At the same time, the new stuff — the unweathered lumber from which barns were built — was available at the mills for thirty cents a board foot! And yet fad-conscious builders continued to buy the more expensive barn board and nail it over outside walls where the new stuff would have weathered to match before the builder could earn the difference in price. These are probably the same people who pay twice as much for pre-faded jeans.

There are fashions even in the secondhand market, but people who buy secondhand to save money should understand the cost of fashion.

Let's Make a Deal

When buying new, you decide what you want, the seller tells you what it's worth, and you decide whether or not you can afford it. As a buyer, your role is mostly limited to saying "Yes" or "No."

In the secondhand market, however, buyers take a more active part. It takes more effort to find what you're looking for, more patience to find the cheapest source, more careful attention to the condition of one thing, and a lot more fun in making a deal. In this market you see, there really is no price. I know, I know, there's often a piece of paper with a dollar sign and some numbers on it. *Forget it.* That's for the carriage trade and the odd tourist who wanders in.

Neophytes to the scene are prone to edging shyly into junk shops and rummage sales. It's unfamiliar territory. Even the dusty, mothball smells are different. Not at all like the Muzak and bright lights of "normal" stores. Finding that the goods don't have a price tag is one more disconcerting difference in this alien culture.

"How much is it?" your spouse whispers, edging around behind you in the narrow aisle.

"I can't find the price tag," you answer.

"Ask the man."

"It's too dark in here to see the price."

"Well, *ask* him."

"It's probably too expensive anyway."

"Here he comes."

"Can I help you folks?" asks the dealer.

"No thanks. Just browsing."

If you are a refugee from Muzak plaza, in a place as strange and foreign as a secondhand shop, finding a price tag is like a welcome sight from home. You can pay it and get out, or you can be righteously horrified at how high it is and walk out feeling comfortable and superior again.

"Did you see that tatty old chair in there for forty bucks? New ones, just like that, were on sale at the plaza last week for thirty-five. Can you imagine!"

When your eyes get accustomed to the gloom and your nose stops running at the whiff of mothball, you'll learn to ignore the price tags. And that's when the fun begins. Anyway, if you've been paying attention to this chapter so far, you won't even go in the door of a secondhand shop until you have some good ideas as to what you want and how much it's worth. You know the retail price of the new ones, how long they last, what is likely to break or wear out, and what possible substitutes might do the same job. You don't need a price tag to tell you what it's worth because you already know.

Then when you find what you want, make an offer. Of course you won't offer what you know it's worth. You'll offer a great deal less. The dealer will be shocked, disgusted, mocking or even gently chiding you for offering such a ludicrous sum. Don't take it personally, though. That's the same reaction you are supposed to have when he or she states the price or shows you the tag. The price starts, of course, at a much higher level than the thing is worth. So you are both in the same game. When you realize that the dealer's offended reaction is part of the sale, it assumes a familiar, almost ritualistic form. A ritual in which you, the buyer, are expected to participate. The dealer doesn't expect to make a sale every time, but there is genuine disappointment when the buyer drops out at the very first salvo without so much as a counter offer.

Despite being strangers on a seller's turf, buyers do bring some weapons of their own to the contest. They are expected to use every visible or imaginable defect to deduct from the price. The scenario goes something like this:

After the dealer has made two or three cuts from his initial price and doesn't appear to go any lower—

Seller: That's it. Take it or leave it.

Buyer: And a fair price, too . . . if it were in good condition.

Seller: They don't come any better than that.

Buyer: The left rear whatsit is worn. *[Rattle it.]*

Seller: Easy to fix.

Buyer: Maybe, but the parts are going to cost me another umpteen dollars *[deduct that from the dealer's last price]*. And there's some rust here. I'll have to clean off the whole thing and paint it *[make another deduction]*. And it looks pretty old. Probably won't last very long.

By now the seller is steaming and sputtering about what great shape the thing is in, and how he never claimed it was new, and do you know how much the new ones cost, and . . .

Buyer: But the new ones are guaranteed. Will you guarantee this old thing? *[Of course he won't.]*

It often happens that buyer and seller get stuck with some distance left between each one's "final" offer. Neither is willing to budge. That is the time to bring up "extras."

Buyer: Well, I'll pay your price . . . but only if you throw in the *[whatever else catches your fancy that might be worth the difference]*.

or. . . but only if you fix the *[whatsit]*.

or. . . but only if you deliver it.

[The Seller protests . . .]

Buyer: Well, knock something off the price, and then I'll fix it *[or pick it up]* myself.

If you're lucky, you'll convince the dealer to accept a price at or below what you know it's worth. A bargain is struck. The handshake is made with both parties protesting at once that they are losing money on the deal.

Will that Be Cash or . . .

The buyer pulls out his checkbook and pen, smoothes out a check, and pauses . . . "Or perhaps you would rather have cash?" The dealer starts to smile.

"Shall we say $X cash?" *[buyer names a sum twenty percent less than the one just agreed to].*

The dealer protests of course, and the haggling starts again. The buyer's line is one of wounded innocence: "Oh, but I thought that saving on bookkeeping and banking, and the risk that checks might bounce would be worth twenty percent to an astute businessperson like yourself." It would be crass to add that cash receipts aren't always reported to the tax department. Crass to say it, but a hint will let him know that you know he knows it.

He will nevertheless continue to protest and may only be willing to concede ten percent or so. If the dealer won't make any concessions for cash, go back to writing out the check (or using your direct debit card), or better still, pull out a credit card. That will cost him up to six percent more to collect from the credit card company. For all those reasons, the seller has more to gain from a cash transaction than you do. Just make sure he pays you for the favor.

Although you will never catch them saying so in public, most businesses would rather see cash than the ubiquitous credit cards. The reason is simple. Every credit card transaction costs the seller a percentage of the receipt. The credit card company takes its cut off the top before it turns your money over to the retailer. Most cash customers, though, pay the same price as the credit card buyers. Cash means up to six percent more profit for the seller. The cost of handling credit cards is passed on to cash and credit buyers alike. It's up to the cash buyer to demand fair treatment. A few establishments advertise discounts for cash. Others will allow cash discounts if a buyer demands them. If they don't, shop somewhere else.

Secondhand Sources

Not every shopper enjoys the mock-serious sport of haggling for bargains. But even shy buyers can enjoy the color and variety of places that deal in "previously owned." The retail stores at Muzak plaza differ in prices and decor: higher prices, thicker carpets and lower lights. A rummage sale, however, is as different from a pawnshop as a garage sale is from an auction. There are a lot more differences between them than price and decor.

Finding What You Want in the Want Ads

Most newspapers have a section of "want ads," properly known as the classified section. Businesses and high-volume dealers use them, but the "for sale" columns are mostly for the little guys — individuals with personal discards to sell.

These can be the best or worst bargains in the secondhand market. It depends entirely on the individual selling the goods. There's no easy way to tell, short of calling the number and asking for details.

The worst buys are often those advertised by inexperienced sellers who simply cannot accept that their nearly new whatsit is no longer worth a little bit less than what they paid when it really was new. This is particularly true of cars and big appliances that may have been bought on credit, and have depreciated faster than the monthly payments. It's hard for the seller to accept that the resale value may be less than the amount still owed.

On the other hand, inexperienced sellers tend to undervalue goods that may require only minor repairs, or older goods that don't depreciate rapidly, like solid furniture, good tools, lamps and dishes.

Sellers differ, too, in their bargaining flexibility. Some have clearly been guessing at prices and are quite willing to consider your view of the market value. Others get stubborn and insist that the asking price is a final price, whether it's reasonable or not.

When shopping in the ads, be careful to follow all possible sources. The big daily papers offer the widest choices, but the smaller weeklies, local neighborhood flyers, and shopping circulars often carry more interesting ads. They may not be as current as those in the daily paper, but prices are often better because sellers place so little value on their goods that they are reluctant to pay for a more expensive newspaper ad. It also pays to check neighborhood bulletin boards for the casual handwritten ads stuck up with a pin. These are often found in places like supermarkets, laundromats and community centers.

In urban areas, there is a particular advantage in following the ads in neighborhood flyers and bulletin boards. It saves you the trouble of traveling all over the city for bargains that may not be bargains when you get there.

Shopping the ads is a popular sport and the best buys are quickly gone. It helps to be the first one on the scene. That means get the paper early (don't wait for home delivery) and start calling immediately. If you do find a bargain, don't dither and think about coming back later after you've checked out the other prospects on your list. The real bargains won't be there when you get back. Offer cash, and close quickly.

When you've been reading the ads for a while, some of them will start to look familiar. Some of them are merely dealers fishing in another pond. Others, however, are genuine, one-time, clear-out-the-basement civilians. Chances are their initial prices were too optimistic. The first rush of bargain hunters said, "No thanks," and now the stuff is still sitting there. When you find an ad like this that has been running for a week or more, call back, even if you tried them on the first day and found the asking price too high. Given time, and the inconvenience of all that unsold clutter, they may come to appreciate your view of a more realistic price.

The Secondhand Shop(pe)

These are the people who buy old junk and sell antiques. The problem, usually, is the price. The range of types is wide, from classy antiques to wreckers' yards. What they have in common is their middle-man status. They buy the goods from the people who have used them, and sell them back to the second rank of users. There's nothing inherently wrong with that position. They do, after all, provide a service in making all those scattered sources more accessible. If you want an old table in a hurry, it's much easier to walk into a shop that may have a dozen tables to choose from than to spend a week trying to track down sellers through the want ads. The secondhand shops are selling convenience.

The thing to remember is that you have access to the same sources as they do. Attending auctions was a great educator in this respect. After a while I began to recognize a few antique dealers and kept an eye on what they were buying. Walking into one dealer's shop on the day after an auction, I was astonished to see a bench with a price of seventy dollars that I had seen him buy the night before for two dollars. A hundred other people could have had it for the same price.

There are no giveaways in secondhand shops, but it is possible to find decent bargains from the dealers. The knack is to avoid the carriage trade. Stick to the low-rent district. Shopping off-season to avoid any tourist traffic helps. So does buying midweek and other slow periods when the dealer has time to haggle awhile.

Remember, too, that even secondhand dealers have waste. An antique dealer, for instance, may buy her stock at auctions or in bulk lots (a whole estate). Only a part of the purchase will be old enough or good enough to display in her shop. The rest is sold to other dealers, sent back to be auctioned off again, or sold from the back room to bargain hunters who wander in and ask for a whatsit even if they don't see one in the window. A goodly chunk of our own home library is from a rare book dealer who casts off the modern paperbacks that clutter up his purchases. Asking an antique dealer, "What's new?" isn't just a bad joke; it's also a legitimate request to see her cheaper goods.

About the best you can hope for from secondhand dealers is to come close to scrap prices: furniture for the price of the lumber in it or metal by the pound.

We set out one year to buy the cheapest old woodstove we could find. All it had to do was make smoke for the smokehouse, and be sturdy enough to be left outdoors. After three days of trekking around sales and stove stores, I finally drove into a secondhand shop. Hope quickened at the sight of hundreds of old cast-iron woodstoves heaped carelessly in the weeds behind the building. The dealer was understanding, but the cheapest relic in the pile would still cost me fifty dollars, broken or not. Scrap iron, he explained, was worth eight cents a pound. The average stove would bring twenty-five bucks as scrap. To pull one out and help me load it would cost another twenty-five. Discouraged, I bought a single door (by the pound) and went home to build a stove from a salvaged oil drum. I was just about finished bolting the door on the barrel when a neighbor, a retired school teacher, stopped to watch.

"Why didn't you tell me you were looking for a stove?" she scolded. "I've had an old one sitting on the back porch all fall. It's too darned heavy to get to the dump. If you can move it you can have it."

The lesson stuck like one of those little light bulbs that pop into the lives of cartoon characters. The heft of an old stove made it valuable to the secondhand dealer, but the same heft made it difficult for others.

Those hundreds of stoves piled up in the weeds must have come from a lot of individuals who were just happy to get the darned things carted away. I was free to use the same sources the dealer had.

Pawnshops

For the buyer, a pawnshop is not much different from any other secondhand shop. In general, the wares are a little more specialized, with emphasis on more valuable and portable items like watches, jewelry, cameras, radios and musical instruments. Pawnshops warrant special mention only because they acquire their stock somewhat differently from other shops.

A pawnshop is basically a lending establishment. They lend cash to customers who are, in turn, required to leave some item of value behind as collateral to secure the loan. If the loan is not repaid, the collateral is sold from the shop.

There's a touch of Hollywood mystery about the pawnshop. Its image flickers in that gray gulf between good guys and bad guys. Maybe it's because of the role it plays in personal hard luck stories, where the loan is not reputable enough to warrant the lower interest rates available at the bank or the borrower is too romantic to sell his collateral outright at the higher prices regular dealers could offer.

Because of its shady aura, some buyers are reluctant to shop at the pawnbroker's. There is no need. The edge of desperation may taint the people who borrow there, but as far as the buyer is concerned, it's a secondhand shop like any other.

Swaps and Exchanges

Anyone with children will understand the very short useful life of anything bought for them: skates, skis, bikes, toys, even clothes and books. The cheap ones disintegrate in their little hands, and the higher quality items are just as quickly outgrown. Parents can't win — except by dealing with other parents.

We started with skates, buying castoffs that were fine for our little ones, but pinching the toes of some older skaters. The skates that we then outgrew were sold back to the exchange for a little less than the bigger ones cost. Then we discovered ski exchanges that work on the same basis. A nearby town boasts a lending "library" for toys, organized by parents. Bikes can be an even bigger problem. Here, local parents have organized an annual trading day at the school. The only bikes that aren't eagerly snapped up are the wee ones, where first-time parents have not yet realized the cost of keeping fast-growing kids outfitted with new things.

The organization of such swaps and exchanges is mostly a local initiative. In some towns, commercial stores operate swaps and trade-ins as part of the business. Sometimes it's a cooperative, ad hoc effort organized by parents or scouts, or done informally on a neighborhood basis. If your area is not already teeming with such activity, it's easy enough to get it started. Just mention the problem to a neighbor whose kids are younger or older than yours and watch the response.

I was tempted to label this a newer phenomenon, an informal offspring of the cooperative movement. Then I remembered that passing around hand-me-down clothes was a regular part of my own childhood. Cribs and baby furniture were rotated around the family and around the neighborhood until they fell to pieces (one reason why it's not a good idea and may even be illegal in your area, to sell old cribs and car seats). And the candy store had a comic rack where used ones were traded back three for two. Swaps are an old idea with modern appeal.

Flea Markets

The good burghers of old Europe, suspecting that the plague was carried from town to town by fleas, kept itinerant merchants (and their flea-infested goods) from entering the city gates. Undeterred the peddlers set up shop outside the walls. The customers came out — caring more about prices than the plague — and thus the flea market was born.

There are few North American towns today that don't have at least one flea market in the vicinity. In most cases, modern city planners still keep them on the outskirts of town, but it's fear of lower prices and not the plague that arouses the enmity of the downtown merchants.

Modern flea markets are as wildly individual as the craftspeople and peddlers within. They range in style from a permanent, indoor, commercial space (that calls itself a flea market only because it is divided into many smaller booths) to the once-a-year neighborhood bash where residents bring a card table and their gleanings from cupboard or basement.

However they may be organized, most flea markets offer a very wide variety of both new and used goods. Prices vary almost as widely as the goods. In general, though, it seems that the more informal ad hoc markets usually have lower prices than those that operate in established commercial premises.

When secondhand goods appear to be too pricey, remember that you can go to the same sources that the dealer has found. And, of course, a flea market is another one of those marvelous places where the buyer is *expected* to haggle over the price. Timing, too, is important, particularly at those markets that don't operate on a full-time basis. At a once-a-week or once-a-month market, dealers are reluctant to leave too much stock unsold at the end of the day. In these places, morning prices may be sticky, but as closing time approaches dealers tend to be more generous with hagglers.

Finally, if prices don't attract you as a discriminating secondhand buyer, consider becoming a seller — even if it's only for a day. In most markets, the manager will rent you a booth, or space to set up a table, on a daily basis. Clean out the cupboard, gather the best of your hobby products, garden surplus, or Granny's butter tarts. Mark every item with an asking price (felt pen on masking tape works well), spread it out on a card table, and you're in business. It may not be Neiman-Marcus, but you'll have all the fun of a flea market and come home a little richer. You may even learn something about the art of selling.

First-time flea marketers invariably find some surprises in the experience. One friend, who was selling all his old paperbacks for a dime each, thought he had the knack as the boxes rapidly emptied. Then he discovered that his best customer — that nice old lady who was such a voracious reader — had a booth around the corner where she was reselling his books for a quarter. Another woman was so delighted with the flurry of interest in her crochet goods that she sold her friend's hat in the excitement.

The nicest surprise of all, however, is when first-time sellers are suddenly struck with the realization that what they produce, collect and have all around them — that might otherwise be put out with the trash — have a value, that somebody wants them, that money can come from someplace other than a paycheck.

Garage/Yard Sales

Garage sales (or yard sales for people without garages) are a great excuse for a neighborhood party. They may also offer good value to the secondhand shopper, as long as you don't have to travel far.

The problem is the limited variety. It's rarely worth the drive across town on the slim chance that someone may be selling just the sort of widget you're looking for. Of course, it's sometimes fun to go just to see what's there, but that's entertainment, not serious shopping. We go if they are close or we happen to be passing by.

Prices are erratic. Since sellers may have limited experience at secondhand values, some goods will be overpriced and others will be cheaper than you could find elsewhere. As with private sales through classified ads, sellers may wrongly assume that resale values are some uniform percentage of what they paid when the goods were fancy and new. Thus modern furniture tends to be overpriced, and older (more solid) pieces are undervalued. Appliances are worth less than most first-time sellers imagine, but small items of household surplus can be genuine bargains such as books, pictures (for the frames), sports equipment, toys, and dishes.

For most families, garage sales are one-time affairs. They may be as interested in cleaning out the garage as they are in the revenues. This has a definite effect on pricing. Although it pays to go early for the best selection, the prices are often lowest at the end of the day when the weary vendors are facing the prospect of stuffing all the leftovers back in the garage. If you see something you like in the morning, but are unable to strike a bargain on the price, try coming back in the evening.

Rummage Sales

These are the church basement and charity bazaar sales, where the goods are usually donated and sold by volunteers. There are two critical differences between this format and a run-of-the-mill secondhand sale that you might find at a garage sale or regular shop. In the first place, prices are generally quite low in comparison with other secondhand sources, and secondly, haggling over prices is *not* usually accepted practice. Without the motive of personal gain, sellers have less interest in maximizing profit margins. So they start low and stay there, for simplicity's sake.

It also seems that donors are more careful of the quality of goods collected for rummage sales. Perhaps it's like listening for the tinkle of coins in the collection plate — one doesn't like to be seen giving less than the best. Whatever the reason, rummage sales rarely offer valuable merchandise, but there's less utter junk than you'll find at other secondhand sources.

Quite apart from the bargains, rummage sales are worth visiting just to meet people. They're invariably staffed by everybody's favorite aunt. It's the one place where I have no qualms about buying used clothing and fresh mince tarts.

Because prices start low and rarely go lower, the best time to visit a rummage sale is in the opening minutes.

Charitable Institutions

Goodwill, Neighborhood Services, Salvation Army, and Superfluity Shops (a favorite, simply because of the name) are all like rummage sales writ large and given permanent status. Like rummage sales, goods are donated, and paid help or volunteers handle the selling. These prices are usually low and not negotiable — unless you are down and out.

The institutions offer good value on smaller items like books, clothing, sports equipment, and small appliances (*sometimes* — always try out appliances).

Because of the larger size and permanent character of these outlets, they do lack some of the qualities of the informal basement rummage sale. Donations are more impersonal, and thus less subject to social comparisons of who has given what. The result is less uniform quality of merchandise than the rummage sale offers — more junk. Furthermore, the large-volume institutions attract more attention from antique and secondhand dealers than the rummage sales do. The competition for things like old furniture gets fierce, and the casual shopper would have to be very lucky to find an antique bargain there.

Trade-Ins

This is a relatively unknown side of the secondhand market that is part gimmick and part real. Everybody knows that most used cars on the market were traded in to dealers for newer models. The "trade-in,"

144 • How to Survive Without a Salary

though, is also used as a sales gimmick by many other merchants. Carpets, appliances, home equipment and other durable items are often sold with trade-in discounts: "Bring in your old whatsit and get fifty dollars off the price of a new one!" Every such ad means that the dealer is going to end up with a back room full of used whatsits. He won't advertise them for sale (it might cut into his new whatsit business), but he will sell them to a used whatsit dealer or to an enterprising bargain hunter who appears at the back door with cash in hand. They are sometimes even given away when the back room gets too crowded. I once carpeted an entire six-room apartment that way — for nothing!

Government Surplus

One of the all-time most popular myths of secondhand deals concerns the army surplus jeep: "Still in the crate and only two hundred dollars"— or fifty dollars, depending on how far removed the seller is from the actual purchase of an actual jeep.

Government surplus of all types is most frequently sold at special auctions. The disposal of U.S. government equipment is handled through the General Services Administration and Department of Defense. To find out more about the GSA Surplus Personal Property Sales, visit www.surplussales.gsa.gov, or their electronic auctions at www.gsaauctions.gov. Or, you can also find out more by calling the National Customer Service Center in Kansas City, MO, at 1-800-488-3111 (U.S. only); or writing to GSA Surplus Personal Property Sales at 1941 Jefferson Davis Hwy, Arlington VA 22202. There is also the DRMS Defense Reutilization and Marketing Services at www.drms.dla.mil.

Call Battle Creek Customer Contact Center at 888-352-9333 (U.S. only). Hard copy catalogs are available by calling 877-319-6030 (credit card payment only), or there's a form to be downloaded and mailed in with a check, or (the best option) they can be downloaded *for free* from the site.

In Canada, Crown Assets Centres sell surplus material at six regional centers across the country. Visit www.crownassets.pwgsc.gc.ca for detailed contact information or check your local phone book under Public Works and Government Services Canada.

Other levels of government may occasionally hold sales of surplus equipment and supplies — watch your local newspaper for announcements.

Unfortunately for the individual, the sheer volume of merchandise falling from the back end of the tax machine demands that such sales be organized primarily for large quantity deals. The system is geared to full-time buyers, wholesalers, or dealers who can buy a thousand desks or pencil sharpeners on a single bid. One gets the impression that dickering over the condition of a single jeep would constipate the entire system.

By and large, the systems in both countries are set up to deal with the middlemen. The merchandise does eventually appear in stores that advertise "army surplus" or "government equipment" or some such thing, but these outlets are run by private enterprise, not by the government. Wares are priced according to what the market will bear, and there are no special deals just because they once belonged to taxpayers.

If you do find such a store, it may pay to keep a few general guides in mind:

◆ Governments buy the best. Even the surplus is usually high quality.

◆ Military clothing is heavy, durable, and well-made.

◆ Not all surplus is used. You may find brand-new discards at less than new prices.

◆ The worst buys will be on the most popular items: desks, furniture, filing cabinets, etc. But if you want a terrific bargain on parade gaiters . . .

And Last But Not Least

The very best secondhand source, for sheer entertainment as well as for bargains, is the auction. That's a chapter all by itself . . .

Auction Buying

The long-haired woman in the purple jacket spent last Saturday standing in a drizzly rain, trying to buy a little wooden storage box and a picture frame. She had made her choices earlier, rooting through boxes of attic gleanings piled on a stranger's lawn. Now she was trying hard not to look at her picks, lest she draw attention to them. Bidding, she knew, was competition. And the fewer interested buyers in the game, the better the price would be. That's the only reason she didn't mind the rain.

The antique dealer, alas, was equally well-prepared. Armed with a waterproof slicker and a thermos of tea, he too was ready to weather the day. And his pile of buys was already beginning to grow into a heap at his feet. The woman gave him a worried look.

As the auctioneer worked his way closer to Ms. Purple's box, her disinterested act began to come undone at the edge.

"How much to start on the caesar salad bowl?" sang the auctioneer, holding a plain china chamber pot over his head.

"Caesar salad? That's a pee pot!" she blurted. And the dealer bought it with a barely visible flick of his thumb.

"Mr. Shrewd, there, is going to get my box," she muttered. And he did. Ms. Purple set her limit at twenty-five dollars, gritted her teeth and passed it, and finally dropped out at forty dollars. Mr. Shrewd added the box to his pile for forty-two dollars.

Determined not to lose the picture frame too, she stuck her arm up in the air to start the bidding. Her rival flicked his thumb and the fight was on. She finally outbid the dealer at fifty dollars. Not a bargain, but a nice picture frame. The Lady in White, sharing a butter tart with her little beige dog, stopped to say so. So did Stylish Blond Streaks, though Streaks was distracted by the task of convincing her husband that, as a big city fireman, he really didn't need eleven milk cans and a horse-drawn plow.

Ms. Purple finally got her bargain near the end of the day: a seventeen-dollar antique wash stand, older, nicer, and bigger than the plain little box that had gone for more than twice that price at the beginning of the auction. By the end, Mr. Shrewd didn't have room on his truck for any more big stuff. And most of the other bidders had already taken their wet feet home.

Live auctions (as opposed to the Internet variety, which are discussed at the end of this chapter) are entertainment as well as business, and variety is a part of their charm. The goods and the actors are different at every sale. So, too, are the quirks and corny jokes of the auctioneer. The unwritten rules, and even the bidding systems, change.

There are "Dutch" auctions, where the auctioneer starts with a high asking price and gradually reduces it. The first bidder wins. In progressive bidding, prices start low and bidders compete by increasing the price. The last bidder wins. In a mail auction, the highest bidder wins, but participants submit only one bid. There is no second chance to outflank the opposition.

If you already have a nodding acquaintance with auctions, chances are you'll be most familiar with the system of progressive bidding. The auctioneer asks for a starting bid and would-be buyers keep topping it until no one is left to raise the price again. The auctioneer says "Going . . . going . . . gone!" (or some such thing) and the goods are sold to the last and highest bidder. That's the usual approach to auctions.

Auctions are used to sell everything from antique things to zirconium rings. Ordinary bargain hunters, however, will most often be involved in a few common types:

Estate Sales

It usually happens that our possessions outlive us. Unable to take it with us to our retirement haven in Florida — or to even warmer places

— we leave it behind for the next generation. The next generation would rather have the cash, thank you very much, and so the auctioneer comes in to convert all those family heirlooms and broom closet leavings to nice long green for the next of kin.

Estate sales are more than appendices to a wake. They also happen when people move, divorce, or just clean out the basement. What makes them different is that they commonly include everything from the family car to the kitchen sink, and the half-finished jar of shaving lotion. Such variety is not only the spice of life, it's also a great advantage for the secondhand shopper. Specialized sales, like those that concentrate on cars or building materials tend to attract large crowds of buyers interested in those particular things. The competition pushes up the prices. The estate sale, however, may offer only one used car, or a single roll of roofing felt — not enough of any one thing to attract the dealers and big money buyers from miles around. You may be the only one at the sale interested in a car or a roll of roofing felt. When that happens, you can virtually name your price.

Estate sales do often attract the interest of antique buyers, and competition can be fierce for anything old and collectible. But if you need a kitchen sink or half a jar of shaving lotion, it's hard to beat the prices at an estate sale.

Farm Auctions

A farm auction is no more than an estate sale that happens to be on a farm. They usually offer an assortment of farm tools and machinery, and sometimes livestock and land as well. The crowd is different from those at a run-of-the-mill estate sale, too. Farms are often harder to find than numbered houses on well-marked streets, so farm sales tend to attract a higher proportion of locals, and fewer day-trippers from the city. The antique dealers still manage to get there if the sale is a large one. In general, though, as sales become smaller and more remote, the competition and prices diminish as well.

Get yourself a good, detailed map, one that shows all the dirt roads and lanes. Look up some small-town weekly papers at the library or online (farm auctions aren't always advertised in the big city dailies), and make a day of it. Take a hat and a folding chair for comfort, and a picnic basket if hot dogs and homemade pies aren't your fare.

Livestock Sales

There was a time when the meat-packing companies sent buyers around from farm to farm to pick up livestock. Prices were as low as the buyers could get away with, and with only a few buyers in any one district, farmers were usually faced with take-it-or-leave-it propositions. In self-defense, many rural communities have sales barns now where local farmers bring their stock, and buyers (in theory) bid against one another.

Sales barns operate on a regular basis (once a week is common), and are usually not advertised, or even very well identified. You are supposed to know where and when the sales barns are in session. Ask a local farmer.

Some farmers add to their herds by picking up bargains at a sales barn, but it's a risky business for neophytes. Animals can be inspected before a sale, and with a practiced eye, you might be able to spot most of the sickies, runts, and genetic defectives. Those who don't know scours from scabies, however, might be better off buying from places where there's time to ask questions.

Meat is a different story. Even apartment dwellers are free to buy the family bacon from the same source the meat packers use. You don't even need a farm. Haul your walking bacon straight to the nearest slaughterhouse, and then take it home all cut and wrapped for the freezer. Do make arrangements with a slaughterhouse *before* splurging on a four-footed steak, however. The butchery may be closed that day, or booked by appointment only. That predicament is hard to explain to landladies.

Specialty Auctions

Some large-scale auction markets specialize in a single commodity group: cars, construction equipment, coins and works of art are just a few examples. Government surplus is often disposed of at specialty auctions. Advertisements for such sales can be found in the classified section of most big-city newspapers.

These sales attract dealers and professionals. They know the market value of everything on the list. Consequently, it's next to impossible to find the real giveaways that happen when there's no competition. On the other hand, these pros and dealers are buying to resell (at a profit) in another market. A clunker at a car auction won't be a steal, but chances are you can buy it more cheaply there than you could at the used car lot.

(Look over your shoulder — that's probably the used car dealer standing beside you stocking up for next week's customers). Check with a local auction house to see if there are restrictions on public attendance. Some car auctions, for example, are restricted to dealers only.

New Goods

Not all public auctions are part of the secondhand market. Retail businesses rid themselves of slow-moving or out-of-season stock by turning it over to an auctioneer. Bankrupt businesses can be liquidated by selling off whole inventories through auctions. Some centers have established auction halls to handle such sales. In other places, the auctioneer goes to work in the parking lots or warehouses of the firm being liquidated.

These sales are usually well-advertised for the convenience of the general public. Consequently, they are also well-attended — always a disadvantage for the bargain hunter.

Functionally, it's an auction like any other. In reality, it's quite different. because of the type of crowd it attracts — people who are looking for new things cheap. Their benchmark is the usual retail price; anything less than that will be considered a bargain by someone. In the usual auction crowd of dealers and secondhand scroungers, anything more than half the retail price is exorbitantly expensive. Dedicated secondhand buffs don't find much to get excited about at new-goods auctions.

One other difference bears watching. Unlike estate sales or farm auctions, liquidation and clearance sales frequently offer multiple quantities of whatever happens to be in stock. At an estate auction, you may find one bidet and two people bidding on it (and the price goes up). When the plumbing factory goes belly up, the inventory sale may offer a hundred bidets — one at a time. The two civilians who are interested will bid up the price of the first two fixtures, get what they came for, and then the rest will be sold to dealers at prices that resemble wholesale. Just remember that bidding patterns change whenever a number of identical items are offered.

Police and Customs Auctions

The law regularly finds itself overstocked with orphan goods. Customs seizures and unclaimed stolen property are common examples. These goods are periodically auctioned off at public sales. Police auctions are good sources for tape and stereo equipment, bicycles and cameras. Customs auctions are less predictable. All such auctions are advertised in the classifieds. Remember, though, that they will attract large crowds, and you will be competing against wholesale buyers again.

Charity Auctions

These are the ones that get all the publicity. They offer name-dropper gimmicks like the mayor's necktie or lunch with your favorite movie star — fun for fans and uninspired feature writers, but not a fruitful place to look for bargains.

Prices are high for the same reason that rummage sales have higher quality junk: at a rummage sale the wares are publicly donated and donors want to be known for the quality of their discards; at a charity auction it's the buying that takes place in public and the Joneses don't like to be seen as cheap. The only advantage to this type of auction buying is that some purchases can be deducted from taxes as charitable "donations."

Consignment Sales

This is the essence of the ordinary, run-of-the-mill auction hall. Sellers arrive through the week with boxes of old paperbacks, granny's fur, the broken TV, or the heirloom chest. On auction night, everything is sold, the auctioneer collects the money, takes a percentage off the top, and returns the rest to the sellers.

The auction halls are normally set up to handle small estates and liquidations, as well as the consignment trade. It makes little difference to the buyer, however. There are three features of these "bits and pieces" auction halls that are particularly attractive to bargain hunters:

1. The wide variety of goods offered makes it more likely that you can always find at least a few of the items on your "things we need to buy" list. Even if the entertainment value begins to pall, the outing remains worthwhile as a regular shopping trip.

2. As is the case with regular estate sales, there is rarely enough of any one line to attract dealers or specialist buyers. The antique buyers are omnipresent, but otherwise the competition is scattered. When only one kitchen sink is being sold, and only one buyer is interested, the buyer can name her price — literally. I have seen perfectly good stainless steel sinks sold for less than one dollar.

3. Most consignment auctions operate on a regular basis — an indoor hall with parking, seats, and a regular weekly schedule. Unlike farm sales, you don't need a map and an entire day to attend.

But Don't Scratch Your Ear

Given the entertainment and bargains to be had, I'm always amazed at the number of people who have never been to an auction. They all know the myths, though: scratch your ear and unwittingly buy the nine-foot, glow-in-the-dark plaster Elvis statue and coin bank. Get carried away with the competitive spirit and pay twenty bucks for the tacky lamp that Wal-Mart couldn't flog for ten. The myths do have some small basis in fact, and perhaps it's the fear of committing such *faux pas* that keeps the uninitiated away.

For the stout of will, the best advice is to attend a few auctions determined not to buy a thing. Watch. Listen. *Don't* panic when the gorgeous old cuspidor (that's probably brass under all that green paint) is practically given away to the klutzy couple who bought the Elvis statue. Let them have it. Keep your hands in your pockets and watch.

If you're like me, though, you can't be trusted in such situations. I can last a month without so much as a tickle in the throat, then go to a concert and (in that dainty pause before the music starts) have an absolutely uncontrollable urge to cough. And I still can't go to an auction without developing an overpowering itch somewhere on the top of my head. If that's all that's keeping you from the auction halls, first spend a little time here to find out how they function, and *then* go to a couple of auctions with your hands in your pockets.

The Auction Hall

The mechanical functions of the auction hall are simple enough. The auctioneer and the owner of the goods agree on the auctioneer's commission. These are usually posted in the hall and will read something like this:

Commissions

    15 percent on furniture

    25 percent on small items

    10 percent for whole estates

The goods are given a "lot number," which identifies the owner. It helps the bookkeeper, but means little to the buyer unless you need some help to track a specific item.

On sale night, buyers register as they arrive. That just means find the office, sign your name, and take a number. The number is on a card. You'll need it to bid and pay up at the end of the evening. Your bidding number is so that the auctioneer and the bookkeeper can keep track of who buys what. No money changes hands until you are ready to leave. Then you go back to the office, or the registration desk to turn in your number. The cashier tallies up your purchases, you pay your bill, load up the Elvis statue and leave.

Have a Good Look

Part of the hall, and likely the outside space as well, will be given over to displaying the goods to be sold. It won't look like the nice displays at Muzak plaza. More like spring cleaning day at the dump. Don't despair. You're about to save whatever it cost the mall to make those arty displays. The goods are the very same ones that made their debut in the plaza.

Here, buyers are free to wander around before the sale, to have a closer look. When an item is on the block (being sold), there won't be time to take a peek underneath, open the drawers, or read the label; it's going, going, gone before you can really judge its condition. The pre-sale examination is vital unless you really like surprises. Don't be shy. It's not like peeking in the neighbor's drawers. Take a tape measure to be sure the table will fit the dining nook, and a retail catalog to check what the new ones are worth. Poke, prod, plug it in if it's electric, count all the pieces to be sure they're there, and try out the chairs for comfort. The only thing you cannot do is ask the salesperson for help. The hired help at the auction hall are mostly furniture movers. All they know about the stuff being sold is how heavy it is. The salespeople are all back at Muzak plaza where the money is. These are the cheap seats.

Don't Ask Us, We Just Work Here

They don't sell programs at an auction, and the only ones wearing numbers are in the audience. How do you identify the players?

The cashier you met when you first arrived. That's where you got the number, and that's where you come back later to settle the bill.

The auctioneer is obvious. He's the one doing all the talking. His role is to conduct the bidding. Since his commission is a fixed percentage of the final sales price, his chief interest is to coax the bidding up to the highest possible price. All the jokes and cajolery are most disarming, but never forget that he is on the seller's side, not the buyer's. When the auctioneer tells you that the clock used to work, don't assume that it probably still does.

Within whispering distance of the auctioneer will be the recorder, a silent presence with clipboard and pen. Her job is to record each purchase, the winning bid, and the person who bought it. If you can't control your arm and do end up buying something, show the recorder your number.

The other semi-official types fluttering around the action are the auctioneer's helpers. They fetch and carry, and hold up the item being sold. If you can't always tell from the auctioneer's babble just what it is that's being sold, it will be whatever the helper is holding up for display. If that's something like a fridge, he may just be holding the door open and looking tired. It's perfectly kosher to ask the helper to turn it around for a better look (not the fridge though), open the drawers, or read out the brand name. It's better if you've already done that inspection yourself, but don't hesitate to ask if the helper isn't displaying it clearly enough.

What Did He Say?

The patter of the auctioneer can be difficult to follow. Complaining is pointless. It took the poor fellow years to learn to be that incomprehensible and he's not about to revert to articulate speech now. Relax. The ear gradually gets accustomed to the rhythm and starts making sense of the nonsense. It helps if you know what he is supposed to be saying.

He first establishes what it is that's being sold. If in doubt, see what the helpers are holding up or pointing to. At this stage, the auctioneer should also clearly state the *units* of sale. If, for example, the helper is holding up one of six chairs, the auctioneer might say

"How much am I bid on *this* chair?" — you're buying only that particular chair.

"Next we have this *set* of chairs." — the price will include all six chairs.

"How much for *choice* of chairs?" — the price is for any one chair. Take as many as you want.

"So much apiece, take them all." — the price is for one chair, but you must take the set.

Likewise, the auctioneer might indicate that he is selling an entire tray of small items, the suitcase *and* its contents, the rabbits but *not* the cages, and so on. Do pay attention to exactly what is being sold. I once saw a woman dancing about in great delight at the fabulous bargain she had just obtained on a dining room suite. Then someone told her she had only bought one chair.

If you are not absolutely certain just *what* and *how many* are being sold, put your hands in your pockets — or lash yourself to the mast and listen more carefully to the siren's song.

The auctioneer is next obliged to suggest a starting bid. He may rattle off something like, "Gimme ten ta start 'er!" or, "Who'll say five for the three-legged chair?" Many auctioneers will suggest a starting price in the range of what they expect the item to ultimately sell for. There is absolutely no reason to be the first bidder into the fray. The starting bid will drop. The auctioneer will lower it himself to get things going, or a buyer will offer a starting bid at some lower point.

When he finally does get a starting bid, the auctioneer double clutches and puts his patter into high. If you thought he was incomprehensible before, wait until he really gets going. You'll know the real bidding is underway when it sounds like Alvin and the Chipmunks singing an old Philip Morris commercial on the trading floor of the stock exchange. But even that can be understood if you know what to listen for.

In spite of the auctioneer's frantic pace, you are not being left behind. The actual bidding moves much more slowly than the auctioneer's tongue. The chant you hear is mostly the singsong repetition of a number — the asking bid. It means the auctioneer has a bid from someone in the audience, and is asking any other bidder to top the last price with the higher number being repeated in the chant. He may also occasionally repeat the bid already given. Thus if $1.50 has been bid, and the auctioneer is asking anyone in the crowd to raise the bid to $2, his chant might be: "I have one and a half, gimme two, gimme two, gimme two . . . one and a half gimme two [someone nods], two and a half, have two, gimme two and a half." If at this point, the bidding ends, the person who nodded at two has won the bidding and pays $2 for the article. Of course, I can't write those bids as fast as he can chant them, and you'll have to let your ear get used to working at 78 rpm. But if, out of all the patter, you can hear a number being repeated, chances are it's the asking bid.

When the bidding ends, the auctioneer will often repeat the winning bid more slowly for the recorder's benefit. The last exchange may end with something like, "Sold to number 79 for $2." It's a good time to check your first impressions of what you *thought* he was saying in the chant.

The hyperactive singsong of the auctioneer's performance is not just an oligarch's exclusion of the unchosen, like a doctor's Latin or a bureaucrat's jargon, but is a deliberate sales technique. The whole intent is to speed up the action, create the impression of frenzy, the possibility of being left behind. It's opportunity knocking, so move quickly before you miss the fleeting chance at a real bargain. In fact, the underlying message is: Don't stop to think about it! Don't stop to consider whether you *really* need a nine-foot Elvis coin bank. It's so cheap! Get your hand up! Now! Before it's too late. "Sold!" Argghhh. Impulse buying incarnate.

It's mesmerizing. One night there was a five-piece silver tea set that glittered enough to catch everybody's eye, and that's not easy at the auction hall where I often loiter. There are usually a hundred or more people there, gossiping, lying, trading amongst themselves, starting up the chain saws, and yelling at the kids. The kids are under the metal folding chairs, competing with a fat old beagle for unattended hot dogs. It is, in short, an audience not easily rapt. Anyway, the tea set glittered and turned every head in the first ten rows. The opening bidder was a middle-aged woman with an instant just-what-I've-always-wanted glaze across her face. She just kept nodding excitedly in cadence to the auctioneer's own frenzy. She ran out of competition at $150. "Sold!" She held up her number for the recorder, then seemed to come out of her trance.

"How much did I pay for that, anyway?"

"$260," said the auctioneer, deadpan. (Hisses and boos from the audience.)

"$150," said the auctioneer, turning the faintest shade of pink. (Clapping and cheering from the audience.) The woman looked relieved.

Few are totally immune to the mesmerizing effect of the chant. I still have nine steel steps from a playground slide. They were a fantastic buy for a quarter (just get that hand up quickly before somebody else takes them home.) Someday I'll figure out what to do with them.

When You Can't Hold It Back Any Longer

So you want to join the action? Sooner or later the urge to bid overcomes all restraint and the arm snaps up in a Dr. Strangelove salute. Here's what to do:

First of all, catch the auctioneer's eye. He's babbling away with both eyes fixed on the person he's trying to persuade to raise the bid (the bidder who's "out"). The auctioneer totally ignores the person who has just tendered the latest, highest bid, (the one who is "in"). As soon as the object of the auctioneer's attention nods, winks, or otherwise agrees to the asking bid, the auctioneer sets a new asking bid and swings back to cajole the former bidder, who is now "out." The auctioneer's head is turning back and forth between the active bidders, always fixing on the one who is "out." If you want to be "in," you may have to speak up or raise your arm.

Once the auctioneer does notice you, he'll immediately ignore you again. You know he has taken your bid when his chant jumps up another notch, repeating a new, higher asking bid. Now you don't have to worry about being ignored. You're "in." You're holding the highest bid (until another bidder tops it), and the auctioneer won't waste his time by looking your way again. If you still aren't sure that he saw you, you can always try waving again. An honest auctioneer will refuse your second wave and remind you that you're "in." One with fewer scruples might accept your second wave as another bid, letting you bid against yourself (or trump your own ace, in bridge player's jargon).

Better to trust that he's seen you. When a competing buyer tops your bid the auctioneer will turn back to you with full, unmistakable interest. He's eye to eye, allegro pitch until you indicate (with a shake of the head) that you won't pay that much, or you bid again . . .

When there is only one bidder left, the auctioneer scans the audi-

158 • How to Survive Without a Salary

ence, making one last plea for another bid. Nobody else interested? "Sold!" The last bidder "in" holds up his card and the auctioneer tells the recorder, "Sold to number 79 for $2."

The closing ceremony — trying to coax one last bid out of the audience — is a variable routine. If there's a lot of money at stake, the auctioneer may plead and wheedle for several minutes before declaring it sold. But if it's a set of dishes and he's trying to raise the bid from two dollars to three dollars, the last bid will be accepted quickly, bang, and on to the next item. For twenty-five percent of that last dollar, it's just not worth his while to prolong the sale —the moral of that distinction being: on the expensive stuff, you'll have lots of time at the end to think about whether or not you want to get back in (make another bid), but on the cheaper goods, those who hesitate will go home empty-handed.

More valuable items may also be sold with a prior warning that there is a *reserve* or *advance* bid. A reserve simply means that the owner of the goods has instructed the auctioneer to refuse to complete the sale unless the bidding reaches some predetermined minimum level. The audience is not told what that minimum is, only that there is a reserve. An advance bid is tendered by someone who may be absent, or someone who wishes to remain anonymous. He gives his bid to the auctioneer in advance, and the goods are sold to the highest bidder, present or not.

The audience's role is not entirely passive, accepting or rejecting the auctioneer's asking bids. It's quite common for a buyer to verbally suggest his own starting bid if the auctioneer starts too high. Or, if the increment is too large, the bidder may signal a reduction. For example, if the price has reached fifty dollars and the auctioneer is asking for sixty, you may see a bidder hold up two fingers and get "in" at fifty-two dollars, or make a horizontal slash with his hand (a common signal for half) as a bid at fifty-five. The *jump* bid is a double increment (in the last example, going straight from fifty to seventy dollars), intending to scare off casual competition early.

Who to Watch

An auction, like professional wrestling, is one of those sports where the audience is part of the entertainment. Knowing who's bidding against you is an essential part of the action. At a general goods auction (an estate sale or consignment hall) the crowd will be filled out with a lot of casual bargain hunters and curious neighbors. The key players, however, will be the dealers: antique dealers, secondhand dealers, and special interest buyers.

The dealers are easy enough to spot. They're the ones doing most of the buying. After the fourth time the auctioneer says, "Sold to number 79 for X dollars!" look around for number 79. If a distraught spouse isn't glaring at him, chances are he's a dealer. Watching *what* he buys will soon tell you whether 79 is an antique dealer, secondhand dealer, or specialist in some other line (a bicycle repairman buying all the old bikes, a watchmaker looking for parts, someone buying only books, or only glassware).

Picking out the main players, post hoc, is easy enough. Keeping track of them, and spotting the participants *before* the bidding is over can be a little tricky. They have a habit of moving frequently, and the dealers are always trying to hide their bids from one another. That's why they're addicted to furtive bidding and elaborate signals that would be the envy of any third-base coach.

Dealers hide from one another because they're competitors. No businessman likes to let the opposition know what he's stocking and how much he's paying. Moreover, knowing whom you're bidding against can affect the final price. And that is the major reason that even casual bargain hunters should keep an eye on who is bidding, as well as on what is being sold.

The first thing you can learn is a lesson on prices and quality. The dealers make their living at this sort of thing. If the dealers have been buying wooden chairs all evening at a steady twenty to twenty-five dollars each, and then refuse to go over five dollars for the next chair in the bunch, don't assume that you've caught them napping. There is likely a very good reason for their reluctance. Have a better look. Is the seat split? A rung missing? Is it plywood under the paint instead of solid wood as the others were?

Quality means different things to different people, though. In the last example, if the chair buyers were all antique dealers, the five-dollar chair may have been shunned because the rungs had been replaced with newer wood. If you are mainly interested in finding something to sit on, new rungs won't matter a bit. It may very well be a bargain.

The other reason for watching the bidders is to predict where the bidding is likely to end. Let's take bicycles to illustrate the point: say there's a decent 15-speed mountain bike that might sell, retail, for around $200. Secondhand, and in good condition, that model might sell for $100. Now when you see such a bike come up for sale at an auction, the bidding depends entirely on who wants it. The used-bike dealer might bid it up to $50 or so. He can resell it for only about $100 in his shop, and must leave a margin for profit and handling costs. A casual shopper, wanting a bike for herself, might bid as high as $100. She knows she would have to pay at least that much at the secondhand bike shop, and anything under $100 is a bargain for her. If you were a dealer, you would probably let the causal buyers fight it out until they each get a bike and drop out of the bidding, and then you would buy the rest of the bikes at $50 or less. If you were a casual buyer, you would jump up and down on your chair, wave your arms, and give every indication you were ready to pay any price. Then, when the dealers drop out at $50, and you scare the other casual buyers off at $60, you might get the thing for $60. Maybe. It all depends on how wily the other bidders are. Which is all the more reason to keep an eye on them.

Finally, there is the bladder factor. Auctions can go on for hours and the players wander in and out, go for a drink or a de-drink. If you are bidding against Jones for the whatsits, watch for the moment he slips away. The whatsits might be selling for considerably less while he's off stretching his legs.

Knowing When to Buy

Unfortunately, you can't always rely on nature calling your competitors away. Luckily, there are other elements of time that may also work in your favor.

Most bidders hang back for the first half hour of any auction, waiting to see how prices develop. And lots of the competition will leave early. My best bargains have always been in the last half hour of an auction, when the crowd is rushing off to pack the junk into the truck and get the bill paid before the lineups start. That's when the pine table in our kitchen was bought for three dollars!

Pay special attention, too, when there are a number of similar items being offered. When a group of lamps, for instance, is being sold on a "first choice" basis, the winner of the initial round of bidding is entitled to take his pick of the lamps — any one or all of them at the same unit price. If you think you want a lamp, it pays to make a quick assessment of who is bidding and what they are likely to choose. If there is one old lamp in a pack of newer ones and the bidders are antique dealers, the dealers are likely to choose the old one and leave the rest to be auctioned again. Second choice, or even third choice, will be considerably cheaper. On the other hand, if the bidders are all secondhand dealers and there are no possible antiques amongst the lamps, then there's a chance that the winning bidder will take them all. If the bidders are casual buyers, like you, they may want only one or two of the lamps. Let them fight it out for first choice, and wait for the cheaper ones on a subsequent round.

Some actual numbers may help to illustrate the point. A few years ago, at a local auction, five doors were offered on a "choice" bid. They were all solid, five-panel, pine doors. One was different — it had a bevel on the panels and it was older than the rest. There were four bidders, an antique dealer and three casual buyers. First choice went to the dealer. He took only the oldest door and paid $3.50. Two doors went on the second choice for a dollar each. The third bidder paid fifty cents for the last two doors. They were indistinguishable from the dollar doors. Similar doors at a building supply store start at $100! Oh yes, the doors were sold in the closing minutes of the auction. Most of the evening's crowd had left to pay their bills and get out of the parking lot.

Setting Limits

A trip to an auction should begin like any other secondhand expedition, with a well-considered shopping list. And a conserver's shopping list, remember, is not merely a list of what you need, but also a clear indication of what you are prepared to spend for it. (See chapter 6.)

Spending limits are essential at an auction. The auctioneer's skill is in hurrying things along, getting buyers caught up in the rapid fire, competitive spirit of the thing. When there is little time allowed for thinking — for trying to remember how much that was at the "nearly new" shop — it's too easy to let the hand fly up and stay in the bidding for just one more round. It's better, and cheaper, to set some limits on each item before you start. When there isn't time to make well-reasoned decisions, better to let your preset limits put you out of the bidding when prices go too high.

I like to keep two limits in mind: an upper limit and bargain limit. The upper limit is, roughly, the cheapest price from any alternative source. If two-by-four lumber, for example, is four dollars at the lumber yard, two dollars at the mill and one dollar at demolition sites, then one dollar would be the upper limit on two-by-fours at the auction. When the price hits the limit, drop out no matter how badly you need the lumber. If you can find it more cheaply elsewhere, quit bidding.

The upper limit is for things we really need. Like many, though, we keep a second mental list of things that we will eventually need, or things that we might profitably use if the price were right. Those things we buy only if they are real bargains. Doors for instance. When we needed doors, we would pay up to one dollar each for them. That was an upper limit. Now we have a cache of doors on hand, however, and occasionally buy them only for other uses. Now the limit is fifty cents. That's the bargain limit.

Too many bidders get caught up in the competition, forget to set limits and lose sight of the alternatives. One auctioneer tells me that fresh-baked goods are the best (or worst) example. "I can auction off a pie for seven or eight dollars," he says, "when they're selling the same pie at the back of the hall for five dollars. People get caught up in the bidding and forget."

Look Again

Auctioneers don't like to argue with customers. It spoils the happy frenzy that keeps the prices high. They try, therefore, to describe the goods with some care. Few would tout an appliance as being in working order if they knew it was not. They might say it "used to work" or it "worked the last time it was used," but few would knowingly lie about the condition of articles being sold. Many auctioneers begin each sale with careful disclaimers to the effect that all goods are sold *as is* — no guarantees.

Nevertheless, anything bought at auction should be examined immediately. If electrical goods have been described as being in working order, plug them in and be sure. Check glassware for cracks and chips. Look inside to make sure all parts are present. One sad woman bought a beautiful, and expensive, grandfather clock. When she got it home, she looked inside and found she had bought an empty case.

If you feel there has been a misrepresentation, the time to argue the point is then and there, not after you get it home. Explain your case to one of the helpers, or take it right back to the auctioneer. Depending on the auctioneer's style, and on the state of his disclaimers, you may not win every appeal on the condition of something bought, but if you have any chance of winning at all, it can only be by making the complaint immediately, when everyone still remembers just how the goods were described.

Auctioneers are mostly reasonable types and are as capable as any of making an honest mistake. A reasonable complaint about an honest mistake is easily made and easily settled.

An audience, too, can help to keep an auctioneer on his toes — sometimes. I do recall one young auctioneer selling gallon cans of paint to an audience of a hundred or so neighbors. He held up a gallon of "ebony enamel."

Three of four bids had already been made when one of the bidders asked, "What color is ebony anyway, Jim?"

"Brown!" shot back the auctioneer, scarcely missing a beat in his patented chant.

"No it ain't," shouted someone else from the audience. "It's sort of an off-white."

Commerce ground to a halt while the crowd divided into three equal factions: pro-whites, pro-browns, and undecided. The few who were pretty sure it was black kept quiet and let democracy run its course. The auctioneer took a vote. "Light brown" was the winner by a narrow margin. The happy buyer, content with the people's verdict, didn't bother to open the can until he got home.

When There's Really More Than You Want

It frequently happens that goods are sold in large, mixed lots. A box of tools when you need a hammer, a ski outfit when you only want the poles, a dozen pigs when two would be plenty. And, for the same reason toast lands butter-side down, these awkward lots always seem to be the cheapest. Fate.

At a regular consignment auction, the solution is simple enough. Just buy the big lot, sort out the portion that you wanted, and leave the rest to be auctioned again later. You will have to pay the auctioneer's commission on the resold excess. If there are only a few small things involved, you may prefer to take the leftovers home until you've collected enough to justify a consignment. In either case, if the price is right, don't worry about the quantities being wrong. You can be a seller as well as a buyer.

Alternatively, you can let the big lots go, then deal privately with the winning bidder. Make him an offer for the part you wanted. Private trading, done discreetly (remember there's no profit in that for the auctioneer and it is his hall), is an accepted part of the auction scene.

Choosing the Sale

If you've never been to an auction before, your first surprise may be the realization that there are so many to choose from. You will find them advertised in local newspapers or on community notice boards. The ads often give a partial listing of goods to be sold. Even so, you may want a few criteria by which to winnow out the better prospects.

Ironically, it's often the sale with the least interesting list of wares that offers the greatest bargains. The reason is simple: an auction is a competitive event. Fewer competitors result in lower prices.

In general then, bargain seekers look for sales that don't attract large audiences, and buy things that are of little interest to other buyers there. An auction-wise car buyer would avoid the "monster auto extravaganza sale" where prices and crowds would be wholesale and up. He would look for a small, out-of-the-way estate sale where one car might be hidden in the list of doilies, hearing aids and china.

The value of being the odd one out cannot be too heavily stressed. Even the classy antique auctions may offer bargains in newer goods. The price is lowest when you are the only one in the audience who wants it.

When the idea of "health" food was still a novelty in North America, I saw one old auctioneer come across an electric yogurt maker in a box of consigned goods. He had to put on his glasses to read the label. "It's a yo-gart maker," he announced to the roomful of farmers assembled to bid on the tools that comprised the main agenda.

"What the hell's a yo-gart maker?!" somebody yelled from ten rows back.

"Makes yo-garts!" the old man shot back. "Now what am I bid?"

One woman there did know what a yo-gart maker was, but wisely kept out of the ensuing debate and quietly bought it for a quarter.

Location is another useful criterion. It doesn't have to be far away — just hard to find. Get a good map and hope that no one is following you.

Timing, too, is of great importance. Again, the idea is to find the auctions that are too inconveniently scheduled to attract many buyers. Auction crowds — and prices — rise and fall with the seasons. Summer is the busy season. Tourists and day trippers from the cities swell crowds at country auctions and push the prices higher. Weekend sales are worse than midweek ones, and holiday weekend sales are worst of all.

Weather plays a big part. Nice sunny days must lull customers into a defenseless state. There always seem to be better buys when it's steamy hot, or — better still — too cold for other bidders to bother with taking their hands out of their pockets.

The ideal sale, in my book, takes place off an unmarked country lane, sixty miles from the nearest city, at five o'clock on a Wednesday morning in January. With any luck, the weather will be terrible and the auctioneer will forget to advertise it. Perfect!

Online Auctions

When all the hype about the Internet burned out, one of the few online businesses left standing, and even thriving, was the online auction. EBay is the most well-known example but there are many others. Some offer every product imaginable, while others specialize in certain categories of items, like used cars or musical instruments.

If you have access to a computer that is hooked up to the Internet, you may be able to find some real bargains at online auction sites. Even if you don't care to bid on anything the auction sites can be useful research tools for gauging prices of items you wish to buy or sell. The computers at your local library will suffice for this. However, if you decide you want to take the plunge and start bidding on items yourself, you should not use a public-access computer for this purpose. Most sites require you to provide credit information in order to register and it can be risky typing in private information like this on a public computer.

Since different auction sites have different procedures and formats,

I will stick to the basics here. When you start looking at online auctions you're going to be sorely tempted to bid on some item or other. But as with live auctions, you should do your best to restrain yourself until you have a good understanding of how a particular site operates. The good sites document their rules and procedures in clear, understandable language and offer tutorials. Read these thoroughly, as well as the FAQ (frequently asked questions) list and any "tips" pages offered.

Now "lurk" for a while — watch how bidders and sellers use the site. Some online auctions are run along the same lines as live auctions but as you explore various sites you'll discover that many of the more popular ones have some important differences. First, the eBay type of auction site — sometimes called a "person to person" auction — does not have an auctioneer talking up the item. Sellers and bidders deal directly with each other. Sellers describe their own items and it is up to bidders to evaluate that information before placing a bid. Winning bidders make the arrangements with the seller to pay for the item and have it shipped.

Even more so than in live auctions, the onus is on bidders to find out what they're getting into when they bid on an item. While most transactions work out fine, there is always the chance that you may be dissatisfied for some reason and want to get your money back. This can be a real challenge any time but especially if you're dealing with someone hundreds or thousands of miles away. The best approach is to do what you can to avoid getting to this point. Most of this is common sense but it is surprising how many people do things on the Internet that they would never risk in the "real" world, like handing substantial amounts of cash over to complete strangers. Be aware that the anonymity and immediacy of the Internet can really break down your impulse control. Though there are some exceptions, you can't retract a bid once you've hit that enter key. In many jurisdictions you are considered to have entered a binding contract when you successfully bid on an item, so don't be casual about these things.

Many of the precautions I suggested in relation to live auctions apply to online auctions as well. When you're confident you know enough about the ins and outs of the site, start by bidding on low-cost items so the inevitable missteps you make won't be too costly. Research the item you wish to bid on so you know what a fair price is. Have a maximum price in mind and don't bid above it. If you've been lurking on the site for a while, you know that the type of item you want will come up again some time and you stand a good chance of getting it at your set price or less. This will also protect you against "shills" — bidders planted by the sellers (or the sellers themselves with a different user identification) to artificially push up the bids.

Your research should also tell you about potential problems to watch for. Don't assume anything about an item's size, working condition, color or any other factor that is important to you. Many sellers provide pictures of their items but these can be misleading — some will use a picture from a brochure or magazine rather than one of the actual item. Some pictures are deliberately blurred to cover a flaw. Be prepared to ask the seller pertinent questions about the condition of the item if the information isn't provided in the description or isn't clear from the picture. If the seller is non-responsive or vague about these details, scroll on.

Get to know the sellers in the categories of items you're likely to bid on. Although all legitimate auction sites make an effort to keep fraud artists at bay, they generally rely on users to report any illegal or unethical behavior or just plain poor customer service. Most sites have a review function that allows bidders and sellers to report their satisfaction or dissatisfaction with transactions. Some sites use this information to create shorthand ratings for participants, but you shouldn't rely on these ratings alone to evaluate a seller. Instead, read some of the comments themselves. Some users use multiple IDs or friends to post positive comments about themselves and thus artificially inflate their rating; others are very picky and will post negative ratings for things that might not bother you.

Ask about the seller's preferred payment method. Avoid sellers who will only accept cash or want you to send payment to a post office box. Checks offer some protection in that they can usually be traced but it'll be tough to get your money back if you don't receive your purchase. Credit cards and payment services such as PayPal provide you with some protection if the deal goes sour. For higher priced items, you might use an online escrow service (this involves a fee, however) which holds your money for the seller until you receive the item in satisfactory condition.

If shipping and handling costs aren't mentioned, ask for a precise fee. In most cases the bidder pays these costs and should take them into account in the price of the item. Some unscrupulous sellers will bump up these costs to an unreasonable level to squeeze a bit more profit out of the deal. Bidders should also have the shipment insured, another cost that has to be factored in to the final price of the item.

If your bid on an item is successful, send an e-mail to the seller shortly after the auction closes to confirm the price, shipping and handling costs, and any other details you have discussed with the seller, such as condition. Include your shipping address and remember to ask that the item be insured. Send another e-mail promptly after you receive the item, especially if you discover any damage or unexpected problems. Keep copies of all this correspondence, as well as a copy of the auction page showing the description of the item.

Most of the time, online auction transactions come off without a hitch and you will be delighted with your purchase. If you do encounter a problem, try to work things out with the seller. Many difficulties arise from simple misunderstandings that can be cleared up with more e-mails or a phone call. If you're still unhappy with the service you've received, give the seller a negative review on the feedback page. Don't get nasty — just explain why you won't do business with that seller again.

If the situation is more serious — if you think the seller has defrauded you — notify the auction site's customer service department. You can also contact the police in the area where the seller lives. But if you take the suggested precautions it's unlikely to ever come to this.

~ 8 ~

Alternatives to Buying

The rules of normal economic behavior ask only that we sell our labor in the marketplace and buy what we need in return. *Quid pro quo.* If we are lucky, we come out even. We work. We earn. We buy. We consume. The rich and the poor are born to their fates. The rest of us try to break even.

The millions who plod through life in quiet conformity to those rules are the redcoats — rank on rank in rigid order. They have pretty clothes and plenty to eat. The economic guerrillas ignore the rules and survive. And the rules, remember, are not rules of right and wrong. No one is suggesting that the economic guerrillas should steal, or live on government handouts (like an aircraft company or an auto maker). The guerrillas merely refuse to accept the regimental uniform, deciding for themselves what their needs ought to be, and meeting those needs in efficient ways, conservative ways, *conserver* ways . . . all right, I'll admit it — CHEAP ways. Any way except whipping out the credit card and buying it shiny new at the parking lot plaza.

When wars were fought by ranks of redcoats lined up neatly on the field, the rules were made to suit the officers who could direct the thing in a safe and gentlemanly way from the shade at the top of the hill: "King's bishop to knight four . . . Oh, well played chaps!" It's no different in economics. Rules of *normal* behavior, from plastic money to fashion, certainly aren't set up to profit the poor schmuck who has to pay the bills. You want to know who decides that skirts are shorter this year? That the candy case is open at nose level for a three-year-old? That pulling something useful out of the neighbor's garbage is socially unacceptable? That fixing a car can cost more than replacing it? You want to know who makes these rules? Look up on the hill . . . There! In the shade. *To hell with the rules!* There are enough redcoats in the world already.

Rent or Own?

The decision to rent or buy has become a cultural decision rather than an economic one. Renting a home is socially acceptable in Paris or Manhattan. In Los Angeles or Cleveland or Scarborough it's strictly déclassé. Renters are people who can't afford to buy.

There's nothing wrong with ownership. It's just that it doesn't always make economic sense. Take this housing situation as an example:

The Smiths have a home that suits them fine. Just what they always wanted. The only problem is that it doesn't belong to them. They pay $1,500 a month in rent and the regular obligation irks them. The landlord is willing to sell for $180,000. The Smiths work hard and save their pennies to someday realize their dream. And the dream comes true. They finally have the $180,000 saved. The stash has been carefully invested to yield six percent, and thus earning a helpful $10,800 a year on its own.

When the big day comes, they sign the papers, hand over the cash, and become owners. No more rent to pay. That's $1,500 ahead each month! There are some new expenses of course. Property taxes come to $3,000 a year. Repairs and maintenance add another $3,000. Insurance is another $2,500. Altogether, their new expenses add up to $8,500 a year. Then, of course, their savings are gone, the $10,800 a year in interest is lost. Ownership, for the Smiths, will cost them $19,300 a year — $1,300 a year *more* than they paid in rent!

Even if they hadn't saved a penny, the result might be the same. If they borrowed the whole $180,000 and paid six percent interest on the mortgage, the cost of ownership would still be $19,000 a year:

$10,800 capital costs (mortgage interest or lost investment)*

  3,000 taxes

  3,000 maintenance and repair

  <u>2,500</u> insurance

<u>**$19,300**</u> **Total annual cost of ownership**

compared to:

$18,000 **Total annual cost of rental**

*In areas where mortgage interest can be deducted, a real comparison would require that this tax advantage be subtracted from "capital costs", making borrowing preferable to investing.

It's not that simple in real life, of course. Inflation complicates the calculation. In the year after the Smiths bought the house, let's assume that inflation pushes housing costs up by three percent. The Smiths' house is now worth $185,400 at newly inflated prices. The house has *earned* $5,400 in appreciation. Had they decided to keep their money and continue renting, the rent might have been increased by $540 a year. That would suggest that, for the Smiths, ownership was a better choice than rental by a margin of $4,860 in the second year. Does inflation always serve the owner and punish the renter?

Not always. The $4,860 in inflationary "earnings" is mostly illusion. In order to collect such earnings, the Smiths would have to sell the house. Any comparable house in the area would also have inflated by three percent and their advantage would disappear as soon as they tried to buy another house.

Renters have some additional protection against inflation in areas where rent is controlled. The protection may only be temporary, since sooner or later rents have to be adjusted to the owner's costs, but such protection must nevertheless be considered in the decision to rent or buy.

People buy houses for all sorts of perfectly valid reasons that have nothing to do with financial advantages. For independence, security, the freedom to build or expand, or just to have an investment that can be seen and cared for. Oil stocks may pay better returns, but their values go up and down for reasons that are totally beyond the investor's control. Mowing the lawn or painting the kitchen doesn't help a bit if you put your money in an oil well.

The decision to rent or buy should not ignore the human factors. Such preferences are at least as important as the financial criteria. But *do* get the financial part of the decision straight by including capital costs in any comparison, regardless of whether the capital is yours or the bank's.

Finding the Cost of Ownership

When considering the purchase of anything other than a house, the questions most often overlooked are: How often do we need it? For how long?

Everybody asks for the initial price. Few consider the cost per use, or the cost per year. It's these costs that must be compared to the rental cost before a truly sound decision can be taken.

Take garden tillers for instance. The cheapest, full-sized new ones start at about $500. Vibration takes a heavy toll on such machinery, but if they're very well cared for they may last for years. I'll be generous and say that with luck and some repairs we might keep one going for twenty-five years. The initial investment would be used up at the rate of twenty dollars per year.

Initial cost ÷ expected life = Annual Cost

or

$500 ÷ 25 years = $20 per year

Now if I weren't buying a tiller, I might leave that $500 invested and earn, let's say five percent, or twenty-five dollars a year. So, buying the tiller will also cost twenty-five dollars a year in foregone interest. Maintenance costs might add another ten to twenty dollars. Operating costs (gas and oil) depend on how much it's used, but let's say that the couple of hours it would take to do a big garden would use about a dollar's worth of fuel. Owning a tiller would therefore cost us a minimum of fifty-five dollars a year, plus a dollar every time we use it:

$20	initial cost per year
25	foregone interest
10	maintenance
$55	**Total annual cost of ownership, plus $1 each use**

The alternative is to rent. The local tool place rents full-sized tillers for twenty dollars for the couple of hours we need it. That includes gas and oil, and they look after the maintenance. For one use a year — to turn the soil in the spring — it would cost fifty-six dollars to own the tiller and twenty dollars to rent it. Granted, we might till more than once a year if we had the machine sitting here. However, we would have to use it more than three times a year before owning became as economical as renting. And we would have to be pretty confident that we could keep it running for twenty-five years.

Renting and owning aren't the only two choices of course. A high-cost, low-use item like a tiller is just the sort of thing that can be profitably shared amongst neighbors. Spread the capital costs, and use the machine more intensively. That, however, is a guerrilla solution that your redcoat neighbors might find hard to accept.

Cost of Owning a Car versus Transportation Alternatives

My urban friends made much the same sort of calculation in deciding not to own a car. They started by estimating their total transportation needs, and the cost of meeting those needs in various ways:

Commuting to work. They both worked in the city center, three miles from home. When driving, they shared a ride and paid $7 a day for parking. Mileage: 1,410

Evenings out. They went out about 50 evenings a year. Most of their outings were into the city, a six-mile round trip. Free evening parking. Mileage: 300

Shopping and appointments. They make 150 trips a year back into the city, or to a nearer shopping center. Five miles is an average round trip. On half the trips they pay an average $3 parking fee. Mileage: 750

Weekend Excursion. Twenty-five times a year they go skiing or out to cottage country. Ten of those trips are overnight (for a total of 35 days). The average trip is 200 miles. Mileage: 5,000

A new car would cost them $18,000, if they don't splurge on the extras. If they took the money out of savings, which were earning five percent a year, they would lose $900 a year in interest. The car depreciates by thirty percent a year, so it will lose $5,400 of its value in the first year, $3,780 in the second year, and so on; but let's say it lasts ten years and the average annual loss in value over the entire life of the car is a simple one-tenth of $18,000, or $1,800 a year. Insurance adds $1,200 a year, maintenance $500. The total parking fees are $2,045. Total mileage is 7,460 miles a year, which would take about $650 in gasoline. Altogether, the cost of ownership comes to $7,095 per year:

Cost of Car Ownership

foregone interest	$900
average depreciation	$1,800
insurance & license	$1,200
maintenance	$500
parking	$2,045
gasoline	$650
Annual Cost of Ownership	**$7,095**

Cost of Alternatives

Taking public transit to work/shopping: 1,240 fares or 2 X $75-a-month transit passes (150 X 12) =	$1800
Taxis for 50 evening outings (approximately)	$800
Renting a car on weekends:	$2,500
Annual Cost of Alternatives	**$5,100**
Savings of using alternatives over owning:	**$1,995**

The simple arithmetic says that using public transport and rentals would save $1,995 a year. In real life, of course, it's never that simple. Depreciation is heavily loaded onto the early years of a new car's life. You could cut the cost of ownership by sticking to used cars. But on the other hand, maintenance gets more expensive for older cars and used car savings might disappear unless you can do some of the repairs yourself. Interest rates might vary considerably over the ten-year life of the car. So could fuel prices, transit passes and insurance costs.

Many drivers like the idea of jumping in the car and being on the road with zero waiting time. But convenience, too, can cut two ways. Bus commuters wait to get on, but step off at the other end without circling the block three times to find a parking spot. Drivers like to be in control; bus people are happy that the flat tire on the freeway is somebody else's problem.

My friends decided that the convenience of having a car on hand was offset by the inconvenience of traffic jams, breakdowns, and parking problems. Being true conservers, they also decided to rent out their empty parking spot at home for thirty dollars a month. Over twelve months, this will add up to another $360. Total advantage to giving up the car: $2,355 a year!

Another option available in a growing number of cities is car sharing. Car-sharing systems vary — some are co-operatives, some are privately owned enterprises. They tend to involve paying a membership fee or a refundable deposit of a few hundred dollars. Shared vehicles of different types are parked in spots all over the city; members can reserve cars over the Internet for even short periods of time (one advantage over car rental agencies that usually won't rent vehicles for less than a day). If your city has a good public transit system and you don't need a vehicle for your daily work, this can be an economical and convenient alternative to car ownership for many households.

Now those circumstances won't apply to everyone, and many families with different needs may find more financial advantages in owning a car. But the example does show how a careful look at costs (in any purchasing decision) may undermine the accepted wisdom that renters are people who can't afford to buy. That's a redcoat rule. Sometimes you are better off not to buy.

Barter's Better

The last time Colby tried amateur wiring, he was sharing a tiny two-room flat with a fellow student and seven cats. Since the landlady was not aware he lived there, he was hardly in a good position to ask her to turn off the electricity while he moved a few outlets around. When the landlady finally did arrive at midnight, to replace the fuses that were mysteriously blowing, she found poor Colby crouched in a corner, trying to splice two smoking wires in a dim little pool of candlelight. The rest of the room was dark as pitch. Even the halo of candlelight was dimmed with a haze of electrical smoke. The room was filed with a hulking mountain of furniture, pushed away from the walls and entwined in a hopeless tangle of disemboweled wires. In the darkest corner — opposite Colby — one of the cats was giving birth and obviously having trouble, screaming and shrieking in an unearthly way that was more like a banshee than a cat. Colby swearing at the wires, and the landlady yelling at Colby (whoever he might be), and the banshees screaming from somewhere in the smoky depths, and a tipsy visitor (awakened by all that screaming) trying to crawl out from under the furniture knocked the pile over in an avalanche that snuffed the candle and finally sent the landlady sobbing into the night. Colby vowed he was through with home improvements.

Years later, when Colby had a house of his own, he broke his vow and built a large addition. He balked, however, when it came to the wiring of the fuse box. He decided it would be sensible to have the wiring done by a professional this time. So he called in a carpenter.

Carpenters, he explained, were so much cheaper than real electricians. Besides, this particular carpenter was also skilled at home wiring. Better still, working without a license himself, the carpenter was more amenable to Colby's unsanctioned shortcuts — like the absence of permits, inspections, and the innocent belief that the building code was some kind of street directory.

Colby might have been safer with a real electrician. His intent, after all, was to short circuit the marketplace, not to hot-wire another house. Electricians understand barter, too, and even carpenters have to be paid.

Colby's carpenter got four loads of firewood, a used lawnmower, and the loan of Colby's cement mixer. Both got fair value. The carpenter had $200 worth of firewood, a lawnmower that would have cost him $50, and a mixer that normally rents for $25 a day (and he kept it for three months). The carpenter, who makes $18 an hour, normally would have been paid $432 for his three days work. After taxes and deductions, however, his $432 would have shrunk to $259 — less than he got from the tight-fisted Colby.

Had Colby been a redcoat, the idle mixer would have stayed in the garage until he needed it again, the wood might have stayed in the forest, and the lawnmower would have gone to the dump. In order to pay the tradesman a regular wage, Redcoat Colby would have called a contractor. The contractor might have paid his tradesman $18 an hour, but he would have charged Colby twice that. Redcoat Colby would have to come up with $864 for the contractor. And in order to have that much after-tax money to spend, he would have had to earn $1,440 himself.

If Colby and the carpenter both earn the same wage, Colby would have to work ten days in order to buy three days of the carpenter's time. Barter, at one-for-one, is a better deal. The "normal" way is like feeding the horse to feed the sparrow — a lot of the value disappears between the beginning and the end of the deal.

Barter has one fundamental advantage over the redcoat economy — it eliminates the middlemen. When you eliminate the paper-pushers, politicians, financiers, administrators, agents, salespeople, organizers, consultants, foremen, brokers, inspectors, investors and profit-takers from the picture, and get right down to the nitty-gritty of a producer and a consumer who can look one another in the eye and make a deal, one-for-one, *then* economics makes sense again.

What Will the Tax Collector Say?

The guerrilla economy, though slowly becoming socially acceptable, still teeters on the edge of official approval. Specifically, the tax department. Strictly speaking, the tax collector sees no difference between earning a paycheck and earning goods or services in exchange for your work. It's all subject to tax.

Although I would not have been so rude as to ask, I expect that Colby's carpenter dutifully listed the value of the firewood, the mower, and use of the mixer as "other income" on his annual tax return. And Colby, I'm sure, detailed the exchange on his tax form. Keeping tabs on the guerrilla economy is a lot more difficult than taxing computerized paychecks, but the law, after all, is the law. Right? Right.

The bureaucrats are happier when barter is done in an organized way. Many large-scale barter clubs and commercial "exchanges" have sprung up in recent years. Members, or participants, earn *credits* on a predetermined scale for services they provide to other members. They may then spend those credits by buying goods and services from other members. The clubs have the advantage of giving access to a wide variety of willing traders (not everyone happens to know a carpenter who can wire houses and needs a lawnmower).

Barter clubs have several disadvantages, however. Most add an administrative fee to each exchange. Eight per cent is a typical charge, and that must usually be paid in cash. Secondly, an organized exchange can put a disproportionate load on some members. A dentist, for instance, in a club with fifty writers and violinists, would earn far more credits than she could reasonably spend within the group. For that reason, some clubs allow participants to demand a share of the exchange in cash as well as barter. Finally, the greatest disadvantage of the clubs is precisely the feature that so delights the tax men: *all those vouchers and credits are easy to count and value and report and tax.* "Line up there, you redcoats!"

Because the barter clubs can only eliminate *some* of the middlemen (and the smaller ones at that), the real guerrillas make their barter connections one-to-one with friends and neighbors. Frankly, it is harder that way to find the goods and skills you may need, but it does seem to be worth the extra effort. The bureaucrats have not yet figured out how to tax the mutual benefits of friendship. After all, who is to say what a friendly favor is worth?

Making Connections

The easiest way to find a barter partner is the direct approach. Ask! The next time the dentist looks in your mouth and phones her yacht broker, ask her if she would be interested in something other than another load of mere cash. Some needlepoint for the chair perhaps? A painting for the ceiling? Polish the yacht? Offer whatever you can provide. And don't be shy on the presumption that a dentist would not be interested in something as, well, *base* as bartering. Chances are her income bracket is higher than yours (unless you happen to be a plumber) and she thus has even more interest than you in something as base as barter. You, of course, will remind her that the value of your yacht polishing must be reported to the tax department. Of course.

Barter starts with need. Decide what you need, find out who can supply it, and ask them what they would take in lieu of cash. The only general advice that applies is to avoid the middlemen and the hired help. It's futile to ask the salesclerk in the department store about barter. If it's furniture you want, ask the man who makes it, or the man who owns it. Deal with smaller firms where the owners talk to the customers, and with tradespeople who can moonlight on their own time.

Barter works in the city as well as in the country. I know of one apartment dweller with a sixteen-foot canoe. He stores it in a colleague's garage. He gets free storage. His friend gets a free canoe, fifty-one weeks a year. Urbanites trade rent-free living for "house-sitting" services, potted plants for records, and car repairs for home cooking. I've seen babysitting swapped for a computer printer, a basement "rented" for a share of the wine fermented there, and theater-goers who buy cheaper season subscriptions and swap unwanted tickets for tickets to concerts and ball games. Nearly every service or ware that can be bought can also be bartered. There are exceptions; public utilities and the tax collector still insist on cash. But by and large the things you can get with barter are almost limitless. I once got the local blacksmith to make up a little part for the pump. Cost me a dozen beets. Try getting blacksmithing done on your American Express card.

The best bartering is that between friends and neighbors. However, when you need something that your own acquaintances can't provide, don't hesitate to ask strangers to barter. Chances are they already know the advantages — just as the redcoats knew the guys behind the trees were better off than they were. The difficulty in dealing with strangers is not in convincing them to barter, but in finding out what they want and agreeing on the value of exchange.

How Many Apples is an Orange Worth?

In the redcoat economy of middlemen and taxes, all goods and services are given a dollar value, and the handy green units will tell you at once how many apples and oranges it's worth, or how many hours of labor it takes to equal a TV set. A dollar is a dollar is a dollar. When everything has a dollar value, exchange is greatly simplified.

The guerrilla economy is a little more complicated. Equivalents are easy enough, in theory. Just trade on the basis of theoretical dollars. If filling a tooth is worth seventy dollars to the redcoats, and yacht polishing pays seven theoretical dollars an hour, then the filling is worth ten hours of polishing. The problems arise when the units are not easily divided. You cannot trade a canoe for a tenth of a car. Nor is it easy to persuade someone to take ten canoes for this car, even if the values are equivalent. Then there's little choice but to trade other things, or look for other traders (or, God forbid, make up the difference in cash).

When negotiating equivalent values, both traders should value their goods in the same price system. A dozen eggs and a loaf of bread might both be worth two dollars at supermarket prices, and a fair trade one-for-one. But if the egg man claims that a fancy restaurant gets eight dollars an egg (served on silver, one at a time), and his dozen are therefore worth ninety-six dollars, he cannot trade them for ninety six loaves of bread. He can try, but it won't often work. If he's going to value his eggs at fancy restaurant prices, then the bread should be valued that way, too.

Choose the price system that seems appropriate — retail, wholesale, bulk, or individual. Keep it fair and be consistent. *And*, if the tax collector's looking, keep to the lowest valuation. For example:

Smith is a plumber, Jones an accountant. They agree to trade ten hours of moonlight plumbing for ten hours' work on the tax return. During regular hours, both earn thirty dollars an hour doing work for which their employers charge customers fifty dollars an hour. So, if Smith had hired an accountancy service in the normal way, he would have paid $500, but only $300 of that would have gone to Jones. Likewise, Jones would have paid $500 if she had called in a plumbing firm, and Smith would have received just $300 for his ten hours' work. Instead, they barter. No money changes hands, but legally each must report the value of service received in return for the labor. Each must report an equivalent dollar amount under "other income." Should they report a value on the barter of $500, the amount they would have paid? Or $300, as the amount they would have earned? Or would they have been better off agreeing to trade labor arbitrarily valued at some lower wage? The trade-off is exactly the same in any case. The question is whether to pay income tax on $500, $300 . . . or $30.

Cooperation and Cooperatives

It can be as simple as borrowing a cup of sugar from the neighbor, or as complex as the billion-dollar system of retail co-ops. Whatever the style of cooperation, it nearly always leads to savings for consumers.

Consumers save by cutting out the overhead and the middlemen. So simple cooperation, like sharing a lawnmower with a neighbor, saves more than buying your own private lawnmower at the co-op hardware store. Bigger isn't always better.

Neighbors feed one another's pets, take turns driving the kids, borrow tools and boost one another's batteries. At the same time, there are kennel services, taxicabs, tool rental firms and tow trucks all willing to sell the services that some neighbors give and receive for nothing. The only price on the cash-free way is that you are expected to give as well as receive. It seems such an obvious and natural way of life that I'm always surprised that kennels, rentals and other businesses like that exist.

It's no contradiction that a tight-fisted skinflint like me would counsel sharing freely with neighbors and friends. That kind of generosity is nearly always repaid in full. When our two tikes wanted to play store one summer, they made a sign, picked bunches of wildflowers, and set up to sell them beside the road. Old spoilsport pointed out that they weren't really giving fair value, since anybody was free to stop and pick flowers themselves for nothing. It was more of a game than a business anyway, so they shrugged and got the crayons out, changing the sign to "free flowers." Not only did they stop a lot more customers that way, but they soon came bounding home with pockets full of "tips," delighted with the joys of giving. I'm neither small enough nor cute enough to get away with that, but I've rarely been disappointed with the rewards for being neighborly.

Neighborliness can become more organized when the group gets too big to remember what's been done and owed, or when friends and neighbors are too mobile to sustain that kind of interdependence. Many urban neighborhoods operate simple cooperatives for common services. Baby-sitting, for instance. The one I know best began when Ann and a few friends were discussing the costs and perils of hiring sitters, particularly in a big city neighborhood like theirs, where people moved too often to get to know the local teens on more than the briefest recommendation. It wasn't the money so much as the idea that strangers were taking care of their kids — strangers with teenage appetites and boyfriends. They decided they would feel better sitting for one another. Ann bought a ledger book (the only expense the group ever made) and asked if Martha was free to sit that night. Martha spent four hours at Ann's that night, and earned a four-hour credit in the ledger. Ann's page showed a four-hour debit. They took turns making appointments and keeping the ledger, and the system worked so well that dozens of families got involved. They could always get a sitter at a moment's notice, and never again found an empty fridge at the end of the evening.

Other families cooperate to buy meat in bulk, share the cost of vacation cottages, own tools in common, establish schools, or make larger-scale investments than any of them could afford alone. In every case, they could act alone and find what they wanted on the retail market, but they gain financial advantage by acting as a group.

One of the newest forms is the cooperative garage, owned by members who hire mechanics to do honest, non-profit auto repairs and assist members (with tools and advice) with their own repairs.

Many of the larger co-ops were formed as protection against the outright exploitation of individuals in the marketplace. Western agricultural co-ops, for instance, were formed by farmers fed up with selling wheat at give-away prices to the few big buyers who dominated the market. The big co-ops look like any other business, though, with charters and shares and voting rights and dividends, and all the consultants, accountants, lawyers, and other non-producing middlemen that go with size. The big co-ops are in the phonebook under "C."

The biggest savings, however, are usually found in the smallest groups, where overhead is zero, middlemen don't exist, and members can make decisions over the backyard fence — without a lawyer to complicate the situation.

Getting It Free

If you're reading this book at the public library, you already have the idea. Go to the head of the class. If you bought the book, I thank you. The publisher thanks you. But pay attention: you have a lot to learn about guerrilla economics.

"There's no such thing as a free lunch," according to some forgotten philosopher.

It's true enough in the larger economy, but the individual is surrounded by a veritable sea of freebies. I know, I know, *someone* has to pay, but as long as the redcoats are convinced that freebies are for the lower classes, it only seems fair to let them get their jollies by picking up the tab.

I'm not talking about food stamps, pensions, or other official aids for those who might need them. I'm referring to the cornucopia of give-aways that are freely available to all. Here's a tiny sample.

Tools. Need a sewing machine to finish the wardrobe, or fancy saws and planers to build a dining suite? Sign up for an evening course at the local high school. There's usually a nominal fee, but you can get access to a roomful of the finest equipment for a fraction of the cost of buying or renting. And if you don't know what you're doing, there's an instructor to help.

Books. There's the library, of course, and most of them also offer music and movies to borrowers. But if you want new books to keep, join a book club. The introductory offers (you know — four books for a buck and that sort of thing) are reasonably good value. When you've finished the obligation, there's no reason why you can't quit and join again for another introductory offer. And once you join the club you're on everybody's mailing list for books. You'll get free samples, special offers, "Take the first volume free and cancel the rest if not completely satisfied" offers. You can collect Volume 1 of every do-it-yourself set published and still not spend a penny.

Fruit. Most city parks plant ornamental fruit trees. Apart from being pretty, they bear edible fruit that clutters up the grass if someone doesn't pick it. Check with your local parks department to be sure they won't object, and that they don't spray the fruit with objectionable chemicals. In the last city we lived in, I picked crabapples, rose hips and cranberries, just on the path home from the office. We make up to thirty gallons of wine each year, and every drop comes from free fruit.

Garden Soil. Need fertilizer, potting soil, or just some good rich fill for the lawn? Make your own by composting manure, kitchen scraps and leaves. If it's mixed in a pile, watered and turned occasionally, it will be ready in a couple of months. Suburban riding stables will give away manure; free leaves cover the sidewalks in many neighborhoods, and — if you ask nicely — the local market or restaurant will save vegetable wastes for you. A smelly nuisance? One fall, we made over five tons of compost on a tiny city lot, and the only hint the neighbors had was when they saw me raking leaves a block away from home. And the head swami guru at the vegetarian café began to suspect that I was feeding a pig on their daily pail of kitchen wastes — now there's an idea!

Meat. Free meat? It's not impossible. Groundhog is delicious if you remove the musk glands first (they're in the "armpits"). Farmers are delighted to get rid of all the groundhogs you can take. Christmas dinner at our house one year was a succulent haunch of beaver — fur trappers throw the carcass away. Squab and pigeon breasts are gourmet delights and cost a fortune in fancy restaurants — and yet they're free for the taking in every rural barn. Fish belong to those who catch them, and sometimes those who catch them are happy to give them away once the pictures are snapped. Small slaughter houses give away soup bones and unsightly pieces that other customers don't want (ask about pigs' heads). Free meat isn't the exclusive preserve of hunters and farmers either. My own introduction was in the busy metropolis of Cleveland, when a friend arrived at the door wearing a black, three-piece suit, carrying a briefcase, a rolled umbrella and a dead rabbit. He was walking past the opera hall, it seems, when this rabbit hopped out of the bushes. The brolly was faster than the bunny. Delicious.

Commercial Samples. The givers expect the getters to feel obligated and buy a lot more after getting the freebie. That's a cardinal redcoat rule. We took our free 8 x 10 family portrait as advertised and the salesman seemed genuinely surprised that we didn't also feel obliged to take the thirty-seven-dollar package of copies that accompanied it. Soaps, toilet articles, new snack foods, cleansers and many other products are commonly given away as gimmicks. The only cost is the will to say *no* to the ensuing pitch to buy some more. The kids' favorite family outing is our annual free tour of the chocolate factory — free samples in the sales room afterwards!

Government Services. Want to know how to skin a rabbit, cook a pigeon, pan for gold or fix your car? Chances are there's a bureaucrat somewhere responsible for that. Federal and local governments are a mine of information. Your local librarian can steer you to the right department and of course there's the Internet — which you can also access for free at many public libraries. We set out to find some information on planting windbreaks, and stumbled across a government nursery selling seedling trees for a dime apiece, and a trained forester full of free advice on how to do it. *Ask.*

Some of the Nicest People Shop at the Dump

Even the Lone Ranger and William Tell were kindred spirits in my affection for adopting orphaned goods. All together now: *To the dump, to the dump, to the dump dump dump . . .*

Amazing what the redcoats will throw away! I wrote several books on a desk that was once a door that went out with someone's renovations. The lamp came from a motel — thrown out when the shade got bent. The little file box is walnut, decorated with hand carved inlays — it was an old sewing machine top, thrown out when the handle broke. The big filing cabinets were government surplus. The credenza was discarded because it was the wrong color for someone's decor. I sit on an antique walnut and leather swivel chair. A doctor threw it out when his teenagers broke off the armrest. With a little glue and the leather restored it's magnificent. If it were for sale I couldn't afford it.

The house is full of it: a walnut dresser, pure wool carpets, antique chests, rockers, chairs, beds, cupboards, lamps, windows, books, doors and even a piano bench. All of it thrown out for lack of a bit of glue and the elbow grease that restores it to life again. We have an easy chair in the living room that is broken beyond redemption. The original plastic cover leaks stuffing from every crack and orifice. Some inner collapse has left it listing, ready to spill unwary guests. It really is an offensive thing in an otherwise pleasant room. We keep it because it's the only piece in the house that someone didn't first discard. We actually bought it new, and leave it there now as a monument to the folly of our old redcoat vanity, when we believed that one had to go to the store to pay for nice things. First-time visitors, who know our reputation for shopping at the dump, usually avoid the chair. I mean, it's so obvious — isn't it?

Treasures don't turn up every week in the curbside heaps of green plastic bags. And many large municipal dumps won't allow scroungers wandering around serious, big-time, burn-'n'-bury operations. Where then? If you don't have access to small rural dumps, you're left with only four good sources: neighbors, special junk days, industrial waste and re-use depots.

Conservers play a curious symbiotic role with "normal" friends and neighbors. Not closet conservers who do their scrounging furtively in the dead of night, but full-flown, honest-to-God, up front, here-I-am, out-of-the-closet addicts to the re-use of refuse. Junk junkies. Word gets around. Before long, friends and neighbors will be seeking *you* out:

"I'm clearing out the basement. Would you like to help?"

"We bought a new fridge: do you have any use for the old one?"

"It's a perfectly good coat; it just doesn't fit anymore."

Truly! It happens! It isn't charity. The scrounger does provide a service more personal and useful than the garbage collector. How many garbage collectors will help you carry your junk out of the basement and then split a bottle of dandelion wine in the bargain? More than that, the scrounger brings some measure of entertainment to the serious business of being a consumer. The game is: "Throw it out — not even Charley could find a use for twelve old shingles *[doghouse roof]*, or a piece of iron bedstead *[barbecue grill]*, or a broken sheet of cork board *[soundproof the pump]*, or a carpet with a hole in it *[a smaller carpet with no hole]*, or the upper half of a boot *[leather hinges]*." That's a lot more fun than seeing their expensive consumer affluence scrunched to a green plastic mush in the jaws of a garbage truck.

Most towns that offer garbage service limit the kinds of things you may set out for the weekly pick-up. No appliances, furniture, lumber, brush, etc. Nothing but old chicken bones and disposable diapers (not even Charley wants those). But once or twice a year such towns relent and have a special collection for "spring cleaning" or some such euphemism. The towns that don't relent find the bigger junk dumped along the roadsides anyway, so it's cheaper to relent officially. When the clear-up days are announced, the piles of furniture, lumber, fridges, and bedsteads start to grow beside the curb and on the lawns of suburbia. And as the sun sinks slowly into the West, the parades of trucks and commandeered wagons start cruising slowly past the piles, ever alert for carelessly discarded treasure. It pays to be early — the best stuff goes first.

The very best junk often comes from industrial garbage. For all the propaganda about the efficiency of private enterprise, there's an enormous amount of perfectly good garbage going out the back doors of North American industry. Admittedly, some of it is sold (steel barrels for three dollars each, and sawmill slabs at five dollars a load, for example), and the best refuse is picked over first by the people who work there. Ask your friends who work in factories or in warehouses about the kinds of things that are normally thrown out. A lot is still left for the taking. In steel-making areas, many a drive and path is paved with slag from the furnaces. Just outside a nearby marble crushing plant, nearly every driveway is paved with pure white marble dust. Fruit and vegetable packers throw away tons and tons of perfectly good food, culled for appearance's sake (crooked carrots, blemished apples). One friend heats a large house with the hardwood packing crates that are discarded at the neighboring snowmobile sales lot. We have pig pens and gates from trucking pallets, workbenches from an instrument factory, and the stone walls are reinforced with broken crane cables discarded at the auto-wrecking yard. (That was something of a coup — finding a use for the junkyard's junk!) Find out what your local factory throws away and ask (at the back door) if you can help get rid of it.

Re-use depots are a relatively new light on the environmental front. Some have been sparked by "green" groups, others by municipalities running out of room in the landfill site. They're like permanent community garage sales, without the prices. The idea is that you leave your discards, and take away anything you like. My favorite is in the posh Boston suburb of Wellesley. Anyplace else would call it "the dump," but Wellesley calls it the "Recycling and Disposal Facility." There's a quaint wooden sign under the tree at the gate that says so. Not a single whiff of *eau de Glad* on the air. This "facility" is the ultimate in eco-chic.

It's more like a park than a dump: shade trees, lawns, and a smooth paved road that winds through the greenery and emerges above a row of dumpsters. There is a separate dumpster for every sort of recyclable, and a few for just plain garbage. Patrons back onto the lip of a dock, so the top of each dumpster is at trunk level. There is finished compost for sale, and a tidy open-air book department offering long shelves of quality hard-covers for recyclers, browsers and takers. The book department even sports a sign-on list for those who wish to request a special title: "Need Volume 3 of *Decline and Fall,* please phone . . . ."

On fine weekends, the "facility" hosts art exhibits and outdoor concerts on the lawn. No low-brow street music here, however; this is strictly string quartets and your finer class of freebie.

Do-It-Yourself

By far the most satisfying freebie of all is to find that you can do it yourself. That advice seems almost gratuitous given that over fifty percent of building supplies sold are now going to amateurs doing it themselves. That's a fact. The suspicion is that a major part of those home projects involve kits and assemblies, glue-on bricks, and self-stick tiles. All very admirable efforts I'm sure, but not really in keeping with the intention here — saving money.

When conservers do it themselves, the end result is meant to be cheaper than the commercial version. It may also be better and more fun than buying, but the point is to spend less, to cut out some more of those middlemen. The ultimate in ridiculous do-it-yourself gadgets is the electric cream-maker. You take a pound of butter, stick it in this gizmo, and make your own cream. Truly! I do not tell a lie. They sell such things! A conserver would set out a pan of milk and take the cream off the top with a spoon. The middleman economy would have us separate the cream, churn it into butter, and then buy a machine to turn it back into cream again.

Do-it-yourself, in this book, means doing it with less — less money, less energy (either the world's energy or yours), less fuss and less claptrap from the middlemen about how only a machine or a skilled, licensed, and regulated specialist can do it properly.

My idea of do-it-yourself is illustrated by one young family not far from here. They completed the building of a two-story house with 1,700 square feet of brand-new space. It took them two years and $10,000. That's right: $10,000! They didn't want to start off life with the handicap of a mortgage, they explained. They started with neither experience nor skill in building. They didn't even have a plan. They copied the outside dimensions of another house down the road, and made up the inside layout as they went along. Nor was it done with kits, pre-built trusses, snap-on siding, or glue-on bricks. Bought materials were just too expensive. The walls are cement and local cedar, and cost just $500 to raise.

Not everyone has the confidence to start a house from scratch, but millions of ordinary people have discovered that they can bypass the middlemen with results that are profitable, and often up to professional standards as well. Here are just a few examples.

Haircuts. The last time I paid to sit in a barber's chair, the price was fifty cents and included a touch-up with a razor and a squirt of toilet water. The minimum trim is now eight dollars, and you'll pay twelve or more to be "styled." If you can press a spouse or willing friend into service, it's a simple job that takes less time than finding a parking spot at the barber's. The barber's skill is in knowing how to cut many styles on many different types of hair. With only one or two heads involved, the knack can be learned in a few practice sessions with scissors and comb.

You may look a little funny for a couple of months, but when a trim costs twenty dollars and you can look back and remember when you hated to pay eight dollars, you'll forget all about the practice cuts.

Legal Fees. The Utopians, Thomas More wrote, had no need of lawyers since their laws were clearly written and based on simple reason. We, unfortunately, have left the writing of law to lawyers, so that it is neither clear nor simple. There are cases, however, that are common and simple enough that the law is applied repetitiously, by rote and formula. An uncontested divorce or a straightforward will, for instance, is processed in the courts like a Big Mac. The language is still mumbo-jumbo, but it varies little beyond the personal data of the participants: Name? Address? Who gets the house? Fries with that? It's about as complicated as applying for a driver's license. Most towns have at least one firm selling "legal forms." It's often a stationery store you'll find in the yellow pages. Most now sell kits to individuals wishing to act as their own lawyers in simple cases, all forms and instructions included. Don't try it if you want to leave your fortune to the canary, but neither should you waste the expense of a lawyer to fill in your name and address.

Plumbing. Like many expensive tradesmen, plumbers use their experience and skills on a tiny fraction of the jobs they do. Most of those fifty-dollar-an-hour bills are for simple things that even a teacher or a writer could master. Putting a washer in a leaky tap or installing a shower over the tub involves a few techniques that a layman could figure out from a how-to book in ten minutes or less: joining copper pipe, gluing plastic drains together, where to screw it off and on, and where to smear the gunk. If you can't figure out the how-to book, the plumbing supply shop will explain it. Even the nasty jobs, like getting the toilet to flush instead of erupting on the bathroom floor, involve more mess than know-how. The expensive tools (like drain augers for the toilet) can be rented. Beyond that, there's little point in paying a plumber fifty dollars an hour to mop up the bathroom floor. Save the plumber for the really tough problems, like where to eat in Nice and whether to be bullish on gold.

Sales Agents. Selling the house? Trading in the car? Getting rid of Grandpa's boat? Do you call in the agent or sell it yourself? Of course the agents will tell you that they earn their fees in the higher price they can get for your treasure. Consider this: most markets for expensive items vary widely over time, or from city to city, but at any one point there is a standard set of values that is easy to establish and hard to buck, no matter who your agent is. If you're selling a three-bedroom bungalow on a forty-foot lot, look at similar properties in similar areas and see how much they are selling for. That's the "market price." You can get less (quickly) or more (with hard work and patience), but chances are you, or your agent, will have to sell pretty close to the market average. The agent's fee is a percentage of the sales price. It varies, but let's say five percent. If the market value is around $100,000, the agent expects a $5,000 fee. If she is in a hurry, she can get $4,800 by finding a buyer at $96,000. Or, she can spend ten times the effort and perhaps get a buyer at $104,000. The difference to you is $8,000; the difference to her is $400. Doubtless, many agents are scrupulous enough to hustle all those extra buyers on your behalf, but there may be one or two who would just as soon take the $4,800 for a sure quick sale. You, the owner, have more at stake and a greater incentive to hold out for the best possible price. On an hourly basis, your return for the extra effort is twenty times more than the agent's.

Car Repairs. Understanding the internal combustion engine is as easy for me as water divining or telling if the goat is pregnant. The color-coded, cut-away drawings were clear enough in the textbooks, but a real engine is closed up and covered with all sorts of mechanical red herrings that weren't in the drawing. Deciding what might be wrong under all that greasy tangle, has, I'm sure, more to do with alchemy than science. The cost of auto repair, however, leaves conservers little choice but to do what they can themselves. When our friendly neighborhood garage merged with the drive-in bank, we knew it was time to dig out some how-to books and start looking for the engine. It's still not easy and I still hate it, but knowing how to unstick the choke, change a tire, adjust the battery and wire the muffler back in place has saved us many a dollar. Moreover, it's car repairs that convinced me that lack of knowledge and talent still can't stop us from doing it ourselves. If I can make a Ford start, anybody can do anything.

And Anything Else You Can Think of. Liz, who learned nothing more practical than Latin in school, has taught herself how to fix the washing machine, tan a hide, knit left-handed, castrate a pig, upholster a chair, spin, cure ham and make three kinds of cheese, lasagna noodles and rugs. Do-it-yourself can get to be a habit. Even my pal Colby, the amateur electrician, eventually found the nerve to try again.

Most of us are capable of doing far more than we ever attempt. We don't trust ourselves to do it right, we listen too much to the self-interested claptrap of the specialists who want to be paid to do it for us, and we give up the effort when the first trial run doesn't come out as a picture-perfect copy of the commercial version. We end up being specialists ourselves as we gradually give up the idea of doing all those other things we're capable of. As Robert Heinlein wrote in *Time Enough for Love,*

> A human being should be able to change a diaper, plan an invasion, butcher a hog, con a ship, design a building, write a sonnet, balance accounts, build a wall, set a bone, comfort the dying, take orders, give orders, cooperate, act alone, solve equations, analyze a new problem, pitch manure, program a computer, cook a tasty meal, fight efficiently, die gallantly. Specialization is for insects.

~ 9 ~

Cheap Tips

A confession: the first draft of *How To Survive Without a Salary* didn't include this chapter. Adding "Cheap Tips" was the publisher's idea. I argued that paying less does not fit into a broad prescription. It has more to do with local sources, personal choices, and one-of-a-kind solutions to one-of-a-kind problems. He argued that readers would want cheap tips regardless, so we put them in. And then we heard from readers. We heard from Nova Scotia and British Columbia. From West Virginia and Washington. From Tauranga, New Zealand, and a bus station phone booth somewhere between Idaho and North Dakota.

Every tip was one-of-a-kind. But most were quick to counter with their own advice. *We don't all live in the country/have kids/write books/etc. — here's how we do it* . . . . And then they proceeded to offer cheap tips from their own local sources, personal choices and one-of-a-kind solutions. Some of these are included here. And we'll soon have the satisfaction of hearing from a whole new generation of one-of-a-kind conservers who will tell us: *We don't all live in the city/love opera/travel/etc. — here's how we do it* . . . .

This cannot be an exhaustive list of all the ways that all readers can cut the cost of living. We don't *know* all the ways. And, so far, we've heard from only a fraction of the clever conservers out there, and only from those still extravagant enough to spend money on a stamp or phone call to volunteer new ideas for the list. Every market and every situation is different.

The starting point is always the same, however. It is not where to buy — it's *whether* to buy. The best cheap tip is not to buy at all. Scratching around for bargains can be a pain in the neck. It's easier to decide that you don't really want the thing after all. It's easier to decide to wait for the cheaper, lusher, vine-ripened summer tomato than it is to scour the market for a bargain tomato in January.

It's not *where* to buy — it's *whether* to buy.

Nevertheless, the time does come when there really is no choice but to pull out the wallet and pay. How and where you perform that fiscal amputation is what distinguishes a conserver from a consumer. How and where to spend is what this chapter is all about.

Food

The obvious way to eat like a king for little or no cost is to raise it yourself. And that doesn't require a farm and a tractor either. Fruit and vegetables can be grown in the smallest city plot. Even an apartment balcony can grow most of a family's salads. Sprouts and mushrooms can be raised in a basement or closet. Rabbits, pigeons, and poultry can be kept almost anywhere (though in some cities you may have to give names to these "pets" and have leashes handy if the zoning inspector calls). Shortly after the first edition of this book came out, I heard from a family who kept a goat for fresh milk — in New York City!

No growing space at all? Try renting a garden plot outside the city and tending it on weekends. Many towns maintain community allotment gardens, marked off, plowed and fertilized. It's an old idea in Europe, but increasingly popular here as North America goes green.

One apartment building in a nearby town used to pay a contractor to look after a few flower beds and mow a large patch of grass behind the building. When a tight maintenance budget forced a reconsideration of the flower beds, the landlord asked if any of the tenants would be interested in keeping them up. Not only did the tenants want to look after the flowers, they convinced the landlord to dig up some of the grass and divide it into vegetable plots for the tenants. Even those who don't like to garden enjoy the inevitable surpluses.

City neighborhoods present lots of opportunities for cooperative gardening. Often — by age, occupation or preference — backyard owners find gardening to be more of a chore than they can manage. Conservers who want to grow free food can find a ready partner in front of many neglected backyards. Ask the busy or the elderly on your block if they would like you do some free gardening for them.

What's the worth of garden output? Well, that depends on whether you grow truffles or wheat, but consider the products of our own small plot. This fifty by seventy-five–foot patch produces the entire year-round supply of vegetables for a family of four, with enough left over in the summer glut to send friends and visitors home with all they can carry. Another plot, fifty feet square, provided most of the feed to produce six hundred pounds of pork each year. That was all we could eat and enough excess to pay the expenses. All together, in a space little bigger than a suburban lawn, we have grown all of our vegetables, meat, milk and eggs. Most of our fruit is homegrown as well. And, a short walk away, nature provides the makings for all the jams, wines, and syrups we can use. We do need cash for coffee, tea, flour, and sugar, but most of the rest can be free.

Anybody growing grass in the backyard can't be serious about the cost of food. Get a good gardening book and discover what a *real* tomato tastes like. Saving a fortune is just a bonus.

If you have no access to the earth and sun, buying food may be inevitable. Spending a fortune at it is not.

◆ Some shoppers save money by making use of discount coupons and refund offers. We don't often bother with these ourselves, because most of them seem to be discounts on junk food, snacks, and convenience foods that we wouldn't buy at any price. However, if your tastes run to coffee whiteners and sugar snacks, they are cheaper with the coupons than without.

◆ Shop for specials and loss-leaders, which are products priced at or below the supermarket's cost just to get you in the store where you'll buy all the non-specials too. Don't. Stock up on the specials when the price is right and don't be tempted by the more expensive stuff beside it.

◆ Generic products and store brands are consistently cheaper than the advertised brands you recognize from television. Even the basics. It's amazing that plain old packages of butter that have "creamy" or "farm fresh" printed on the wrapper are always more expensive than the identical ones labeled "plain old butter."

◆ Food co-ops and "no-frills" stores are sometimes (not always) cheaper than the ones with Muzak and uniformed bag packers.

◆ Always shop with a list prepared at home. Impulse buying is expensive. In fact, some stores have found they can improve their profits by providing larger shopping carts. Impulse buyers keep going until the cart is full, and a bigger cart keeps them going longer. Stop when you've finished your list.

◆ Buy in bulk. If you can't freeze or store a year's supply of a super bargain, get several families together and share the bounty. With several families sharing the work and investment, it may be worthwhile to branch out: take turns driving out to the country for a trunkload of potatoes, windfall of apples, or a neighborhood steer.

◆ Use farmer's markets. The food is fresher (and often cheaper) than the packaged stuff in the supermarket. If the price isn't right you can bargain.

◆ Cities, too, have public markets. Some are more urban chic than others, but most offer fresh, cheap food. The freshest is at the beginning of the day, the cheapest at the end. One reader in Winnipeg visits "The Forks" market on Sundays, when the last of the weekend stock gets sold off at fire sale prices: a dozen peppers for a dollar, bananas or tomatoes for twelve cents a pound.

◆ Get wholesale prices by buying in larger lots: a case of soup, a seventy-five-pound bag of potatoes, a bushel of apples. Just make sure the goods are non-perishable, or that you can use them up before they go off.

◆ Make the fullest use of leftovers. When Liz can't take anymore meat off a bone, it goes in the pot with some beans or any other left-over bits and pieces. The pot goes on top of the furnace and spends the day bubbling quietly away. By evening it's ambrosia. What people can't eat, the pigs happily clean up.

◆ Look for big discounts on seconds: bruised fruit, day-old bread, tins with torn labels.

◆ Check out the cheaper cuts of meat. The most expensive turkeys, for example, are those injected with butter or oil. Get a plain one and do the job yourself (with an inexpensive syringe from the drug store). Better still, get an even cheaper "utility" turkey — an expensive one with a broken wing or tear in the skin. Save a bundle and entertain Thanksgiving guests by explaining how your prize was injured.

◆ Buy in season. Unless you live in Florida or California, having lettuce and tomato salad in February is for the birds (who can fly down there and get it fresh). Bean sprouts, shredded cabbage, raisins, currants, cress, carrots, celery, apples, or any of the more easily stored winter foods make interesting substitutes in salad. If you absolutely must have Southern produce in a winter salad, do it the cheap way: get green tomatoes in the fall (gardeners are happy to give them away at the first sign of frost), wrap them in newspaper and store them on a dry, cool shelf. They'll ripen slowly and still be good in January, when supermarket tomatoes are fifty cents a piece. And grow the lettuce in a flower box that can be brought indoors when the weather gets severe (though I've used an ax to chop a perfectly good head of lettuce out of the ice in December). Having a diet with a seasonal rhythm of its own is more than just a money saver. Nothing tastes as fine as the first crisp apple of fall, or strawberries in spring. That pleasure is greatly diluted when taste buds are jaded by eleven months of cardboard imitations brought to you by California Chemical and Teamster.

◆ Your stomach will thank you for buying in season, but your wallet will be doubly grateful if you buy the very cheapest produce at the *end* of the season and store it for the future. Late-fall potatoes, summer beans, winter fruits (in the South) — prices are at their best when there is a spoilable glut and growers face the cost of storing or shipping any unsold produce.

◆ You can save the grower one more cost and get food even cheaper by picking your own. Since labor costs began to climb, more and more market gardens are switching to the "pick-your-own" system. Even the hardier vegetables, like potatoes, are being sold this way around major cities.

◆ Whenever possible, eliminate the middlemen and buy direct. Get fruits and vegetables at the farm gate or from home gardeners. Even if they are not "commercial," most backyard gardens produce a glut of something in every season. Sports fisherman and hunters often lose interest in their catches after the photos are taken. Ask — these sellers rarely put up a sign.

◆ If you live in an area where food is produced or processed, the commercial wastes are often free for the asking. Fruit and vegetable packers discard perfectly good food on cosmetic grounds: crooked carrots, lumpy apples, and so on. I've watched Florida packers bulldoze aside piles of beans simply because they fell off the trucks. Smaller slaughter houses often give away soup bones and dog food just to get rid of it.

◆ Wild foods should not be dismissed, even in urban areas. You'll need a first-rate guide to be absolutely sure of what you're picking, but the fare can be far more exotic than the stereotyped image of dandelion greens and blackberries. One spring, a local newspaper columnist wrote of being tempted by a four-ounce tin of morels (fancy mushrooms), imported from France and "discovered" in a gourmet shop two hundred miles away. The price — twenty-nine dollars and change for the tiny can — deterred him. That week our eight-year-old staggered home with a two-gallon pail full of fresh morels, picked less than a mile from the journalist's home! Fried with wild leeks and followed by bowls of succulent wild strawberries with lashings of maple syrup, we gorged on free food that only an orthodontist could afford to buy.

◆ The greatest savings don't come from coupons or red letter specials, but from basic changes in your eating habits. Avoid nutritionless snacks and expensive convenience foods. Drink more water rather than bottled drinks. Make more meals from scratch, which can be as simple as scrunching up your own dry breadcrumbs to shake on chicken, or using your own leftovers to "help" the hamburger, although at today's prices it shouldn't need any help! Substitute cheaper protein for expensive red meat by using more poultry, eggs, fish, pork, and beans.

◆ Don't be fooled by the "budget" image of some pre-packaged foods. One popular brand of macaroni and cheese is practically synonymous with welfare and student diets. And yet nobody bothers to point out that macaroni and cheese, bought separately, are cheaper and potentially more interesting than the glutinous dinner combo.

Heaven forbid you should ever be reduced to the theater caper, but voluntary penury does not mean you have to quit eating, or even quit eating well. Apply the usual principles of doing it yourself, bypassing middlemen, buying when things are cheap to store for the lean times, seeking out alternative sources, and not scoffing at the freebies. That approach won't do for those addicted to microwave trays, McBurgers and beef, but more discriminating shoppers can eat better for less.

The theater caper? Well . . . there was a year when a few enterprising fellows (whose budget rarely covered meals, much less theater tickets) discovered that the box office closed at the second intermission. They saw the third act of every new show in town and ate royally at the opening night parties that followed. The cost? A borrowed suit and an appetite for salmon mousse.

Clothing

Like most consumer items, clothing costs are more easily trimmed by simplifying needs than by finding bargain sources. As usual, though, we will try to do both.

Now, make a quick inventory of the complete contents of your closet and drawers. Add everything in those boxes under the bed, suitcases, attic trunks, and Goodwill bags. Every bit of clothing you own. How many suits, shirts, skirts, sweaters, shorts, shoes, sandals . . . ? Of all that, how many items have you worn more than three times in the last year? Take those off the list. How many items are worn out beyond repair? Take those off the list. What's the value of all that's left? All the clothes you bought but didn't really need? If you want to save money on clothing, *first quit buying what you don't need.*

A conserver wardrobe is basic. It's warm, durable, simple (to survive the vagaries of fashion) and neutral in color (to match anything else you might add to it). If you want to be noticed in a crowd, shave your head or get a tattoo — impressing with your clothes is expensive.

A conserver wardrobe is also deliberately small. Just enough to get down to your last clean set of everything by washday. Everything gets worn regularly and thus gets worn out before molding at the bottom of the drawer or being left totally behind by the evolution of fashion. It's also easier to plan replacements in a small wardrobe. When socks go on sale, I know exactly how many pairs I'll need in the next twelve months. I know that my only pair of shoes will need laces soon, and then should last for at least three more years (for a total of twelve years of service). I doubt if I'll be able to find another pair like them for six dollars, but I've got three years to look.

When you've established a minimum, basic wardrobe, you can maintain it inexpensively if you:

◆ Start with the most durable quality goods, even if you have to pay a little more. Wool, cotton, and leather generally outlast the cheaper synthetics. Well-made clothes have heavy seams and are reinforced at stress points. Don't assume, though, that the highest price buys quality. Fourteen-ounce denim is fourteen-ounce denim, whether you pay twenty-five dollars on sale or seventy-five dollars for the fashionable ones with a logo on the bum.

◆ Wear them out — completely! Then repair them and wear them out again. My first sports jacket — a heavy, hand-woven, all-wool Harris tweed — set me back twenty dollars! With the help of two replacement linings and two sets of leather patches, it survived thirty years of regular wear. Shirts are worn until the elbows go. Then they become short-sleeve shirts. Long trousers become shorts. When clothes are worn beyond repair, they become work clothes, and finally rags.

◆ Imperfect clothes, or "seconds," are often first-rate value. The imperfections don't always affect the real quality of the garment. It may be a misaligned print pattern, a color fade, or a stitch over-run. Look for quality-brand seconds at discount stores and factory outlets.

◆ Factory stores offer discounts of up to fifty percent over regular retail outlets. Better still, it's a good place to find seconds.

◆ Wait for sales at end-of-season clearances and on out-of-fashion bargain tables. Back-to-school sales are good times to buy casual wear. Winter clothing is cheapest in spring.

◆ The cheapest source of quality clothing has to be a handy set of non-conserver friends with a closet full of clothing that is out of style, out of favor, or out of room for an expanding midriff. It would be bold to ask, but when word gets out that you won't be offended by the offer . . . well, it would be a shame to throw out those perfectly good trousers just because the waistline has shrunk.

◆ f you don't get the closet discards, chances are the rummage sale will. Look for them there. It will cost you some change, but the quality's the same.

◆ Making clothes from scratch is relatively popular, but not always as financially rewarding as it ought to be. The catch is the price of the materials. But that's only a problem if you buy new material. Old clothing, drapes, or linens, which can be had for pennies at auctions and rummage sales, can be recycled to make "new" clothing. Sewing skills are equally useful in repairing existing clothes.

◆ Children's clothing should never be a problem. They keep growing. Awash in North American affluence, there are always more hand-me-downs than hand-me-downers.

Furniture and Appliances

As the last chapter indicated, conservers should never need to buy furniture, as long as the Joneses keep buying the good stuff and throwing it out. I used to think that interesting used furniture gathered in our house because of something we did, like some Midas touch with other people's junk. But now I'm beginning to see that it's not us, it's the society we live in. There's something about life's little changes — marriage, divorce, moving out, moving in, mid-life bubbles or simple boredom — that compel those around us to make new lives by molting their old stuff here. Maybe it's because we have lots of storage room. Maybe it's because I'm too soft to say no when anybody asks for help with a move. Whatever the reason, the result is Charley's Law: *furniture will expand to fill the space available.* The trick is to see furniture in what others see as a disposal problem.

The trick is to see furniture in what others see as a disposal problem.
•••••••••••••

If you must buy furniture, shop secondhand sources, avoid any hint of the antique trade, and haggle. One good source that's often overlooked is asking at small hotels and boarding houses. They replace their furnishings regularly, and small shoddy places often discard older, better-quality furniture. That's how we got an antique chest of drawers for four dollars.

Appliances are a little harder to come by. Their mechanical bits are prone to fail. If you're handy enough to fix them, you can pick up small appliances (kettles, toasters, irons, radios) for a dollar or two at auctions and rummage sales. Try them out on the spot if you want to be certain they work.

It's harder to be sure about the big appliances. If a kitchen stove has a dead burner, you can't be sure if it needs a fifteen-dollar element or a fifty-dollar wiring job. One way is to buy privately, through acquaintances or the classified ads, and take the time to ask all the necessary questions or poke around until you find out *why* the thing is being sold, and what exactly might be wrong with it.

When buying new seems the safest course, go about it slowly and carefully:

1. Use consumer guides to find out which brands are most functional and durable.

2. Ask a repairman about the strengths and weaknesses of different brands.

3. Remember that the simplest models are not only cheaper, but have fewer parts to break. The more gadgets, the higher the cost of maintenance.

4. Remember that the cheapest model is not always the greatest bargain. It's the cost per year (including energy and maintenance costs) over the expected life of the appliance, that you should try to minimize.

5. When you know exactly *what* you want, wait until the price is right.

6. Clearance sales (after Christmas or Mother's Day for example) are good occasions to find lower prices on appliances.

7. Discount stores and mail-order distributors can often undercut prices in regular stores. Knowing exactly what you want makes it easy enough to pick up the phone and compare prices all over town.

8. The Joneses worry about the appearance of appliances. They won't take anything that's marred. If your only concerns are function and durability, scratch and dent sales offer terrific savings.

Entertainment

I neglected entertainment in the first edition. But since the kids grew up and we re-discovered the joys of going out to a movie or a play. We also re-discovered the cheap detours at the box office.

Mid-week tickets are usually cheaper than weekends. Many movie houses have special cheap nights during the week. Better still are the "rep" or "art" cinemas that are always cheaper because their films have been around for a season or more. Best of all is the film club we found, which shows the best in the world for less than two dollars a film, with a wine and cheese party thrown in.

Plays and concerts also have cheaper mid-week tickets. Review performances are cheaper than later in the run. Subscriptions, or season tickets, are cheaper (per performance) than single ticket prices. If you have more tickets than you want with a subscription, make a deal with friends to subscribe to some other series and then swap — more variety at the low price of season tickets.

Big name acts are almost always more expensive than new plays, young actors, and musicians at the hungry beginnings of a career. The big names, though, we can see on television. The new acts are often more exciting. We enjoy free "debut" concerts by professionals trying to build performance credits. And almost-free midday concerts being taped for national radio broadcasts are also good.

If you live in a major city, you can find festivals of national music, film or theater sponsored by a foreign embassy or consulate. They're usually free but not well advertised. Look for announcements on cultural bulletin boards, at an arts school for example.

I thought I had most of the angles covered until I heard from a theatre buff who volunteers to usher. He spends an hour before the performance, handing out programs, and then gets the best seats in the house, absolutely free. His latest was volunteering to be a "supernumerary," non-singing extra (spear carrier) at the opera. He had to be on stage for the first thirty seconds of Carmen, but watched the rest from a seventy-five-dollar seat.

Readings by published authors at bookstores and libraries have become popular in many cities and are usually free.

On a smaller scale, neighborhood dances, parties and sports can be some of the best entertainment going, and the cheapest.

Travel

In the halcyon days of low-priced energy and high-priced dollars, bargain travel was a breeze. Europe on five dollars a day was a matter of simple meals and the right hotels. Cheap travel is still possible, but it takes a lot more sacrifice and ingenuity to do it these days.

Getting there commercially depends on where "there" is. See a travel agent to get the latest on competitive fares, low-season discounts, stand-by rules, charter savings, rail passes, and other internationally advertised bargain schemes. A travel agent will give you the latest rules and rates for nothing. The agent's profit, however, is a percentage of the ticket price. The carrier pays the agent. Don't, therefore, expect the agent to be full of helpful advice on how to get there for nothing. If you learn how to use the Internet to do your bookings, you may not need a travel agent at all and can find some real bargains. But it can take many hours of research and very careful planning. Some travelers have saved on fares by using the various travel web sites but then ran into trouble on their trips from miscalculations in travel time from one connecting flight to another. They then ended up having to pay a full fare for the final leg of their trip and little or no saving overall. Travel agents have the know-how to avoid these glitches.

It's not as easy as buying a ticket, but many conservers have used these alternatives:

- ◆ Working passage on a ship. Commercial ships are tough to crack — a maritime card, union membership, a long wait, and a contract to complete the round-trip voyage may be necessary. I've heard more success stories from those who hang around yacht harbors, checking notice boards, and making friends until they find a private yacht in need of a crew.

- ◆ Walking holidays. It's undoubtedly slower, but you can see more sights and meet more people than you can at 35,000 feet. Take a tent, or rest your feet in inexpensive hostels.

- ◆ Take a bicycle tour. Get all the rewards of walking with less effort and more speed. Even we older types can cover fifty to a hundred miles a day with a little luggage on the back, and the boring stretches can be beaten by hopping a train — some carriers will allow the bike on free as baggage.

- ◆ If a tent's not your style, use hostels, pensions, or bed-and-breakfasts. Outside the major cities, prices are quite reasonable. Check with the national tourist office of the country you're traveling to for price brochures and booking information. Then make arrangements yourself since the agencies tend to prefer the big hotels.

- ◆ Drive someone else's car. When the Joneses fly off to Miami for the winter, they hire car delivery firms to get the family car there too. The delivery firms get cheapie travelers to do the driving. Look for ads in the classifieds of the nearest big-city paper.

- ◆ Get a job. I know, I know, that's what you're trying to get away from. But some jobs entail being sent abroad. It usually takes a trade or special skill to land a foreign contract.

◆ Volunteer. Aid agencies, churches, unions, and professional organizations sponsor volunteer working visits or exchanges. Some even pay fare and a stipend. Even if you have to pay some of your own expenses, however, a volunteer job is a great way to meet people outside the tourist industry.

◆ Working holidays are common fare around the British Commonwealth and in much of Europe. The idea is to pick a spot, get yourself there, and then find a job — any job — to pay living expenses and to find out how the other half lives. Write ahead to be certain that work permits are not a problem and to get some advance leads on the temporary job market. If language or credentials are barriers to practicing your own occupation abroad, you can always pick fruit, cut cane, or wash dishes in any language.

◆ Meet people. Be nice to foreign visitors wherever you encounter them. Such meetings are prone to end in the swapping of addresses. Many folks have traveled the world by dropping in on such acquaintances.

◆ Join an organization that swaps addresses for you. Most universities have a foreign students' club where contacts can be made.

◆ Swap houses. If you're traveling someplace to stay awhile, make advance arrangements to trade houses with someone who lives there. You can find private swap offers or organized swaps advertised in the classifieds, under travel. If you can't find what you want, place your own ad in a newspaper from the city you want to visit.

◆ Know what to take. Embassies or large libraries can provide newspapers from the places you're going. Read the ads and find out what's expensive there. That's what you should take. To be duty-free, such "imports" are supposed to be for personal use (that's why there is a limit on quantities). But personal use can include gifts — like gifts to innkeepers, who might wish to return the gesture in some way.

◆ Students and pensioners qualify for all manner of reductions on fares, museum passes, entertainments, and other assorted tickets. You'll need an ID card to prove your status (though if the language gap is wide enough, a driver's license or library card works just as well).

◆ Go native. The Hilton, Kodak, Club Med, Intourist, English-spoken-here vacation is for thumb-suckers and the elderly rich (the richly elders go native). Take one small suitcase, local buses, a short walk down the hall to the can, and a wide, wide detour around anything with an American Express or Diner's Club sticker in the window.

Our North American obsession with tidy toilets and turnpike familiar fare leads to the spending of vast un-neccessaries to duplicate our cultural environment halfway around the world. Anybody who insists on a McBurger in Paris or a shower in Japan could have saved the airfare and sent away for the souvenirs by parcel post.

My all-time favorite train ride (not for scenery but for the lesson learned) was on the Trans-Siberian railroad. Booking ahead, we faced a choice of:

"Hard class" — Not recommended for more than commuting distance. Seats can be wooden, and hard!

"Soft class" — Cushioned seats, a dining car, and sleeping berths. The native way to go.

"Deluxe class" —The usual tourist choice.

At the time, deluxe fares were fifty percent higher than "soft." For no other reason, we immediately chose the soft class. It was a pleasant surprise. Coaches were modern and clean, meals were sumptuous and our traveling companions delightful. We shared the compartment with a mother and child from Vladivostok. In the rest of the car were soldiers on leave, holidaying workers and a friendly attendant who kept the tea pot humming. It was a linear party, and, as the only non-Soviets aboard, we were treated like welcome guests.

We were amazed then, at sundry stops, to overhear bitter complaints in a familiar language about lousy accommodations, suspected "bugs," and even pancakes. "You know, PANCAKES!" he shouted, making a six-inch circle on his plate with a fingertip. Mystified, the waitress served him a steaming bowl of soup with a whole chicken breast swimming in cream. The pancake man refused it.

Our interest piqued, we decided to see how the other half lived, and at the first opportunity slipped into the "deluxe" coach at the end of the train. It was truly a tsarist relic, a joke on cultural pretensions, a neat little touché of irony that only a Russian could devise. The "deluxe" coach was exactly that — in 1917. By now, the Rubenesque seats were oozing stuffing onto the floor, the French paper was peeling off the walls, and all the twiddly bits of Victorian decor were moldering in the dark, stuffy exclusivity of class. Whether or not there were "bugs" in the walls, there were certainly plenty of bugs. There wasn't a native in sight.

Much later, we were swapping Siberia stories with fellow travelers.

"The worst thing about traveling in Russia," the woman lamented, "is that they never let you actually meet the ordinary people."

She heartily agreed when I added that the pancakes are terrible too. Thank God for Howard Johnson's.

It isn't necessary to go exotic distances, either, to avoid the expensive tourist traps. One set of sun-kissed isles is so close to Ho-Jo land that shivering northerners threaten to sink it every winter. Pink and white bellies squeeze in between the casinos and souvenir stands that line the beach. What the travel agents don't tell northerners is that they can get a list of all the accommodations by writing to the island government. Picking the cheapest rooms in the book — at a village too small to be seen on the map — we ended up right on the beach, under the coconut palms with miles and miles of clean empty beach in either direction. The innkeeper was so surprised to see a family of five outsiders that far from the casinos that he moved into the room we had reserved and insisted we take over his house. Oh, yes — there was one other outsider there, an anthropologist studying the natives. He, of course, had us beat — he was being *paid* to be there.

~ 10 ~

Caesar's Due

Being a financial anarchist is fun. Like the Marx brothers snipping off the world's necktie, I enjoy walking into the stock broker's office with holes in my pants, writing personal notes to bureaucrats on the tax return, and disputing the gas company's right to round off the bill to the nearest penny. Twenty-first century Luddites break conventions for the fun of it — because they're there.

It began as high camp, but the resulting lesson was clear enough the day the Yippies "raided" the New York Stock Exchange. Led by Jerry Rubin and Abbie Hoffman, the costumed freaks wheedled their way up to the visitors' gallery and began tossing cash over the rail. *Wheee!!* Millions of dollars of trading went by the boards as the stock wizards stopped their dealing to scramble after the dollar bills wafting down from above. The traders were down on their knees, scrabbling for bits of paper before they realized they had just had their ties snipped off.

To a certain extent, we can isolate ourselves from the tragi-comic farce of a glutted consumer economy absorbed in its own importance. We can walk right by the prepackaged breadcrumbs and the Beanie Babies. We can refuse to have a telephone and let the TV stay broken when we realize that nobody misses it. We can even walk away from jobs and say to hell with all that. But that's a desertion, not a revolution. Caesar lives, and the necktie economy keeps right on rollin' along, with us or without us. Even Jerry Rubin eventually put on a tie and went to work on Wall Street. Sooner or later, there are points at which we have to coexist. We don't have to get right down on our knees and fight over bits of paper, but there are some arrangements we have to make with normal society, whether we like it or not. The object of this chapter is to plan those arrangements to keep them as simple, as cheap and hassle-free as possible. Please be note, though, that I am not an accountant or financial advisor. The information below will give you an idea of where to look for tax savings but is subject to change and strategies will vary greatly according to individual circumstances.

What To Do 'Til the Tax Man Comes

The surest way to save money on income tax is to lower your income. Sounds facile, but it works. In the U.S. married couples with incomes of less than $14,000 (2003) paid no income tax. Basic personal tax credits for a Canadian couple add up to a tax threshold of $15,268 (at the time I'm writing this). Add on other credits and deductions for children, certain forms of income, allowable expenses, sales tax credits, property tax or rent credits — and the point at which you break even with the tax collector rises even higher. Anyone who can't live on less than that just hasn't been paying attention. Although taxes may be complex, they are certainly not onerous for low-income families.

In chapter 4, we dealt briefly with tax opportunities that arise before you leave your job. The general approach is to invest the maximum amounts in deferred tax shelters, often associated with retirement plans. The rules can get complicated but the essence is to put money into the shelters now (when you are in a high tax bracket), and take the money out after retirement (when you will be in a lower bracket). In the meantime, any return on the investment compounds tax-free. You will eventually have to subject these funds to taxation, but at a much lower — or zero — rate. It's a form of income averaging.

The variety and complexity of different investment/tax plans keeps thousands of lawyers and accountants busy. It would be futile to attempt a useful detailing of plans here. In any event, the rules and pay-offs change so often that all investors should do some up-to-the-minute research of their own before investing a cent. Here's how.

Deferred tax investments of various types may be offered through the company pension plan. Check first with your personnel office. Remember, though, that your employer may assume that you will be staying in the harness until the age of sixty-five, and a company plan may prevent you from cashing in a deferred tax investment until you reach a certain age. Company plans may also have various limits on portability before retirement.

Whether or not you're worried about starting rumors of your imminent departure in the personnel office, dig up some details on non-company plans as well. Generally speaking, banks, brokerage houses, and "near banks" (trust companies, credit unions, savings and loans) all have investment plans to sell and will provide free information on them. As a potential early retiree, you will primarily be interested in these five characteristics:

1. The degree to which the investment is tax deductible. Some, like the U.S. Keogh plans, or RRSPs in Canada, are 100 percent tax deductible. If you put $1,000 into the plan, you subtract $1,000 from total income before calculating your tax. In a 25 percent tax bracket, that's a $250 payoff. Even if the investment pays zero interest, you've effectively made 25 percent in the first year! Other investments allow partial tax write-offs under different rules. Real estate depreciation, capital gains or dividend plans either reduce taxable income or tax the income at reduced rates. Some, particularly the 100 percent deductible pension plans, have upper limits on how much can be deducted in total. Only the portion within the limits is 100 percent deductible. For any plan, find out the percentage of the investment that can be deducted, the allowable limits, and the actual tax advantage — within your own tax bracket.

2. Redemption rules. The usual assumption of pension plans is that the investment will remain untouched until the worker retires at a normal age. That's why IRA plans, for example, don't normally allow withdrawals from the investment until disability or the age of fifty-nine and a half. "Premature distribution," or cashing in early, is penalized by including the withdrawal in your gross income for the year and also taxing the withdrawal an extra ten percent. Even with a penalty, the tax break may be worthwhile. An American worker in the 25 percent tax bracket, putting $1,500 a year into an IRA for four years, saves $1,500 in taxes. In her first year without an income (and therefore below the tax threshold), she withdraws the entire $6,000 and pays a $600 penalty tax. She's still ahead on taxes by $900.

Canadian RRSPs have no lower age limits. You can cash them in anytime; the only penalty is the regular tax bite at the time of cashing in. Again, the regular bite is much smaller in the lower tax brackets, so the trick is to cash them in (or draw them out gradually) to replace lost income when you retire, not to cover some big expense.

Other tax-deferred investments have their own redemption quirks. Real estate investments, for instance, defer taxes by deducting depreciation as a cost. When the investment is ultimately sold or redeemed, the profit is calculated as the difference between the sale price and the *depreciated* cost of the investment. So the paper cost is also counted as a paper profit and is taxed later as a capital gain. The age of the investor is irrelevant. Find out the tax penalties for cashing in each plan under your own particular circumstances.

3. Loading Charges. Many tax-inspired investments add administrative or sales charges either at the time the investment is made (front-end load), or at the time you cash in. Some allow the option of deferring the load and gradually reducing it to zero over a six- or eight-year period. Always ask about charges and include them in any comparison of different plans. Don't automatically assume that a "no-load" investment is a better deal, however. Administrative costs may simply be absorbed by paying out lower dividends.

4. Risk. All investments carry some element of risk. If you are investing primarily to defer taxes, don't overlook the risk of the investment itself in your enthusiasm to reduce what's due to Caesar. Over the years, governments have offered special tax incentives to invest in oil exploration, film development, venture funds, and so on. With initial deductions, depletion allowances, and capital gains breaks, some investors made a bundle with a minimal tax bite. Some also made empty holes in the ground. Less risky plans offer more modest dreams, but with some greater guarantee of performance.

5. Income performance. The income potential of an investment can sometimes be predicted by its past performance and an estimate of the effects of future developments. If you want to invest in rental property, for instance, recent rents, capital appreciation, zoning changes and predicted developments in the neighborhood being considered might all be useful in calculating the expected income from the investment. Term savings and institutional investments sometimes "guarantee" income performance for the future.

With full information on tax and redemption rules, charges, risk and income, you should be well-equipped to judge which tax deferral plan is best suited to your circumstances.

After the Salary's Gone

Unfortunately, your days of dealing with the "revenuers" don't automatically end with the paycheck. Presumably you've set something aside, like a deferred tax investment, to soften the blows of penury, and cashing it in means paying taxes on it. Then, too, there's always the possibility that the Tahitian nudes will start to sell, or the basement inventions actually start to work, and retirement begins to get profitable. In that event, tax hassles and costs may depend to a large extent on what you choose to call yourself and what form your income takes.

If you're truly retiring, and of an age to do so, you've hit the tax jackpot. In addition to pensions, you get tax deductions based on age. And some pension income may be tax-free.

As with pensions, any other form of income that allows deductions will reduce the tax bill. When the tax collector asks your occupation, it's not idle curiosity. A salaried job, small business, commission sales, farm, self-employment, retirement and unemployment are treated differently and taxed accordingly. There are rules by which your category ought to be determined, but with the small-scale enterprises contemplated here, the official distinctions get a little fuzzy.

If your income is going to be big enough to tax, there are definite advantages to finding a category that will allow you to deduct costs from gross income, with the aim of reducing the remaining taxable income to zero. The self-employed, including those who operate farms or businesses, generally have the greatest range of opportunities to deduct all manner of costs from income. A business operated from the home may deduct a share of household expenses, for example. Farmers may deduct fence repairs, depreciation on buildings, and in some circumstances get rebates on property taxes and exemptions on gas and sales taxes.

If you are a former office worker who has just dropped out to raise your own food on a small-scale farm and make pottery in the barn, the decision to call yourself: "not employed," "farmer (sort of)," or "self-employed potter (mostly unpaid)," may be a matter of choice. If you qualify for more than one category, you will have to decide which title suits you best by considering just how much income you expect to have, and thus how many deductions you can use. On a small farm, for instance, if your gross income is expected to be so low that you may need only a few thousand dollars in deductions to cut taxes to zero, there's little point in fussing with the qualifications for farmer status, as long as the needed deductions can be scraped up from personal deductions or other easier routes. There's little to be gained by taking deductions beyond what you need to not pay tax. The exception is if you expect to return to high income levels in future years and are in a category where certain losses can be carried over to offset future profits.

The other purpose of choosing your official "occupation" carefully is the possibility of putting earnings into tax-free forms. A business can use its profits to buy equipment, add to inventory, expand marketing, and go to conferences or anything else that may qualify as a cost. That use of earnings is usually considered to be tax-free re-investment. If, on the other hand, the proprietor takes a "salary" from the business, it's taxed at the full rate — even if you intend to save it and ultimately re-invest it in the business.

Even ordinary taxpayers can convert some of their earnings to tax-free forms. Interest on some state and municipal bonds is exempt in the United States. Canadians pay less tax on capital gains than on earned income. Dividends are taxed less than wages. From the tax perspective, the worst possible way to earn an income is to work for it.

In the lower-income brackets, where there isn't much tax to save by calling yourself one thing or another, you may still wish to choose your official occupation carefully. Businesses and the self-employed are required to report earnings quarterly and make voluntary prepayments. If you think that the once-a-year tax form is a frustrating hassle just to prove you don't owe anything, wait until you're stuck with the job every three months. Worse still, at that point, receipts and a more formal set of books become essential. Unless you're really serious about a business, or really happen to be making money at it, it's easier to be "not employed" but honest enough to report the odd dollar that comes in as "other income."

Most ordinary, no-longer-have-a-paycheck retirees are content to be out of the income-tax game. Paying less is a middle-income concern that no longer bothers the voluntary poor. Getting some back is a different matter.

A Credit Beats a Deduction

At the very best, taking advantage of all possible deductions can reduce your taxable income to zero. You owe nothing. More deductions will still leave you owing nothing. The only way to come out ahead is through tax credits. Most credits can only be subtracted from the tax total. If you don't incur taxes, you can't take any credits. The American earned-income credit, however, was made to order for low-income survivors. Unlike other credits, the earned-income credit can be taken as a refund even if you pay no taxes. Full instructions come with form 1040. In the simple case of a married couple with two children and an income of $13,000, no tax is payable but the earned-income credit comes back as a $4,140 refund check. (Please keep in mind that these rules are subject to change, especially in the early 2000s, when the U.S. government was enacting some rather complex tax reduction legislation.)

Similarly, in Canada, provincial tax credits, federal Child Tax Benefits and sales tax credits can come back as refunds even if you pay no income tax. The other "non-refundable" credits are only useful for reducing the amount of tax owed.

You Can Do It

A final warning: nobody said tax law was simple. The possibilities and rules continue to sprout like dandelions in spring. The complexities expand almost as quickly as the tax preparation firms offering to find the loopholes. Nevertheless, there are two very good reasons why you should consider doing it yourself. In the first place, even if you use a tax consultant, you will still have to do the hardest part yourself, and secondly, you're better equipped for the job than any tax firm could be.

A tax firm can only know as much about your finances as you tell them. You have the information, and the consultant has a blank form to be filled in. He can't *give* you any credits or deductions that you don't tell him about. The forms are free at the post office and all the credits and deductions are listed. Reading the form line by line, you'll trip over every credit and deduction. The guide will tell you whether you qualify. Start at the beginning and follow it through step by step. You'll be ahead by at least the amount of the consultant's fee.

American taxpayers have an additional concern. In 1980, the Internal Revenue Service began enforcing negligence-penalty provisions enacted by Congress in 1976. The effect is to pressure accountants into correcting any errors or questionable items on a return that might otherwise result in lower taxes. Taxpayers can't help but wonder if the hired accountant is on their side, or on the side of the Internal Revenue Service (IRS).

The hardest part of the tax job is the preparation — sorting out the twelve months' collection of receipts, check stubs, and records. Once those are in order, it's mostly a matter of filling in the blanks. And the tax preparation firms won't do the hard part for you. You've still got to amass your own documentation. Once you've gone that far, you might as well fill in the blanks yourself.

Insurance: *What If Something Goes Wrong?*

Insurance, like taxes, is another of those middle-income bugaboos that the voluntary poor can by and large do without. Not all insurance is expendable in every-man-for-himself land, but by looking through a different prism, we can easily see which ones are. The prism, the acid test for insurance needs, consists of these simple questions:

What have I got to lose?

Can it be replaced with money?

Curiously, it often seems that those with the least to lose are the most concerned with insurance policies. It must have something to do with living on the margin of a wealthy economy. When one's financial life is Spartan, even a very small loss may spell disaster. By the numbers, there isn't much room between the conserver lifestyle and what the wealthy around us would consider destitute. Depending on the perspective, life on the edge can be the most secure or the most insecure spot on the continent. It is insecure for those who consider they're just an accident away from ruin; it's secure for those who know they have little to lose anyway, so what the hell.

Things are bound to go wrong in every family. Houses burn, accidents happen, illness strikes, and sooner or later most of us die. Fate besets us. We can't stop it, so we cushion the blow by arranging to receive sums of money whenever bad luck happens. Never mind the fact that it was our own money to start with. It still seems a curious custom when most such losses have little to do with money.

Arsonists might disagree, but the people I've known who have watched their houses burn have always seemed less concerned with the financial loss than with the things that cannot be replaced at any price: the family pet, the photo album, the kids' first paintings, Grandpa's mustache cup. The most macabre of all is school accident insurance — those check-a-box policies that the kids bring home from some corporate friend of the school board. So much for loss of an eye, twice as much if you lose two, $11,500 for an arm . . . but how do you tell a kid to forget the arm, we have $11,500 to make up for it? What's the point? The money is irrelevant in such circumstances. A cash windfall is not to be sneezed at, but there can't be any pleasure in it when it's at the price of someone else's tragedy.

Life Insurance: You Bet Your Life

When a company wagers that you'll live to be old, it's called life insurance. If you grow old, you lose. If you die young, you win. Make sense? Sometimes it does. Let's apply the acid test.

What have you got to lose — besides your life? The standard rationale is that your death will also cause a financial loss for the surviving members of the family. This may be true if you are the main source of income for dependents. But if your survivors are capable of providing for themselves, then nothing is lost, monetarily, that can't be replaced. A single person, without dependents, has no reason to insure his or her own life. Life insurance, for a childless couple, implies that the spouse is not capable of earning an independent living.

Let's assume, though, that you are the sole wage earner, with no financial reserves and a load of incompetent dependents. Chances are, in that position, you won't be interested in surviving without a salary anyway. You really need that paycheck. But never mind, perhaps you misread the title and were looking for guidance on how to have a salary without surviving.

A salary without surviving is only useful as long as your dependents remain dependent. When the children are grown, there's no reason to remain insured other than to insult your spouse's competence. There's nothing to lose by *not* being insured — except your very presence, and that can't be replaced with money, can it? In the meantime, if and while the family needs to replace your salary, how does one choose insurance?

There are two basic types of life insurance: *whole-life* (sometimes called permanent), and *term* insurance. The jargon is clear enough. Whole-life policies are enforced until you die. Whether you die at ninety-seven or twenty-seven, your dependents will be equally well looked after. A term policy, on the other hand, pays off survivors only for a given period. If you buy a twenty-year term policy at the age of thirty, your survivors only benefit if you have the foresight to die before you reach the age of fifty. After that, they're on their own. Most parents hope the kids will be on their own after twenty years in any event. That, in itself, is reason enough to choose term policies over whole-life policies. The fact that term policies are considerably cheaper enhances the preference.

When insurance agents begin to suspect that you might be the type to prefer an independent streak in your grown-up children, or that you have every confidence that your spouse could manage just fine without you, that's when the "guilt pitch" is dropped in favor of the "investment advantage" of whole-life policies. Whole-life policies, you see, earn a sort of dividend. They *grow in value* as the salespeople say, whereas those cheap little term policies just sit there at the chosen level, insuring your income powers.

The problem with the investment pitch is that it's based on a common ignorance of the powers of compound interest. Investing the same premiums at the bank and compounding it over the years will show more profit than whole-life policies. If the salespeople's figures sound impressive, just ask them what the effective *annual* interest rate amounts to. If it's more than your savings account earns, it's time to switch your account to another bank.

Some argument is made for the borrowing capacity of a whole-life policy. It's true that policy holders can borrow against these policies at very attractive rates. The rates should be attractive — after all, *it's your own money*. Had you put the premiums in the bank, you could "borrow" against that for nothing just by withdrawing the funds anytime you wish.

Death has several consequences for families. Among them are personal loss (against which any policy is irrelevant), and loss of essential earnings (which can be compensated with survivors' benefits and death benefits from Social Security or the Canadian Pension Plan, personal investments, or as a last resort, term insurance policies). Judge insurance schemes as you would any other investment — strictly on investment criteria: *risk, return, growth, tax advantage, and redemption features.* Love, guilt and family responsibilities have nothing to do with the quality of investments. Make that distinction clearly before considering any insurance policy.

How do we cope? Well, when needs are so reduced that a salary becomes unnecessary, then it is also unnecessary to insure against the loss of the salaried. Death and finances are unrelated.

The cost of dying need not be a problem. If the family income is guaranteed either by term insurance, personal investments, low cost-of-living habits, or the survivor's own earning capacities, then the tragedies of early death do not have to be financial ones. The other costs are a matter of making the usual conserver decisions. There are cardboard coffins and rental coffins. Cremation saves the cost of plots, markers, and coffins. You can die for free by donating your body to a medical school or to a hospital for its usable parts. Make arrangements ahead of time. Too disrespectful? Unloving? Perhaps to some, but think about it this way. If love and respect can be given through the medium of money, then why give it to the undertaker who has earned neither your love nor your respect? Spend your money and your love on the living, while they can still enjoy it.

Health Insurance: In Sickness and In Health

Dying may be cheap, but getting better isn't. As long as doctors and dentists assume that an hour of their time is worth a week of mine, sickness is a considerable risk. And hospitals are even worse. Not even doctors and dentists can afford to pay their own hospital bills.

How can low-income survivors protect meager resources from ruinous medical costs? Insurance is one possibility. Most Americans carry some form of hospital insurance. Almost 100 percent of Canadians are covered by public hospital and medical insurance, supported through the tax system. Americans of working age are stuck with paying the costs of private insurance. The usual rules apply: shop around, and don't buy more than you need.

The best solution is to stay healthy — and that's not being flippant. Individuals have a surprising degree of control over the state of their own health, and thus over the cost of their medical care. We can choose to stay out of the noon-day sun, practice safe sex, exercise more and smoke less. A recent study concluded that individual habits and lifestyles accounted for a major part of health problems and costs. These "diseases of choice" that spring from careless driving, heavy drinking, smoking, junk food diets, obesity, stressful lifestyles and other self-imposed risks can all be controlled by choosing between healthy and unhealthy practices.

"About half the burden of illness is psychological in origin," the report claimed. And for the physically ill, "diseases of the cardiovascular system were by far the principal cause of hospitalization . . . . " Accidents were second.

The report went on to note that "self-imposed risks and the environment are the principal or important underlying factors in each of the five major causes of death between age one and age seventy . . . . " The five major killers were motor vehicle accidents, heart disease, all other accidents, respiratory diseases including lung cancer, and suicide.

Accidents and ill health can strike anywhere of course. Healthy lifestyles won't ensure the end of medical bills, just as an apple a day won't really keep the doctor away (even when properly aimed). But, statistically, a sedentary smoker-drinker-worrier who refuses to wear a seat belt is guaranteed to die younger and more expensively than he would if he chose healthier habits.

Knowing we can reduce the risks of catastrophic medical bills but can never really guarantee good health, there's comfort in having back-up insurance for major problems. There's greater comfort in knowing that we're less likely to need professional health care. Health-conscious survivors who do not have access to public health plans can tailor their insurance to the possibility of catastrophe, and work on reducing the need for uninsured minor maintenance by taking better care of themselves. In practice, that means brushing and flossing instead of sending the dentist to Las Vegas, taking a cold to bed instead of to the doctor (who can't cure it anyway), or treating your nerves to a day of rest instead of Valium.

Auto Insurance

Doctors aren't the only financial calamity around. Lawyers can be worse. Thus driving can be a financial risk as well as a physical one. Fending off possible disaster with insurance policies is a major part of the cost of transportation.

Auto insurance, like health costs, can be greatly affected by the decisions you make. An inexpensive car is also cheaper to insure. A good driving record reduces costs. Some companies offer special low rates to nonsmokers and nondrinkers. The fastest way to save money, though, is to cut out whole chunks of coverage.

Remember that the greatest risk, the possible calamity, would be a lawsuit to recover any damages you might cause. Insurance to meet that possibility is called "liability" insurance. That part is almost indispensable. In some jurisdictions, it is mandatory. You can save on the liability coverage by maintaining a good driving record, and by limiting the maximum coverage. The safe driving record speaks for itself.

The extent of coverage is a matter of some dispute. Insurance agents, and some lawyers, advise carrying big liability packages, in the range of the highest awards being given by the courts. That's fine for those who can afford it. Those who cannot afford big liability coverage may not need it anyway. Gauge the risk by looking at your assets (remember the acid test — what have you got to lose?). The more you have to lose, the more careful you should be to insure it. The less you have, the less it costs to defend it.

Insuring against damage to your own vehicle is called "collision" insurance. Combined with coverage against theft, injury, fire, brimstone, and marauding Visigoths, it's called "comprehensive" coverage. Again, the most significant question is: what have you got to lose? This time, instead of looking at your assets, look at your car. If it fell under a steamroller tomorrow, how much compensation would the old clunker warrant? Remember that repair costs won't be covered beyond the depreciated value of the vehicle. Also remember that if the accident is your fault, you pay the first $250 (or whatever the deductible portion is) and a claim for the rest will boost your future insurance rates. If the accident is the other guy's fault, you can be compensated through his liability coverage whether or not you have your own collision insurance. Comprehensive coverage seems to be designed for the person who has an expensive new luxury car and who never has to claim on the policy. It was not designed for the person who drives a middle-aged economy model and is inclined to accept a dent here and there as a part of the decor. A woman who drives a car just like that finally accepted my argument that a single insurance premium would cover all the damage her car could suffer without being sent to the junkyard.

Her last defense was the theft coverage. "I need my car. What if somebody should steal it?"

It was a cruel thing to do, but I asked her to look at the car again and pretend she was a car thief. Knowing the penalty was the same, would she steal her own car or the new Corvette beside it?

"I see what you mean," she relented. It suited her own needs just fine, but no self-respecting Visigoth would touch it.

Still in doubt? Look at it this way. Insurance companies profit by the statistical certainty that the average driver, in his lifetime, will pay more in premiums than he will collect through claims. If you are an average driver with an average car, you can put the equivalent of the insurance premium into a bank account or private investment. You can have an average number of accidents, pay for them yourself, and still be ahead by the margin of the insurance company's profit. With a cheaper car and better than average safety habits, you can make even more than the company. In fact, you *are* an insurance company — with a single client. By all means insure against the total calamity of a big liability claim, but the rest you can do yourself.

Risking the Family Jewels

Fire, storm damage, theft and all manner of financial threats beset the family property. What have you got to lose? For most homeowners, the family home is more than they can afford to lose. If it's mortgaged, the lender will likely assist on the property being insured. Make a list of all assets, and consider their vulnerability to loss. The house can burn. The land cannot. Tools can be stolen. The house is usually left behind. Are vandals and Visigoths a problem where you live? Is it a hurricane zone? Earthquake prone? Strike off everything (like land) that's relatively invulnerable, everything (like Auntie's ugly heirloom jewelry) that you wouldn't particularly *want* to replace, and everything (like the wedding rings) that *couldn't* be replaced. The rest should be things that would have to be replaced at a high cost, like the house if it burned. Consider insuring those things with a homeowner's policy. A homeowner's policy should include some liability coverage. The rest? If you or your money wouldn't replace it, there's no advantage to insuring it.

Like other aspects of conserver living, however, the most secure household is not the one with the most insurance, but the one with the most modest possessions, the one with the least to lose. The less you have, the less you have to worry about — and the less it costs to protect it.

Our most expensive theft was a lawnmower. It was relatively new, but no great loss since it never worked right. In fact, I accepted the theft with a surprising measure of relief mixed in with the resignation. I began to understand how Grandfather felt about his Kaiser (the Edsel of its day). He used to park it with the keys left in and fervently hope it would be stolen. When someone suggested the price of gas might be deterring prospective thieves, he took to leaving cash on the seat as getaway money. Anyway, the lawnmower was gone and easily forgotten — until the following spring when the police showed up with it. Not only was the loss replaced, but an obviously frustrated thief — with greater skills than mine — had repaired all its faults.

Pensions: Waiting for the Gold Watch

My favorite retirement story (and I heard it twice so it must be true) was the gentleman who stayed on in faithful service until the company finally pensioned him off with a gold-plated watch and a modest stipend. They had the usual little ceremony in the tea room just before five o'clock. The assistant manager attended (the manager was too busy, but sent his best regards) and cracked a few jokes at the expense of Our Faithful Servant before telling everybody what a great old guy he really was and how the company would find it hard to get along without him and how this gift was just a token of the high regard in which he was held. Our Faithful Servant's young replacement, chomping at the bit for six months past, and already making more than O.F.S., cried "Speech! Speech!" and all eyes fixed on dewy-eyed O.F.S. The hush was expectant. Even the sales staff held their glasses at half-mast out of respect, and turned the hub-bub down to a whisper.

"I'm not much at making speeches," O.F.S. croaked (and the secretaries dabbed their eyes), "so I'll just say 'thanks for everything' and I know you will all understand how I feel about you."

And with that, he held up the new watch for all to see, waved, and strode out the door — a jaunty sprig of mistletoe pinned to the end of his coat tail.

I'm always surprised at the number of people who quietly confide their disenchantment with working life, the dodos they have to work with, or the meaningless nature of the daily chore. More surprising is their reluctance to kiss it all good-bye in favor of some more satisfying task. The usual excuse is the pension — waiting for the gold watch. Even those with the confidence to support themselves today worry about ensuring an income for their later years. The promise of a pension is one of the strongest ties to the nine-to-five labor force.

The Company Pension

There are thousands of variations. The usual form takes a contribution from each employee's paycheck (usually a fixed percentage of salary), adds a contribution from the employer, and places both contributions into a special pension fund. The pension fund is invested where it will earn some interest. When you retire, you begin to receive regular payments from the fund. The size of the payment is based on the number of years of service, and on your pre-retirement salary. The higher the salary and the longer you worked, the greater the total of your contributions over the years, and so the higher will be your pension.

A fair and tidy scenario, but not entirely foolproof. No one can guarantee the future. Here's what can go wrong:

◆ The pension fund's *raison d'être* is security. Therefore the fund is nearly always invested in the safest long-term investments around, and the penalty for being conservative is earning the lowest interest rates around. Pension funds grow notoriously slowly. If they could get their hands on the employer's contribution, the average employees might invest their own pension funds much more profitably.

◆ Employers can, and do, go out of business with alarming disregard for niceties like pension rights and severance pay. If you're hanging around just for the pension, you'd better be confident that the company is going to stick around too.

◆ Some employers have a nasty habit of firing or laying off older workers just before they qualify for full pension rights or early withdrawal rights. What are your own rights to withdraw pension funds should you be laid off tomorrow?

◆ The most serious flaw in the security of pensions is also the most certain — inflation! Some pensions are indexed to the cost of living. That is, pension payments are regularly raised to keep up with inflation. Most pensions are not indexed, however, and that is what makes them virtually useless for long-term security.

A friend of mine (let's call him Joe) turned fifty-five last year. He and his wife worked out a detailed budget and concluded that they need $25,000 a year, after taxes. Joe's take-home pay now covers that nicely. They have a little money in the bank and a company pension plan that will give them two-thirds of Joe's salary when he retires in ten more years. He expects some raises between now and then, and was feeling quite secure about his future. I asked him if he had figured out the effects of inflation on the family budget. No, he hadn't, but he was confident that things wouldn't get any worse, and inflation would likely remain under three percent (Joe's an incurable optimist).

So we took his $25,000 budget and inflated it by a mere three percent a year between now and retirement, ten years away. "At sixty-five, Joe, you are going to need $33,598 a year, after taxes, just to maintain your present standard of living." He was a little shocked, but not too worried, since he expected his salary to keep pace with inflation (in reality, that would be unusual). If everything went according to plan, the company pension would come to about $24,000 after taxes. With their savings, and a modest public pension added on, it sounded like enough — until we figured that he might live for another twenty years after retirement. At age eighty-five, his modest standard of living will require an after-tax income of $60,682, and his company pension will still be providing only $24,000! And that's only if the company doesn't fold, Joe doesn't get laid off, he keeps getting raises, and inflation stays down at the three percent level. Some security!

If he uses savings to augment the original gap between company pension and family budget, the savings won't last, much less stretch to cover the much larger gap at age eighty-five. If he's counting on Social Security or CPP/QPP to fill that hole, he hasn't been reading the newspapers lately. Both public pension plans face possible collapse when the Baby Boomers start to retire, leaving too few workers behind to support too many retirees. The only mathematically possible ways to save public pension plans are a) drastically increase the current contribution levels, b) drastically raise the retirement age, or c) subject the universal pensions to means testing.

A big increase in contribution levels — assuming politicians have the stomach for it — will hit employees and employers alike. If the employer's part of the increase comes out of wages, Joe's raises and ultimate pension level will be reduced, or, worse, Joe might lose his job. If, instead, employers cover the shortfall by raising the prices of their products, then the cost of living goes up and Joe's rosy three percent inflation forecast takes a hike over Heartbreak Hill. Then remember that Joe's part of the pension levy jumps too. That reduces his take-home pay and lowers his standard of living, or it cuts into his savings if he uses those to make up the loss.

Raising the retirement age will hijack Joe's ten-year plan completely. He'll have a few more years to pad his pension, but he won't have as much retirement to enjoy.

Means testing, or limiting pensions to those most in need, won't help Joe much either. He and his wife were planning a comfortable retirement, not a dropkick into penury. The only way they'll qualify for a means-tested public pension is if the company pension collapses.

No matter how the politicians fix the public pension system, Joe's plans fall apart. And if they don't fix the system Joe's plans fall apart for sure.

Check your own situation in the "Inflation Table" opposite. First, follow the life expectancy column down to your own best guess in your personal longevity stakes. Make another bet on inflation (I've worked out the projections for four percent and ten percent inflation). Now look across to the column that approximates your own current spending level. That astonishingly big number you see represents how much you will need *per year* if you live that long, and if you maintain your current spending habits. Thus, if you are thirty-five now and spend $30,000 a year, you will need $144,030 a year by the time you're seventy-five.

If inflation returns to double digits (the norm not that long ago), the future gets bleaker even faster. At ten percent inflation, your $30,000

Inflation Table

Life Exp'ncy in Years	Inflation Rate	Current Annual Spending ($)			
		20,000	30,000	40,000	50,000
10	4%	29,605	44,407	59,210	74,012
	10%	51,875	77,812	103,750	129,687
20	4%	43,822	65,733	87,644	109,555
	10%	134,550	201,825	269,100	336,375
30	4%	64,868	97,302	129,736	162,170
	10%	348,989	523,483	697,978	872,472
40	4%	96,020	144,030	192,040	240,050
	10%	905,187	1,357,780	1,810,374	2,262,968

spending habit will swell to more than $1.3 million a year by the time you're seventy-five.

The obvious question is, can your fixed pension plan compensate for the effects of inflation? If it can't, is it worth hanging on to a job just for the hope of a company pension?

A Way of Life to Beat the Cost of Living

One way to get around this problem is to reduce that budget figure. Let's take Joe's case, as an example. In thirty years with three percent inflation, remember, it will require $60,682 to support his lifestyle. His company pension will provide $24,000, leaving him with a $36,682 deficit to overcome.

Now let's assume that he loses his senses and throws caution to the wind. He quits the job now and abandons the pension. He and his wife would have to trim the spending budget by forty percent, from $25,000 to $15,000 the first year, to end up with roughly the same deficit — $36,450 a year — at age eighty-five that they would have had with the company pension. Most people would find this a daunting task but it is within the realm of the possible for serious conservers, who would do it by moving somewhere cheaper, growing their own food, and doing many of the other things I've described in this book. The trade-off is whether they want to work ten more years for the company pension, or retire now with a budget cut.

Do-It-Yourself Pensions

It is possible to set up your own pension plan in a way that may offset inflationary effects. Directly or indirectly, company pensions are financed by employee contributions. Part of it comes straight off your paycheck, and part of it comes from company profits (which your labor helps to produce). You're buying the pension, but you don't have any control over it. If you want to control a pension — make it grow as fast as the cost of living — you will have to set up your own fund. Subject to certain rules and limits, contributions to your private pension fund can be tax free, and you can invest it in a way that suits you. If you're a worrier, you can pick the same kind of low-interest securities that the company funds are buried in. Gamblers can put their funds into riskier, high-yield investments. Or, you can tie your pension fund directly to the cost of living.

One way is to distribute investments into fields where you may be most vulnerable to price increases. Are you a renter worried about the cost of apartments in thirty years? Buy the building. Invest in real estate, property management firms, or holding companies. If rentals do go sky high, the profits on your pension fund investments will rise with them. Does the future price of food bother you? Invest in the food industry. Your losses in the supermarket will be recovered in the dividend checks. Scared by soaring medical costs? Hospital and drug stocks are soaring just as fast as the costs.

Economists call that *hedging*. Gamblers, investors, and farmers do it all the time. Simply put, it's an offsetting transaction that guarantees the investor cannot lose. A bookie can calmly accept a million-dollar bet that the National League will win the World Series — and not lose a wink of sleep over the outcome. His hedge is to take an offsetting bet that the American League will win. No matter who wins the series, the bookie collects a million and pays out a million (minus a handling charge of course).

Inflation fighters protect themselves by investing in fields where soaring costs will provide an offsetting profit. Motorists who bought oil stocks have been immune to the pain of higher gasoline prices. What they lose at the pumps, they gain on the stock market.

Stocks may be too volatile for many would-be pensioners. If you want to dampen the risks further, diversify a do-it-yourself pension through equity mutual funds, or a mix of equities and interest investments. Remember the tax bite, though, and put the interest investments under the registered retirement plan, where they will be sheltered from tax; and keep any equity investments outside the plan, because capital gains and dividends will be taxed at a lower rate anyway.

My favorite pension plan? A young hardwood forest. A few acres of maple, ash, hickory, and beech. It's mostly young stock now, but by the time we're too infirm to do whatever it is we're doing now, the trees will be worth enough to keep us rocking merrily around the hearth. In the meantime, they get bigger and more valuable every year, pay an interim dividend of winter fuel, spring syrup, and summer building supplies. The price of lumber and fuel inflates along with everything else. There's always a chance that fire and pestilence could cashier the pension prematurely, but that risk is no greater than the company pension disappearing to Rio or into bankruptcy. The future can never be 100 percent assured, but an inflationary future doesn't seem quite so scary with a pension that grows all by itself.

The People's Pension

The Cadillac of pensions is the indexed model. Payments increase with the cost of living. That's peachy for the person who has one, but there's some argument as to whether society can afford to be that generous. Consequently, few North American workers have access to indexed pensions. For most of us, the only thing that approximates self-inflating pensions is the government models: Social Security in the United States and CPP/QPP in Canada.

The first catch, of course, is that *tsunami* of Baby Boomers already starting to upset the actuarial apple cart. As we said a few pages ago, the People's Pensions might not survive long in their present forms. If indexing gives them a Cadillac shine, it's a wheezing old gas guzzler of a Caddie that you might not want to bet your vacation on.

The second catch, for our purposes, is that these plans require that the would-be retiree be a bona fide contributing worker. No problem with that. Fair's fair. However, most workers who can now contemplate some form of unsalaried existence have probably already contributed to the public plan during the years of formal, normal work. What portion of that can be salvaged at sixty-five? Or earlier?

The Social Security system is similar to CPP/QPP in that qualification depends on having had some minimum attachment to the regular work force. Self-employed persons also contribute. Generally speaking, benefits are available to those retiring at sixty-five (sixty-two with lower benefits), provided you have contributed for up to ten years during your career. Survivors and the disabled usually need fewer work credits to qualify for special benefits. The size of the retirement benefit is based on your record of earnings, and is partially indexed to the cost of living. Social Security has an additional advantage for those with a history of low earnings — under some circumstances, there is a Supplemental Security Income that can provide a larger pension than earnings would normally warrant.

CPP/QPP pays a retirement benefit based on a percentage of pensionable earnings over the period of contributions. In other words, the longer you work and the higher your salary, the higher will be the pension. If you earn a small income, or work only sporadically, the pension will be reduced accordingly. If your income is "unearned," from rentals or investments for example, or if earned income is less than $3,500 (the 2003 exemption), then you aren't required to make any contribution — and neither will you earn any pension credit for that year. If you are self-employed and earning over $3,400, you contribute at a higher rate (9.9 percent and rising). You don't have to stay in the plan continuously. Moving in and out depends on the level and nature of your earnings. And when you retire between sixty and sixty-five, your whole work history sets the level of the retirement benefit. After that, it's adjusted each year for cost of living increases.

Canadians who have earned too little to qualify for a maximum CPP/QPP pension can fall back on the two universal pension schemes that are not related to earnings. The basic Old Age Security pension, combined with the Guaranteed Income Supplement, is available at the age of sixty-five regardless of how spotty your work history is. So Canadians who leave the regular work force early may still receive (at sixty-five) pensions from OAS, GIS, and probably a smaller amount from CPP/QPP as well.

Both Social Security and CPP/QPP require contributions in order to maintain coverage. It is very tempting, therefore, to give first priority to a pauper budget and drop out of the contributory plans, hoping that OAS, GIS trees, or whatever else will suffice at sixty-five. There is a strong argument, however, for remaining qualified — if only at the minimum level. Check with your local Social Security or CPP/QPP office to see what it would take to keep your own qualification up. It may be no more than a temporary job every few years, or an occasional burst of self-employment. Minimum qualification may not provide much of a retirement pension (remember it's set according to your average earnings), but it does have these advantages:

♦   The pension, however small, is tied to inflation and will grow.

♦   In addition to retirement benefits, both plans give benefits to widows, widowers, orphans and the disabled.

♦   Not all benefits are earnings-related. Social Security death benefits, and the CPP orphan's allowance, for example, pay a standard amount, regardless of how little the contributor earned.

♦   Social Security qualifiers receive free hospital and low-cost medical coverage under Medicare.

♦   Survivors' benefits, under both plans, are a form of "life insurance" for families. It may be cheaper to qualify for this coverage through occasional contributory work than to pay for commercial insurance policies.

Living for Caesar

It's a circular logic, self-perpetuating, all-ensnaring: the one-eyed notion that one must work to pay the high cost of living, when, in fact, that high cost of living is composed, in some measure, of the costs of earning and maintaining high incomes. Like the cart horse who can't give up the wagon because he needs it to carry all the grease, wheels, and spare parts the wagon requires, the modern worker feels obliged to cling to the highest salary he or she can get in order to support a network of insurance policies, pension plans, and government programs that might offer protection against the loss of a high salary.

The greatest security is not in having the most, but in needing the least.

The greatest security is not in having the most, but in needing the least. A simple lifestyle, with a bare-bones budget, is not only cheap in itself, it's also cheap to protect.

What Do You Do for a Living? (and other difficult questions)

Strangers are the worst. People who have worked beside us long enough know better than to ask. It's the well-meaning strangers, attempting innocent small talk, who become most vexing in this sort of life.

"And what do you do?" they ask, with a brittle little smile that says that any answer longer than a single sentence would severely try the listener's patience.

If there's an exit handy, I can answer cricket player, sheriff or pope. The usual response is, "How interesting." And the inquisitor goes back to the canapés.

Others, whose interest is more genuine, warrant some more truthful explanation. I've tried them all, and none really fit. "Independently wealthy," "independently poor," "domestic economist," "self-employed peasant," all have a measure of truth, but they all begin to sound like smart-assed ways to say that we do nothing at all — and that is certainly *not* the truth.

Are You Working?
The last time someone asked me that I answered (truthfully), "Yes, I'm building a house."

"Where?"

"At home. We're building a house for ourselves."

"Oh, I see. You're not really *working* then . . . ?"

In fact, we were working seventy to eighty hours a week creating something useful from stone and timber. In ten years of various paid labors, I had never worked so hard or accomplished anything as concrete and lasting as that. But in his eyes, and by any economist's definition, it wasn't really work because it wasn't performed in the marketplace. Unlike "real" construction, there was no earning and precious little spending going on. If you don't get paid, it can't be work.

We could dismiss such cock-eyed views as a semantic quibble if it weren't for the fact that this society places the mantle of virtue only on work of the official, paid variety. The rest of us are said to be "housepersons," "unemployed," "dropouts," even "parasites." Regardless of how we may spend our time, if we aren't actually selling ourselves in the marketplace, the implicit question is: "Can you justify doing 'nothing'?" The semantics create a pressure to work only at those things which consumers are said to demand, whether or not it is rational, sensible and useful work. Thus the person who is paid to package "pet rocks" for sale is *working* and is accepted as a useful member of society. The employer who pays the rock packager, and accepts the profit, is a businessperson and is seen to be even more virtuous than the worker. The person who takes the rocks and builds himself a house, however, is doing *nothing* in the economist's eyes. If the builder isn't paid for his labor, then he's unemployed and is subject to conservative scorn and liberal rehabilitations.

Now if I were to go over and build a neighbor's house, while she came here to build mine, I could pay her and she could pay me and we would both be officially working. We would have to settle the question of pay, of course. Since we each want the same type of house, I should charge her what she charges me. As long as the price is the same for each, society should accept the deal as fair and praise us both for seeing the light at last and becoming gainfully employed.

So if I gave her one dollar, and she gave me one dollar, everybody would be happy, right? Well, not really. That would mean that we would both be officially poor — poorly paid and living in cheap housing. Even worse, our one-dollar wages would be too low for the government to tax. And our feeble effort would make no perceptible contribution at all to the growth of the GNP. We would officially be giving little more than stagnation to the economy.

Better all around if we agreed to give each other one million dollars for the mutual building effort (by check of course). Now society would honor us as wealthy and successful people. We might even be appointed to boards of directors and government commissions. Our homes would be considered valuable real estate instead of worthless one-dollar hovels. The GNP would jump by two million dollars and politicians would rejoice that the economy was recovering. They would also send us each a tax bill for half a million or more. Best of all, we could finally retire to our homes without the need to work at all, having justified ourselves in society's eyes as successful people of independent means.

Please note that in that entire farce no mention is made of what the houses might really be like. They could be palaces or mud huts. The economist is totally indifferent to quality. If we trade our labor for a million dollars, the economists add two million to the GNP. If we trade for one dollar, we're only worth one dollar. If we each give up the farce and go home to build our own houses, then neither of us is working, and our official worth to society is zero. In actual fact, what we produce is totally irrelevant. *Only the price is counted.*

Down with the GNP!

To the economist, a $4.95 pet rock has the same value as a $4.95 dose of polio vaccine. Two pet rocks would be twice as valuable as a single polio shot, and, if society were forced to choose between them, the economist would insist on the pet rocks. The vaccine, at half the value, would be dismissed as an "uneconomic" alternative. It sounds absurd when reduced to that limit. And yet society, led by economists and GNP-worshipping politicians, consistently chooses the profits of quantity over the costs of quality.

Consider the arguments over the use of coal to generate electricity. National planners dismiss solar energy as "uneconomic" and accept coal as the more economic alternative. But how do they decide what is economic and what isn't? Coal burning fouls the air with sulfur compounds that turn to acid in the rain. The air, however, is *free.* That is, air is not metered and controlled in the marketplace (yet!). Nobody makes a profit from it. Therefore, say the planners, polluting the air is not to be counted as part of the cost of burning coal. Nor do they count the cost of ruining forests and crops with the fallout — since the forests and crops belong to someone else. If the utility company doesn't have to pay the cost, then the cost does not exist. It could very well be that even if we considered all of the human costs as real and gave them dollar values, coal might still be cheaper than the uneconomic alternatives, but that is not the point. The point is that economics is only *one* of the measures of man, and a very inadequate one at that.

Drive through the commercial zones that serve as fast-food arteries for every North American suburb and start adding up the multi-billion-dollar cost of superfluous baubles. Drive-in burgers, topless bowling, Bar-B-Q, go-carts, thick shakes, mini-golf, donutty, X-rated, pinball smash-em, blinking, glittering, hollow-brained, pimply, masturbating, overweight, gum-chewing, pornographic glut of commerce that makes up . . . *ta da!* . . . the GNP! The Wealth of Nations! The continent could become a coast-to-coast carnival midway and the economists would rejoice at our riches, the politicians would take proud credit for the economic growth. The skies might be hidden behind ochre-colored smog, and the farms that once produced the burgers might be paved, but the economy would be booming. What's good for the GNP is good for the country. The invisible hand of the marketplace knows best. Or does it?

As always, it comes back to choices. I like an occasional burger myself, and I can accept that another might legitimately spend his money on topless bowling, and dismiss the cost of smokestack filters (to stop smog) as uneconomic. Enforcing my values on the economy is no more acceptable than dictating that we must all chew gum or squeal our tires in the parking lot of the McPimple Burger. That's the price of freedom. But that freedom also implies the right to quit spending, the right to quit earning, the right to be "uneconomic," the right to produce what we value and to ignore what the marketplace values. Repeat after me:

"There is no shame in choosing to consume less rather than more."

"There is no shame in choosing to grow vegetables for nothing rather than bowling for dollars."

"There is no shame in producing art that never sells rather than kiddie porn that does."

"There is no shame in subtracting from the GNP."

A woman actually told me once that she was worried about leaving her job. She didn't need the money. She didn't think her job was either interesting or important. She wanted to make time for the things that she did consider important, but those things were not attached to a salary.

"How can I justify not working?" she asked. "Does that make me a parasite?"

I asked her to ignore salaries for a moment and consider whether society would be better served by what she proposed to do with her retirement, or would it be better served by having another publicist, civil servant, hamburger stand, game show host, roller derby queen or anything else that economists value by their salary rather than by their product. If the product was worthwhile in *human* terms, to hell with the money. That alone never justified anything. She admitted then that her job was perhaps more parasitical than her retirement. She left her job. No one else has filled it. Society never noticed the difference. The GNP dropped by $40,000 a year and the world was actually better off.

What If Everybody Did It?

In the first place, everybody won't. The inventors of capitalism knew what they were doing when they selected greed and envy as the fundamental motivating forces of the system. Only sex is a more potent human impulse, and it's not entirely free of greed and envy either. A preference for consuming less must always be about as popular as celibacy.

Secondly, even if the Doctrine of Less does become more popular, it's the shallow end of the economic pool that empties first. With less money to spend, my family and I didn't give up food, clothing, books, music, health care, and the things that really matter. We did, however, give up paying for French wine, credit, life insurance, restaurant lunches, and silly gifts like pet rocks and navel brushes. I daresay half the working population of North America could quit their jobs and the important parts of the economy would keep right on producing food, clothing, health care, and so on. There might be fewer topless bowling emporiums and pet rock sellers as the shrunken economy sets spending priorities more carefully, but the civilized world wouldn't end. It might even be improved.

Finally, there's the Second Law of Thermodynamics. (It's not the final one, of course. There are a third and fourth, but the second law is the only one that matters to our economic future.) The Second Law of Thermodynamics shows that many processes are irreversible. Envisage, for example, a locomotive with a head of steam, parked beside an icy pond. The steam in the engine has a great capacity for potential work: pulling trains, pumping out the pond, whatever. Now, if the locomotive ends up in the pond, the total energy in the system remains unchanged. The steam cools off and the pond heats up. But the system has lost the capacity to perform work. The steam is a dribble of tepid water that couldn't pull the train if it tried — not even with the help of the slightly warmer pond. And nothing can reverse the heat transfer and make it work again without the addition of new, outside energy to heat it up to steam again.

What's that got to do with the economic future? In a word, everything. It means that every industrial conversion we make changes some part of the earth's resource to a less useful state. The plastic box around the pet rock has spent the potential of the oil that made it — forever. That loss is universal, eternal and irreversible. Every bauble or bit of garbage that makes up the world's GNP is a permanent debit against the future. While we go around frantically pushing locomotives into ponds, the economists count and add the activity to the GNP. The politicians cheer the pushers on, since a higher GNP is the measure of their success. No one asks if that's the best way to use locomotives. And those of us who decline the chance to participate in the great mass defiance of the Second Law, thank you very much, are treated as virtual traitors to the capitalist cause — not doing our bit for the GNP.

The Second Law is so important that C.P. Snow called it the scientific equivalent of Shakespeare in explaining the human condition. It was the Second Law that convinced me to stop pushing locomotives, but what if everybody in North America did it? What if everybody began consuming less, deliberately dampening the economy? The consumer diet? The material fast? Would the Western world really collapse under the stress of moderation?

Does the Conserver Have a Place in the Capitalist Economy?

Given the Second Law and a finite world, the most disturbing aspect of capitalism has to be its essential reliance on growth. According to theory, a capitalist economy must grow to remain healthy, even if the growth itself will ultimately prove malignant. Crudely put, the rationale for growth goes something like this:

Assume we have a simple economy that consists entirely of the production and consumption of gizmos. We consume one hundred gizmos a year, and those one hundred are produced by ten machines. One machine wears out each year, so the economy must include another factory that turns out one gizmo-making machine per year. The total GNP will be: 100 gizmos plus 1 gizmo machine (replacement).

Now there's a war or a baby boom to start the economy growing, and consumption increases by ten percent to 110 gizmos a year. But we only have enough machines to produce 100, so the gizmo machine factory has to double its output to cope with a mere ten percent increase in gizmo consumption. Now they must make the usual replacement machine, plus another machine to cope with the growth.

The following year, consumption remains stable at 110 gizmos, and the gizmo machine factory goes back to making the single replacement machine required — one gizmo machine instead of last year's two. So stable consumption causes a fifty percent slump in the machine industry.

The traditional answer to that dilemma has been to encourage continual growth. The overall capitalist economy is stable only when consumption continues to grow. That's why economists cry "recession" even when the economy is producing and consuming more than ever before in the history of the world.

When resources were plentiful and energy was cheap, continual growth was accepted as an adequate short-term solution. Somewhere along the line it got to be a religion and neither OPEC nor Club of Rome calculations (which use computer models to predict *when,* not *if* the earth's supply of commonly required resources would disappear at present rates of consumption) have managed to dissuade Western politicians from accelerating down the road to disaster. Accelerating consumption, fed by natural greed and envy, and officially encouraged by the slavish pursuit of an ever-expanding GNP, is a powerful force to thwart. What, then, can one person do?

Until an economic messiah comes along to forever cast GNP out of the temple, the best we can do is conduct our lives conscious of the

Second Law and the limits of growth. That means living like con-servers, reducing consumption, producing for permanence — even at the expense of short-term profit — putting aside competitive earning and competitive spending in favor of less material measures of satisfac-tion.

Capitalism is founded on greed and envy. That's not a pejorative slur. It's an accepted part of the creed that the economy performs most efficiently when each one of us takes as much as we can get and gives as little as we must. Each of us striving competitively to have more than those around us is supposed to fuel the engine of progress. Greed and envy, far from being vices, are necessary virtues for material success. What, then, is the place of the conserver, who eschews material success? Is the conserver a misfit in a consumer world?

The obvious answer is that only a few can win in any competition. In the competition for material success, there must be losers as well as winners — otherwise, it wouldn't be any fun for the winners, having no one to defeat. So, as long as there have to be "losers," it might as well be those of us who aren't that interested in the game in the first place. I also lose wet T-shirt contests and monster truck competitions — sim-ply by choosing not to compete. Choosing not to compete in the con-sumer game of "who's got the most toys" is equally easy. Those of us with dry T-shirts and tiny trucks are not only part of the system, we're as essential to it as those on top. You can't have mountains without the valleys, and you can't win the consumer game without a few of us down here eating pigeons, getting our furniture from the junk of the rich, and making wine from the sour grapes.

In a more serious vein, it may take a conserver streak in all of us to preserve enough of the earth's energy and resources for our grandchil-dren to live half as well as we have. Under an ethic where each one takes as much as he or she can get, those of us who refuse to take more than we need are a small but unapologetic brake on the wasteful excess of consumption. Like a governor on a runaway engine, far from being dis-loyal to the system, we may, in fact, be helping to save it from itself.

But Isn't It Uneconomic?

This question is usually directed at what conservers do rather than what they refuse to do.

238 • How to Survive Without a Salary

- Isn't raising your own food uneconomical?

- Why stay home with the kids? Put them in day care and get a job.

- Wouldn't aluminum siding be cheaper than stone?

- You're planting trees? There's more money in corn.

The answer to every such challenge has to be, "Yes" — as long as you accept the one-sided system of accounting that ignores quality, counts no input or output whose value is not controlled in the marketplace, and takes no responsibility for the future. Under that blinkered view of economics, yes, we're uneconomic.

Let's take those points one at a time:

Quality (and the term here includes permanence as well as taste): Yes, despite the fact that stone is free and aluminum siding costly, the time it takes to move heavy stones around may well make them uneconomical. But stone makes a better house, a more permanent house — an errant baseball will not dent it. There is, however, no provision in modern accounts for quality — only quantity. Just as well the efficiency experts were not involved in decorating the Sistine Chapel. I can hear them now, clipboards in hand, peering up at Michelangelo on the scaffold above: "Mike! Hey Mike! I'm telling ya that paint would go on twice as fast with a roller!"

Value: How do you count what's "free"? The marketplace doesn't put a price on good health or even on life itself, and if health and nutrition are ignored, then yes, I suppose raising your own food could be uneconomical. The homegrown stuff, however, is free of added sugar, coloring and unpronounceable chemicals that get blamed for everything from cavities to miscarriages. The security of knowing it would never give cancer to a lab rat isn't worth a dime to an economist. If you dismiss that fact, and the terrific taste (which is also free and therefore considered to be irrelevant), then it would definitely be more economical to spend our gardening time earning a salary and leave nutrition in the hands of Dupont, Kraft, and illegal-immigrant labor.

The Future: Finally, accepted ways of deciding what is and what is not economic take no responsibility for the future. Farmers continue to grow corn on shallow topsoil, knowing that the soil itself will be permanently lost or damaged. *This* year's profit counts. Logging companies clear-cut vast tracts of forest, stripping the best and leaving the most genetically inferior species to propagate future forests. Profits are calculated on *this* year's costs.

Even under the current idiocy of ignoring all costs that can't be measured in dollars, many essential activities persist despite their "uneconomic" character. Farmers continue to grow food despite low returns on land that could be turned into much more rewarding malls. Friends give one another free advice that therapists would charge big bucks for. Volunteers keep churches, scouts, amateur sports and charities alive. And full-time parenting is still the toughest job anybody ever did for a hug.

Under the circumstances, I've never felt either foolish or guilty for behaving "uneconomically."

What Does It Feel Like to Be Poor?

Having never considered ourselves poor, the question always seems to be misdirected, and yet folks who have more money than us invariably wonder. Perhaps a better question would be: How do we manage to feel so rich with so little money?

The difference between feeling rich and feeling poor has little to do with how much is consumed and a great deal to do with how it's consumed. Ironically, it's deprivation, more than anything else, that seems to enhance the appreciation of material things. The surest way to appreciate anything is a bit of self-denial — *the material fast.*

One night last summer, we sat down to a particularly sumptuous family meal. The centerpiece was a platter-sized rainbow trout, garnished with cherry tomatoes and salad things. There was hot buttered corn on the cob, peas and tiny green beans, kohlrabi and cucumber — everything taken from the garden less than thirty minutes before the meal. There was a loaf of bread still hot from the oven, a bottle of chilled white wine, and fresh raspberries and cream for dessert.

The highlight of the meal? The choicest morsel at the feast? A few lowly potatoes! Steamed in their skins and served whole, without even so much as a lick of butter and salt to tart them up. We're not addicted to potatoes, and two days later they were just a part of the culinary furniture again — no more remarkable than the butter on the bread. What made them so special in the midst of all that mouth-watering fare? The winter stock of old potatoes ran out in the spring. For four months we did not taste a single spud, and this special treat was the very first batch of new summer potatoes. Tasty enough at any time, but with appreciation honed by a four-month potato "fast," it seemed like the richest food at the table.

Strangely enough, even economists accept this view of wealth as a relative feeling. "Diminishing marginal utility" is one term used to describe the concept. In plain English, that means that a hungry person's first steak is of very great value. The second one served is slightly less useful, and the hundredth steak at the meal earns nowhere near the appreciation that the first one did. At some point beyond saturation, the arrival of still more steaks can get to be an absolute nuisance. It sounds so obvious when stated like that, and yet eyebrows still arc incredulously when I say that it's easier to feel material satisfaction (wealth) by limiting consumption than by extending it. The material glutton has reduced all marginal pleasures to zero. He dines on nothing but the one-hundredth steak and never knows the joys of the first one. How many rich men can enjoy a potato?

Man As Peacock — And Frightened Peacock

Consumption is not all there is to wealth of course. There is also the display of wealth, and the security it purports to bring, that compel some to material success. The display of wealth can be even more important than its consumption. It's what Western society has chosen as the basis of the hierarchy. Conservers have the choice of finding satisfaction at the bottom of the hierarchy, or refusing to participate in the peacock game — displaying something else besides wealth as the measure of their worth.

The urge to display is insidious, partly because it can be hard to recognize. We pretend to shop for quality and satisfaction when the more honest criterion is the social status of the acquisition. Houses, clothes, cars, even holiday destinations are chosen as much for their display value as for their intrinsic value.

Once upon a time, my partner and I considered living on a boat. The initial impetus was pure conserver thinking: life aboard dispensed with the most expensive part of landlubber housing — the need to occupy real estate. Also, boats were cheaper than houses. In the course of this research, we made connections with a yacht broker. A genuine teak and mahogany, absinthe on the poop deck, how are things in Ibiza, yacht broker. It took a while, but we eventually realized that getting mail from our yacht broker (and better still, making mention of the fact) was a lot more fun than the thought of actually living on the water. We kept the broker going for two more years after realizing that he did as much for the sheen on our tail feathers as any old boat could do, and it only cost an occasional stamp.

Preening is part of the impetus for material success. Security, however, is the essence of that drive. For the materially driven, there can be no such thing as having *enough*. The goal is to have more than anybody else, and more again to protect that status from any possible incursions against the wealth. *Enough* means having enough to withstand the loss of income, inflation, old age, recession, black plague and infidels without losing the number-one status. *Enough* never comes, so the materially driven can never stop. And the more they have, the more they have to protect.

I know a man who, at twenty, planned his life so he could retire at forty. The initial plan was to take the highest paying jobs he could find, regardless of whether they were interesting or satisfying. He intended to spend as little as possible, maximize his savings, and invest them. The investment dividends would eventually provide a livable income for early retirement. Gradually the goal changed so that the dividends would have to do more than simply provide for family needs; now it was thought necessary to replace current earnings (which were much higher than needs). Then, as that goal was reached, it was raised again to accommodate the possible effects of future inflation. Each level of success is not recognized as a greater security, but as a new responsibility. The more he accumulates, the more he has to protect by accumulating even more wealth. His fortieth birthday is long past now, and retirement (and the plan to work at jobs he was really interested in) is still a distant dream.

The Tragedy of the Materialist

The drive for material success is fundamentally based on aggressive competition and material acquisition. But true satisfaction is impossible under those rules. Materialists compare themselves to their peers, who always have more than they do. When materialists exercise their greed and envy with greater skill, they achieve even more material success — and compare themselves to a new set of peers. Their new peers, again, have more than they do. Although you may be working overtime to keep up with the Joneses, the Joneses don't compare themselves to you and feel rich. They compare themselves to the Rockefellers and feel poor. Only at the very pinnacle of material success can greed and envy be satisfied. But even there — especially there — at the very top of the money heap, success is incapable of buying peace. For it's never enough to win. Winners must forever defend their spoils from all of the envious strivers beneath them.

Conservers have reached the point of "enough."
• • • • • • • • • • • •

The tragedy of the materialists is their inability to ever say "enough." When material needs are established only in relation to what others have, irrespective of what little is really needed to be warm and well-fed, then needs can never be satisfied. Conservers don't come from any higher spiritual plane, free from greed and envy. They have merely reached the point of admitting that they really don't need more *things*. They have reached the point of "enough."

What Kind of People Would Do Such a Thing?

Greed and envy are powerful forces, not easily restrained. What is it then that is powerful enough to pull us in another direction? To say that material ambition is a futile, or even a silly competition — akin to running the bulls in Pamplona or squealing tires at the McPimple Burger — is simply not enough. What else, besides disillusionment, causes people to pin mistletoe to their coat tails and walk out the door to do something else?

Each of us is driven by our own little engine (or "different drummer" in Thoreau's more poetic world), and these suppositions may only be valid for one, but it seems to be that those who have walked away from salaries and survived have had two characteristics in common: strong personal goals, and a sense of their own mortality.

Personal goals, for a lucky few, can be pursued entirely through paid employment. At some point, however, those who set out to achieve something else in the world feel the constraints of the employer's rules, the employer's interests, and the employer's inarguable right to direct the work towards his or her own goals. Breaking away successfully invariably involves positive rather than negative motives. Leaving a job to devote full time and energy to other goals works. Leaving a job only because the job is a bore leads too often to another boring job.

The only problem with a regular job is that it can begin to get in the way of more important things. Sooner or later, people with those strong personal goals find that evenings and weekends just aren't enough. The choice is to hang on to the job and hope it gets better, or follow the path that interests you, regardless of what — if anything — it pays. Some meet more success by leaving jobs than by keeping them. Babe Ruth could have stuck it out as a bartender, and Howard Cosell was once a lawyer. Albert Einstein was a clerk, Golda Meir a schoolteacher, Dave Brubeck a cowboy. Quitters all. Others of us may never attain that much by leaving vocations for avocations. All we can manage is the joy and satisfaction of trying.

Doing what's important — and damn the pay — smacks of youthful rebellion. It's as likely, however, to strike in middle age. In the first place, it takes years of salaried toil (and perhaps an early taste of material success) to fully realize that that kind of success is not always everything it promised to be. It's hard to abandon financial security without first having had some and seen that it is not enough. More important, the young so rarely have a sense of their own mortality. At twenty-five, there seems to be plenty of time ahead to have a career for money, a second career later for interest, a family, leisure, travel . . . anything is possible. At thirty-five or forty-five, death starts to seem possible — even probable. All the unfilled dreams begin to tickle at the back of your sleep. All the things you were going to do with your life, all the important things, are still waiting for the time to do them, and the future isn't somewhere over the horizon anymore. It's here and now — or never.

Why Bother?
The tragedy of the industrial age has been the overwhelming dominance of consumption as the measure of humanity. Even work — each person's art, creation, and contribution to the world — has come to be measured not by its quality or human worth, but by its commercial value. *What is it worth in trade for consumable goods?* I am what I am paid. I am what I consume. I spend, therefore I am. Like so many

swine, we've allowed the economists to define us and rank us by our basest animal instinct — our appetites.

It's a small act. Each conserver's individual declaration of independence from Mammon's frenetic hierarchy of consumer envy and material ambition is not a world-shaking trend. It's not even a socially responsible act in the eyes of many. They are the ones who cannot believe that work can be done for a spiritual purpose. To them, the material measure is the *only* one. If you don't get paid, it isn't work.

Surviving without a salary is not the denial of work's importance. Quite the contrary. It is the celebration of work — real work — as a human act whose value is intrinsic, irrespective of its value in the consumer market. We do our work in our own small way, not because Mammon pays us, but because it makes us human.

Index

Also by Charles Long . . .

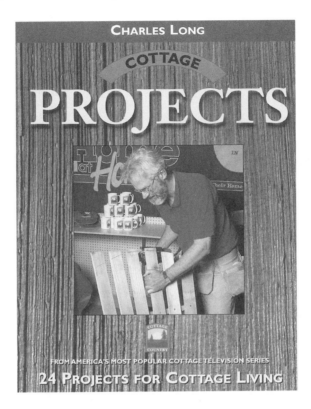

Cottage Projects
24 Projects for Cottage Living

From the popular *Cottage Country* television program, *How to Survive Without a Salary* author Charles Long presents two dozen simple yet affordable projects that can make your summer cottage, camp or cabin more appealing.

Each project includes detailed step-by-step instructions involving woodworking, stonebuilding and cottage maintenance. Color photos and black & white drawings accompany each project.

ISBN 1-895629-75-6

The Vegetarian Traveler

A guide to eating green in 197 countries

If you are a vegetarian who enjoys travel but speaks English only, you know the difficulties of ordering food that suits your needs. *The Vegetarian Traveler* is the answer. Here is the first guide book to the words and phrases needed to order vegetarian food in 197 different countries.

World traveler and long-time vegetarian Bryan Geon gives an informed and witty overview of what to expect when attempting to order meals around the world.

ISBN 1-894020-85-5

The Real Taste of Jamaica

The Real Taste of Jamaica sizzles to life as Enid Donaldson embarks on a tropical culinary journey, exploring the unique flavors that can only be called Jamaican. Taste native cuisine prepared by local housewives, cooks, restaurateurs and road-side "Jerkies" that food lovers savor all over the world.

ISBN 1-894020-86-3

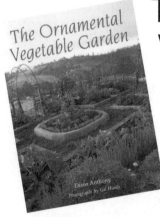